The Cambridge Introduction to
Early Modern Drama, 1576–1642

Engaging and stimulating, this *Introduction* provides a fresh vista of the early modern theatrical landscape. Chapters are arranged according to key genres (tragedy, revenge, history play, pastoral and romantic comedy, city comedy, satire and tragicomedy), punctuated by a series of focused case studies on topics ranging from repertoire to performance style, political events to the physical body of the actor, and from plays in print to the space of the playhouse. Julie Sanders encourages readers to engage with particular dramatic moments, such as opening scenes, skulls onstage or the conventions of disguise, and to apply the materials and methods contained in the book in inventive ways. A timeline and frequent cross-references provide continuity. Always alert to the possibilities of performance, Sanders reveals the remarkable story of early modern drama not through individual writers, but through repertoires and company practices, helping to relocate and re-imagine canonical plays and playwrights.

Julie Sanders is Chair of English Literature and Drama at the University of Nottingham, and currently Vice Provost for Teaching and Learning at its Ningbo, China campus.

The Cambridge Introduction to
Early Modern Drama, 1576–1642

JULIE SANDERS

CAMBRIDGE
UNIVERSITY PRESS

CAMBRIDGE
UNIVERSITY PRESS

University Printing House, Cambridge CB2 8BS, United Kingdom

Published in the United States of America by Cambridge University Press, New York

Cambridge University Press is part of the University of Cambridge.

It furthers the University's mission by disseminating knowledge in the pursuit of education, learning and research at the highest international levels of excellence.

www.cambridge.org
Information on this title: www.cambridge.org/9781107645479

© Julie Sanders 2014

First published 2014

Printed in the United Kingdom by TJ International Ltd. Padstow Cornwall

A catalogue record for this publication is available from the British Library

Library of Congress Cataloguing in Publication data
Sanders, Julie.
The Cambridge introduction to early modern drama, 1576–1642 / Julie Sanders.
    pages cm. – (Cambridge introductions to literature)
Includes bibliographical references and index.
ISBN 978-1-107-01356-8 (hardback)
1. English drama – Early modern and Elizabethan, 1500–1600 – History and criticism.
2. English drama – 17th century – History and criticism.   3. Theater – England –
History – 16th century.   4. Theater – England – History – 17th century.   I. Title.
PR651.S26   2014
822'.309–dc23   2013023081

ISBN 978-1-107-01356-8 Hardback
ISBN 978-1-107-64547-9 Paperback

For John, again, still, always.

'They came in wherries, on horseback and on foot, from Cheapside and White Chapel, Westminster and Newington, Clerkenwell and Shoreditch, deserting for an interval their workbenches, their accounts, their studies, their sports, their suits at law, and their suits at court. They preferred the pleasures of the Globe to the pleasures of Brentford and Ware, and if they did not pass coldly by the ale-house door, at least they preserved enough pennies to pay the gatherers.'

Alfred Harbage, *As They Liked It* (London and New York: Macmillan, 1947), p. 3

Contents

Illustrations

Preface: an outline of approaches taken

This is a study of the early modern drama that was written and staged in England between 1576 and 1642. It is determinedly a study all about making connections. Focusing on the commercial theatre context which arose from the opening of a series of purpose-built playhouses in London from 1567 onwards, and the particular acting practices, companies and residences that they brought into being with them, it nevertheless connects that particular theatrical world with the wider performance cultures of the court, of noble households and estates, and of civic communities, including that of the burgeoning capital city of London itself. Presented in part through chapters organised by genre, the book is punctuated by a series of focused case studies on topics ranging from repertoire to performance style, from political event to the physical body of the actor, and from plays in print to the space of the playhouse. These case studies enable the reader to zoom in on particular moments, attitudes and aesthetic practices that contribute to the overall story of the remarkable body of drama that was produced at this time. The study as a whole, however, asks readers to think about drama not through individual playwrights or plays but through repertoires and company practices, placing those playwrights and their plays into a highly collaborative and competitive environment of cultural production.

Individual chapters are deliberately not organised chronologically, or by strict periodisation, although the relevance of terms like 'Elizabethan', 'Jacobean' and 'Caroline' when thinking about early modern drama will be explored in the Introduction. The swerve away from a neat linear history is performed in order to allow the rich lines of connection and synergy between those plays staged in the 1590s and those performed in the 1630s and 1640s to emerge in fresh and unrestricted ways. Historical context remains important, nevertheless, to the meanings being argued for and the activities being described. This context is accounted for both in terms of defining the broader aspects of the labels we might place on plays dating in composition and first performance from certain decades and identifying key aspects of certain reigns and moments – work done in the Introduction – and in explorations of specific cultural and political contexts in individual case studies. A supporting Chronology is provided at the back of this volume in order to assist readers in understanding and applying that historical context when looking at individual plays.

It is always worth knowing when a play is likely to have been composed and first performed since, as one specific case study will argue (K), there is often much to say about the cultural and political field from which a play emerges and to which it is inevitably seen to respond. For this reason, I have endeavoured to provide a likely date of composition (even though this is sometimes accompanied by a telltale question mark indicating a certain fluidity of view on this matter) on an initial mention of any specific play and this material is repeated in the Chronology. Equally though, thinking in terms of repertoire, as the connective approach of this study invariably does, challenges us to think about plays in an ongoing relationship with a company and indeed with audiences and we would do well to avoid the fetishisation of first performances in any account of a play. Where does the story of the performance history of a single play begin and end? When plays were revived at a much later date in a repertoire, sometimes years, even decades later, parts would be played and indeed reinterpreted by different actors. Sometimes the different print and manuscript versions of these plays are evidence in themselves of this accretive biography, of how a play changes over time. Plays are also likely to have moved even within a single week or month between venues and therefore to different contexts, with court commissions of performances of popular commercial theatre plays being standard practice, and a regular need for provincial touring on the part of companies like the Chamberlain's/King's Men when the public playhouses were closed during times of plague outbreaks and alternative sources of revenue had to be sought; the 'text' such as it was would in these cases undergo further shifts and changes in the process. And it was not always or necessarily only successful plays that got revised or adapted for future performances: some plays find their moment much later in their life cycle. A prime example, referred to in more detail in Chapters 4 and 7, is John Fletcher's *The Faithful Shepherdess*, which flopped in 1608 when first performed (probably by the Children of the Blackfriars) but was revived with huge success by the King's Men in the 1630s when Queen Henrietta Maria's neoplatonic-influenced court proved more receptive to pastoral tragicomedy as a form and influenced the repertoire of public theatre venues in a similar vein.

The print life of a play is another whole new way of being in the world that changes the ways in which a work might be categorised or understood, and could even impact its future fate within the repertoire. Certainly, if a play was a resounding popular success on a first performance, with good box office receipts to boot, it was likely to be revived quite swiftly. That is one way of describing or charting success and popularity, yet we also know of plays that were booed from the stage on their first performances (Ben Jonson's *The New Inn* in 1629 is an all too famous example)[1] but went on to enjoy a recuperative afterlife in print, appearing in private libraries and collections and feasibly even being performed in amateur household performances (for a fuller discussion of this particular phenomenon, see the Conclusion).

By thinking about plays in relationship to each other in repertoire in this way, then, we can also start to make better sense of the collaborative writing contexts of early modern theatre. Professional playwrights wrote somewhat to order; a businessman like Philip Henslowe, entrepreneur-manager of the Rose Theatre in Southwark, could make a case for the kind of work he wanted in a particular season from a Shakespeare or a Jonson. Furthermore, certain writers with specialism and expertise in specific aspects of playwriting and dramaturgy – plotting or comic scenes or spectacle for example – might be combined to write a single play in unison. William Shakespeare appears in this study, then, as part of the broader landscape of early modern theatrical creativity; importantly, not as a standout figure but as one working playwright among others, as someone responding to changes in fashion and styles of writing, to the possibilities and even restrictions of new playing spaces, and to what Rosalyn Knutson has called 'the politics of company commerce'.[2]

In explicating the rationale for the way in which material is selected and ordered here, I need to return to the important if knotty issue of genre. While the Introduction to this volume, and many of the chapters that follow, make the case for the understanding and indeed categorisation of early modern drama through an understanding of issues of space, place and time, the chapters themselves have been organised by genre. Tragedies, histories, comedies and the significant subgenres of pastoral and romance, revenge drama, city comedy and satirical comedy, as well as the hybrid tragicomedy, are significant ways of thinking about the plays that were produced for the early modern commercial theatre. As Jean E. Howard has indicated, 'genre was a key concept for organising textual production in the early modern period'; she continues with the point that 'genre indicated the implicit system that made one kind of text distinguishable from another in the relational field'.[3] Perhaps the easiest way to explain this is to think about a playgoer heading to the Rose Theatre in the 1590s or to the Blackfriars Theatre in the 1620s. Aware that they are going to see a 'tragedy' or indeed a 'tragicomedy', this thought is already shaping their approach to and expectation of the performance before they have even reached the theatre. Many plays openly acknowledged this kind of expectation, sometimes satisfying it: the opening Chorus to Shakespeare's *The Lamentable Tragedy of Romeo and Juliet* tells us after all that the 'star-crossed lovers take their life' (Prologue, 6). A play may equally opt to surprise those expectations; it may find its creative energy from twisting or subverting generic expectations and conventions or from bringing them into sometimes dissonant dialogue with conventions from a wholly different genre (revenge tragedy's fondness for macabre comedy is a case in point). The collaborative writing conditions already described and explored in more detail in Case study J fostered this opportunity for generic encounters as playwrights with skills in tragic and comic writing were brought into conversation with one another (for example, see the relationship between main plot and subplot in Thomas Middleton and William Rowley's *The Changeling* in 1622).

Janette Dillon notes that what we are dealing with most often when attempting to describe genre in the early modern period is 'overlap and blurring of boundaries' but she adds that 'Genre and expectation are mutually shaping.'[4] If we accept that, as Jean Howard puts it, genre was always 'provisional and productive' in the context of early modern theatre, we can nevertheless uncover much about developments, innovations and revisiting of genre and tradition as they were carried out by early modern playwrights in response to new conditions of playing and performance.[5] In chapters organised notionally by genre, that provisionality will be all too evident in the way that this volume as a whole constantly seeks to find overlaps and to blur boundaries in ways that deliberately threaten to undo its own categorisations. While individual case studies can be read for themselves alone, the volume as a whole undoubtedly benefits from being read in a linear fashion since the chapters, like the plays discussed, constantly refer back to each other and make connections. Genres do not respect borders and the reader is advised to enjoy a journey through texts and times that will quite deliberately loop back on itself.

Genre is, of course, just one particular way of organising the material that is presented here. The interspersed case studies are designed to offer a plethora of other ways of working and other ways of approaching these texts. Presenting in brief some of the cutting-edge scholarship of recent years, the thirteen case studies offer a panoply of approaches to apply not only to the texts analysed here but also to those for which there was sadly no space for detailed discussion. I fully expect, having made that bold statement, that individual readers and users might opt for a different route-map to the one I have set out, and may indeed choose different points of entry rather than simply following the chapters in order. On their own perambulation through the material they may well end up in different places to those I imagined. Like early modern playgoing, it may in the end just depend on the weather on the day: the opening case study is intended as an exercise in phenomenological study which suggests and stresses the value of the subjective as well as the objective in scholarship. As long as you enjoy and learn from the process of travelling through this book, it will be a job well done.

Acknowledgements

Thanks are due to: Lucy Munro, as always, for allowing me to see forthcoming work on pastoral drama prior to publication and for endlessly stimulating conversations on early modern drama as a whole; Richard Cave and Brian Woolland for permission to use images from the wonderful *Brome Online* workshops which shaped my thinking in so many ways about Caroline drama in performance; Clare Wright for her invaluable and endlessly gracious work on the picture sourcing and permissions and the Chronology for this volume at a ridiculously busy time in her own career; Sarah Stanton at Cambridge University Press for patiently nodding through a series of emails pleading for time and understanding; all my students, and especially Jemima Matthews for the endless inspiration and kindness; and the wider early modern team at Nottingham who continue to make me glad to be working in this field: Jem Bloomfield, Janette Dillon, Sarah Grandage, Brean Hammond, Mike Jones, Peter Kirwan, Mark Robson and Nicola Royan. I researched and wrote this book while being Head of the amazing School of English at Nottingham, so thank you to all of my colleagues (past and present) for putting up with the stress and strain of that ambition, but none more so than my irreplaceable School Manager, Mari Hughes, and my Director of Teaching, Jo Robinson. They have both taught me everything about good pedagogy, good working practices and good friendship.

And finally, as always, to John – for standing in the rain at the Globe that August Saturday and for being there through every kind of weather . . . *xiè xiè*.

Abbreviations and editions

All quotations from Brome, Jonson, Ford, Marlowe, Marston, Middleton and Shakespeare are from the following editions and are referenced by individual play title in the text.

Brome Online	*The Complete Works of Richard Brome Online* gen. ed. Richard Cave, www.hrionline.ac.uk/brome
CWBJ	*The Cambridge Works of Ben Jonson*, gen. eds. David Bevington, Martin Butler and Ian Donaldson, 7 vols. (Cambridge University Press, 2012)
Ford	John Ford, *'Tis Pity She's a Whore and Other Plays*, ed. Marion Lomax (Oxford University Press, 1995)
Marlowe	Christopher Marlowe, *Doctor Faustus and Other Plays*, ed. David Bevington and Eric Rasmussen (Oxford University Press, 1995)
Marston	*The Selected Plays of John Marston*, ed. MacDonald P. Jackson and Michael Neill (Cambridge University Press, 1986)
Oxford Middleton	*Thomas Middleton: The Collected Works*, gen. eds. Gary Taylor and John Lavagnino (Oxford University Press, 2010)
Oxford Shakespeare	*The Oxford Shakespeare: The Complete Works*, gen. eds. Stanley Wells and Gary Taylor (Oxford University Press, 1988)

The following individual editions of plays are used extensively. All other references to individual editions of plays are provided in notes to the main text.

The Cardinal	James Shirley, *The Cardinal*, ed. E. M. Yearling (Manchester University Press, 1986)

The Duchess of Malfi	John Webster, *The Duchess of Malfi*, ed. Leah S. Marcus (London: Arden Shakespeare, 2009)
Edward IV	Thomas Heywood, *The First and Second Parts of King Edward IV*, ed. Richard Rowland (Manchester University Press, 2005)
Galatea	John Lyly, *Galatea and Midas*, ed. George K. Hunter and David Bevington (Manchester University Press, 2000)
The Lady of Pleasure	James Shirley, *The Lady of Pleasure*, ed. Ronald Huebert (Manchester University Press, 1987)
A New Way to Pay Old Debts	Philip Massinger, *A New Way to Pay Old Debts*, ed. T. W. Craik (London: A & C Black/Norton, 1999)
Philaster	Francis Beaumont and John Fletcher, *Philaster*, ed. Suzanne Gossett (London: Arden Shakespeare, 2009)
The Shoemaker's Holiday	Thomas Dekker, *The Shoemaker's Holiday*, ed. R. L. Smallwood and Stanley Wells (Manchester University Press, 1979)
The Spanish Tragedy	Thomas Kyd, *The Spanish Tragedy*, ed. J. R. Mulryne (London: Arnold, 1989)
The White Devil	John Webster, *The White Devil*, ed. John Russell Brown (Manchester University Press, 1985)
The Witch of Edmonton	William Rowley, Thomas Dekker, John Ford &c, *The Witch of Edmonton*, in Peter Corbin and Douglas Sedge (eds.), *Three Jacobean Witchcraft Plays* (Manchester University Press, 1986)

Introduction: Brick, lime, sand, plaster over lath and 'new oaken boards': the early modern playhouse

Writing retrospectively in his three-volume *Itinerary* (1617) of what he had seen with his own eyes during extensive travels across Britain and Europe in the late sixteenth and early seventeenth centuries, Fynes Morison commented that: 'There be, in my opinion, more plays in London than in all parts of the world I have seen . . .'.[1] It is the task in part of this Introduction to explain why and how by 1617 this was the case. Why had London become the epicentre of an unparalleled theatre industry, with a raft of purpose-built playhouses, competing companies, and playwrights of the stature of William Shakespeare, Christopher Marlowe, Ben Jonson and Thomas Middleton vying for business from spectators and the publishing houses alike? What made this such an exciting moment of discovery and experimentation, one in which acting styles, the reach of dramatic language, notions of genre, ways of writing and working, and ideas about what might physically and intellectually be achieved on a stage, were stretched almost to breaking point?

From the outset, it must be made clear that the early modern professional theatre with which this study largely concerns itself did not appear fully formed from nowhere. There were much longer traditions and legacies of playing and performance on which early modern theatre was founded and to which it constantly referred and alluded. Janette Dillon has written that

> When audiences saw [the star actor Edward] Alleyn wear a false nose to play Barabas in *The Jew of Malta* (c. 1589–90), they were seeing a continuity with medieval devils; when Barabas fell into a cauldron of his own devising they were seeing a continuity with the medieval hellmouth; when the Porter in *Macbeth* (1605–6) came to open the stage-doors in response to the knocking on them, making a stream of jokes about being a 'devil-porter' opening the gates of Hell to sinners, they knew they were being asked to recall the harrowing of Hell plays from the mystery cycles; and when *Volpone* (1606) opened with an image of Volpone surrounded by heaps of gold, they recognised not only Marlowe's Barabas at the start of *The Jew of Malta*, but also the

numerous allegorical images of Goods, Money or Covetousness in early moral plays like *Everyman* (c. 1510–19?) or in later ones such as *All for Money* (c. 1572–7).[2]

These continuities were crucially important and form part of the much larger nexus of intertextuality that in part defined the operations and interactions of early modern theatre, an ongoing stage dialogue where plays and playwrights persistently quoted, and sometimes parodied, each other, where they recycled and remade ideas, both their own and others', and constantly riffed on other dramatic moments and experiments that had worked for paying audiences. This kind of connective thinking will shape much of the analysis and reflection that follows.

What also rendered the moment on which this study focuses different, and perhaps unique, were the places, the very stages, on which this kind of dialogue unfolded. The temporal parameters of this study stretch, seemingly very precisely, from 1576 to 1642. The year 1576 dates the opening of the Theatre in the Shoreditch region of London, often marked as the first purpose-built commercial playhouse in England, though in practice the Theatre built on the precedent of the Red Lion at Stepney which was the work of the same entrepreneurial mind, that of John Brayne the London grocer, and another playhouse at Newington Butts that had been operating in the decade prior to this. The Theatre was rapidly followed a year later by the Curtain, also in Shoreditch, and by the Rose Theatre and the Swan in Southwark in 1587 and 1595 respectively. Equally famous venues such as the Globe (1599, constructed on the Thames Bankside from the dismantled timbers of the Theatre when that playhouse's lease ran out) and the Fortune (1600) followed in due course and in 1614 the Hope Theatre was erected in the southern suburbs of the City on the site of former bear gardens. As purpose-built playhouses proliferated and formalised their operations, there emerged a series of competing theatre companies.

The year 1594 was another landmark date, this time in the history of company formations. Andrew Gurr has recounted in considerable detail the specific impacts and effects of the formal licensing of two companies by the Privy Council in that year.[3] One was under the patronage of the Lord Chamberlain himself, Henry Carey, first Baron Hunsdon, and was linked to the Theatre in the north, and the other under the aegis of another Privy Councillor, Charles Howard, the Lord Admiral (and Carey's son-in-law), at the Rose Theatre in the south on Bankside. Once again, these companies built on previous playing traditions, the practices and aesthetics of the children's companies emerging directly out of the work of the boy choristers who had performed the plays of John Lyly for courtly audiences at Greenwich and elsewhere during the reign of

Queen Elizabeth I, and those of the travelling players who toured the provinces performing in noble households and in inns for payment in the late sixteenth century, the Queen's Men chief among them.[4] It is no mere coincidence that Brayne's Theatre was located on the main road north out of London and that the Newington Butts operation in Surrey was on the main road south. This conscious positioning – the cartography of the professional playhouses as it were – recognised the intrinsic relationship between theatre in a fixed place and theatre in its more mobile touring and travelling identities (for a map of early seventeenth-century London marking the location of the major playhouses, see Figure 1).[5]

These historical legacies and connections are a crucial part of telling the story of what is special or different about the period 1576–1642. Start moments and endpoints will always have an element of the arbitrary about them; as the conclusion to this study will suggest, as well as continuing in a long tradition from medieval and early Tudor performances, early modern commercial theatre did not suddenly and abruptly end in 1642 when an official parliamentary declaration demanded the temporary closure of the public playhouses. The rationale for that closure was initially premised on the grounds of health and safety as tensions grew in the lead-up to what would become the English Civil War, though, of course, there were also underlying religious reasons as the City of London became increasingly fundamentalist in its exercise of the Protestant faith. But theatre did not simply stop because the Globe and its companion playhouses were shut down and eventually dismantled. As usual, deep theatre history reveals a far more incremental and piecemeal narrative of evolution and adaptation as drama found a voice in alternative modes and genres and in alternative modes of performance such as opera.[6] Nevertheless, to my mind, something special does seem to happen between the start and end dates attached to this study and this is directly linked to the construction of purpose-built playhouses and the concomitant professionalisation of the activities of acting, producing and indeed writing plays that followed from that. With so many people taking part in theatre in some way – as commissioners and businesspeople, as performers, as backstage 'hands' producing costumes, feather headpieces, music and props, as writers and adapters, as theatregoers – what emerged was a set of new and ever-growing competencies in this particular art form.[7]

So bricks and mortar do matter very much to this story. The title to this introductory chapter refers explicitly to the extant contract for the building of the Fortune Theatre in Cripplegate. Signed by Philip Henslowe, Edward Alleyn and Peter Street on 8 January 1600 (we will hear much more of Henslowe and Alleyn both in this chapter and in the discussions that follow; Street, a

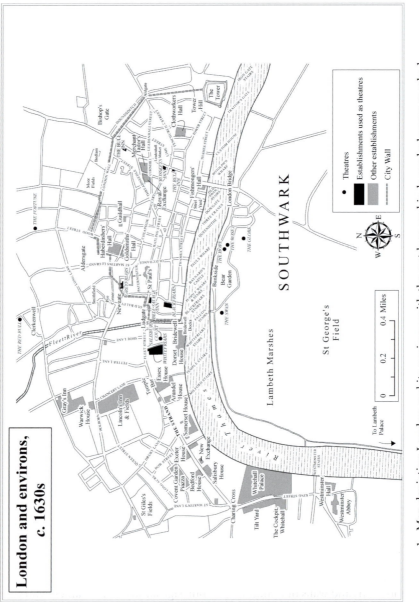

1. Map depicting London and its environs with the outdoor and indoor playhouses marked.

carpenter, was also involved in the building of the Globe from the material remains of the Theatre when that theatre's lease ran out, and reappears in the 1614 contract for the Hope Theatre), it set out the need for 'a good sewer and strong foundation of piles, brick, lime and sand' and a stage of 'good strong and sufficient new oaken boards'.[8] These materials contributed to the sense of permanency that attached to these buildings and which gave them a presence in the physical and cultural landscapes of the fast-growing city of London (the population grew from *c.* 15,000 in 1576 when the Theatre opened to *c.* 200,000 by 1642 when the Civil War led to the closure of the public playhouses).[9] In a very practical sense they contributed to the acoustics and sightlines of the performance spaces and therefore to the sounds heard and sights seen by early modern theatre audiences.[10]

Material conditions and the physical features of the stage matter a great deal, then, as do the social, economic and cultural conditions in which early modern theatre took place. As well as being a tale of artistic process and practice, it is telling how often the story of early modern theatre is also one of economics and entrepreneurship.[11] The life-story of Henslowe, best known to us now as the owner-manager of the Rose Theatre though also heavily involved as we have seen in the building of the Fortune, is a useful barometer in this respect. Described in the *Dictionary of National Biography* as a 'theatre financier', he was a freeman of the Dyers' Company and had several active investments in the pawnbroking industry and in starch-making. Henslowe was through and through a businessman; he would, alongside his Rose activities, keep his hand in several property ventures (inns and houses as well as theatres), and for a time he shared a licence as Master of the Bears that were baited in the nearby Paris Garden on Bankside with his star Rose actor Edward Alleyn (who married Henslowe's stepdaughter Joan in 1592).[12] He also left at his death a remarkable set of papers that constitutes accounts and inventories for the Rose and that has given us valuable insight into the quotidian operations of an early modern working theatre.[13]

There is a strong connecting line between the theatres, their owners and their actors, and the artisanal working world of London. Jonson and Middleton had strong links to the Tylers' and Brickmakers' Company and Jonson was a trained bricklayer, evidence of whose work may still rest somewhere in the foundations and walls of London;[14] the Burbage family, father James, who was one of the co-founders of the Theatre in 1576, and son Richard (the latter is, along with Alleyn, a major stage celebrity in this period), linked to the building of the Globe and the acquisition and refurbishment of the second Blackfriars Theatre, had a family background in joinery; Robert Armin, the Chamberlain's Men actor thought to have played parts like Touchstone in

Shakespeare's *As You Like It* (1600) and Feste in *Twelfth Night* (c. 1601), was a trained goldsmith (and this may explain Touchstone's name, which refers to the way in which gold was tested or 'assayed', and some of the play's more arcane dialogue); John Heminges, manager of the Lord Chamberlain's and later the King's Men, who was involved in the printing of the 1623 folio collection of Shakespeare's plays, had, like John Brayne of Theatre fame, a background in the Grocers' Company.[15] What this kind of detail reveals is how embedded in the everyday operational life of the city the theatre community was and this in turn underscores the value implicit in reading the plays produced by them against the daily life of the city, its practices, its customs, its concerns, its knowledges, its pleasures. The bricks and mortar that built the early modern commercial playhouses direct us back to this sense of a vibrant, working city in significant ways. But, of course, this is only in part a story about brick, lime, sand, plaster and oak. This is also crucially a study of what populated those spaces: companies, players' bodies, costumes, objects and props, music, food sellers, audience members, words, ideas... sometimes, as we shall see, even the weather (see Case study A). The story begins, then, with the outdoor theatres, often referred to as amphitheatres and mostly circular in shape (the Fortune and the Red Bull are exceptions to this rule). The repertoire of one particular open-air amphitheatre, the Rose Theatre, home to the Admiral's Men company, is explored in detail in Case study B. Roofless constructions, they could hold up to 2,000 audience members and performances took place in broad daylight and were open to the weather. The stages of these outdoor theatres were largely minimal; with two or three doors at the back enabling entry onto the stage, a gallery space above, and in some cases a trapdoor onto the main stage, what was mostly visible to the eye were the bare boards onto which actors, costumes and props would be transported to make meaning at any given time in the performance.

Henslowe's papers list all the props in the ownership of the Admiral's Men, including the following items:

> The Enventory tacken of all the properties for my Lord Admeralles men, the 10 of Marche 1598.
> Item, j rocke, j cage, j tombe, j Hell mought.
> Item, j tome of Guido, j tome of Dido, j bedstead.[16]

These are large-scale rather than handheld properties (though Henslowe's papers also evidence plenty of the latter in the Admiral's Men repository). We might imagine the cage being deployed in a performance of Marlowe's *Tamburlaine* or the bedstead in the first-act scenes in *Volpone* where the magnifico feigns his sickness in order to gull fellow Venetians of their wealth or from which he tries to rape Celia in 3.7. The 'Hell mought' is yet further evidence of those continuities with medieval moral drama that we were exploring a moment ago. Later in Henslowe's list we find: 'Item, j caudern for the Jewe' which is clearly the cauldron into which Barabas falls in Act 5 of *The Jew of Malta* and which has been read by scholars like Dillon in the earlier quotation as a direct throwback to medieval hell-mouth traditions. A later Case study (F) will use a single stage property, a skull, to explore the ways in which objects made meaning on the early modern stage. Henslowe's papers are also testimony to the importance of costumes in the company holdings, and the resonance of this is returned to at several points in the study, when looking at the work of the boy actor (see Case study H) and at the traffic of dramatic materials between public and courtly stages (see Conclusion).

What Henslowe's inventories and accounts help to unveil are the practical elements that make up theatre: props, but also fabrics, craft and the sheer labour that went into the making of these things. In this way we are encouraged to read artisanal as well as authorial presence in the collaborative making of commercial drama at this time. Equally important in the co-production of meaning in the theatre were spectators, and the architecture of the outdoor theatres seems expressly designed to capitalise on this fact. Audiences could see each other during a performance as much as they could observe the actors onstage. They were either seated in galleries or standing in the pit area directly in front and to the side of the stage as 'groundlings' and paid ticket entry prices accordingly. We can see a version of all these particular architectural and socio-spatial details in the much reproduced Johannes de Witt 1596 sketch of the Swan Theatre which depicts a single bench onstage around which and seated on which are two actors in conversation while a third appears to be carrying a halberd (a weapon that has an axe-head mounted on a long wooden shaft) and to be bending over in a gesture of deference which might suggest he is a messenger or visitor of some sort. There are few spectators visible in the de Witt drawing, which has led some to speculate that it is a sketch of a rehearsal, but contemporary accounts flesh out how the theatre might have looked during an actual performance, describing, for example, how food and drink sellers moved around the audience during performances.[17] We need to think what goes on *on* but also *around* a stage when making sense of a live event.

Later discussions of particular plays will consider the impact of the fluid stage space of the outdoor theatres on particular dramaturgic decisions and effects (Case study I), but Stephen Greenblatt captures something important about the exciting sense of sheer possibility it created in his account of the plays of Marlowe:

the scene changes so quickly at times that Marlowe seems to be battering against the boundaries of his own medium: at one moment the stage represents a vast space, then suddenly contracts to a bed, then turns in quick succession into an imperial camp, a burning town, a besieged fortress, a battlefield, a tent.[18]

The opening Chorus of Shakespeare's *Henry V* (1598–9) alludes to something similar when it demands of the audience:

> Think, when we talk of horses, that you see them,
> Printing their proud hoofs i'th' receiving earth;
> For 'tis your thoughts that now must deck our kings,
> Carry them here and there . . .
>
> (*Henry V*, Prologue, 26–9)

These brief examples are evidence enough of the importance of the commercial theatre audiences, who were invoked, spoken to, by means of soliloquies and asides, asked questions of, sometimes even co-opted as citizens and soldiers in scenes needing to provide a sense of critical mass (see a modern reconstruction of this in Figure 2). Active examples might be Mark Antony's funeral oration in 3.2 of *Julius Caesar* (1599), or Henry V's address to his men before the Battle of Agincourt in Shakespeare's eponymous history play (4.3.20–67); the direct address of clowns, fools and malcontents in everything from comedies to the darkest and most macabre of revenge tragedies; the witty and subversive servant Mosca's conspiratorial soliloquy at 3.1 of Jonson's *Volpone* or the cynical monologues of Barabas in Marlowe's *The Jew of Malta*. The list is potentially pages long but combining these particular moments of audience participation with conventional dramatic devices to mark the threshold into and out of plays, we gain a genuine sense of this as theatre interested in, indeed invested in, the art of frame-breaking. The love of 'plays within plays' and other forms of inset drama – for example, in *The Spanish Tragedy* (1585–6), *Hamlet* (1600–1), *The Taming of the Shrew* (1590–2), *Volpone*, *The Revenger's Tragedy* (1605–6), *The Roman Actor* (1626), *A Jovial Crew* (1641–2), to name just a few – is yet another example of early modern theatre's wish to heighten spectators' awareness of their own position as audience members, as part of the show.[19]

Having thought about the interior space and appearance of the outdoor theatres, it is equally important to register their urban spatial location in London and its adjoining suburbs and the contribution this made both to the experience of theatregoing and the reputation (for good or ill) of theatre as a commercial art form. The newly built commercial playhouses tended to cluster in certain locales: in the suburbs to the north and south of the City, and in

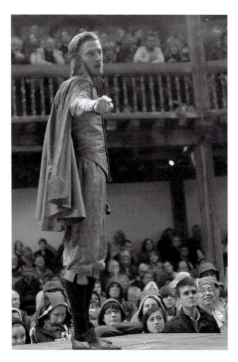

2. A moment of audience participation in a reconstructed outdoor theatre space.

the liberties that existed within the City walls. Liberties were demarcated areas outside of formal civic jurisdiction and so, like the suburbs, allowed for easier planning permissions and enabled the theatres greater freedoms of operation. As already noted, the Theatre and the Curtain were close to each other in the Shoreditch area to the north and then a series of subsequent theatres were built in Southwark in the south, where Paris Garden, known for its bear-baitings and nefarious happenings, and the Clink, with its prison, were both officially liberties. Henslowe would reside near the Clink all of his working life, evidencing the important point made by Dillon that 'Players gradually became an integral part of the parishes where playhouses were constructed.'[20] Arthur Kinney has also noted the convenience of the Thameside location of the Bankside theatres in particular, observing that the Globe was located outside the City walls at Southwark but was a good location, drawing as it did 'on the crowded suburbs and just upriver from the houses of nobility and the palace of Westminster and downriver from the royal palaces of Hampton Court, Greenwich and Richmond'.[21]

At the turn of the century, a new type of purpose-built theatre venue added to the diversity of venues when, firstly through the work of all-children companies, a number of so-called 'indoor theatres' were erected. These are sometimes referred to as 'private playhouses' by scholars; something of a misnomer since in reality they were open to the paying public. St Paul's and the first Blackfriars date from 1575 and 1576. These were across the water from the Bankside amphitheatres and often located in the City itself but were also initially sited in liberties. The Blackfriars precinct, site of former religious houses, is a prime example of this. Dillon notes that the two indoor theatres that emerged on that site (the first Blackfriars in 1576 and the second in 1600, following initial thwarted attempts to open a playhouse there by James Burbage in 1596 when he realised that the Theatre as a playing locale was under threat) converted different parts of the site including the buttery and the dining hall.[22] Burbage had become interested in this location as an alternative to the Bankside theatres since it offered the opportunity for indoor winter performances but he was initially thwarted by opposition from the neighbourhood. This was a wealthy district that was distinctly unsettled by the idea of what a playhouse might do to the tone of the area and organised an oppositional petition accordingly which was submitted to the Privy Council in November 1596 and which spoke of the 'generall inconvenience' a local theatre would represent.[23] Ironically it was the more elite atmosphere of the environs of the Blackfriars precinct that had made this an attractive business proposition to Burbage since it promised a more upmarket and higher fee-paying audience than the open-air amphitheatres in the south. His adult company (by then under the name of the King's Men following the accession of James VI and I in 1603) would eventually take up residency there in 1608 but not before the enterprise threatened to break the Burbages financially. What saved him was the decision in 1597 to dismantle the Theatre wholesale when its lease expired and reconstruct it as a playing space in Southwark close to the Rose Theatre and which he called the Globe.

By the first decade of the seventeenth century, there was also the Whitefriars, where in its opening year 1609 Jonson's *Epicene* was played. Then there followed those indoor theatres that were built and developed their reputation and repertoire towards the end of our focus period, largely during the reign of King Charles I, such as the Phoenix (*c.* 1616, also known as the Cockpit) and the Salisbury Court (1629).The indoor venues were smaller, more intimate, covered and therefore candlelit. They had access to a permanent troupe of musicians, which also impacted on the inclusion of instrumentation and song in plays after 1608 when the Blackfriars began to be the second permanent home of the King's Men.[24] Much useful research has now been done into the ways in which the use of interior illumination (and some of the practical needs created by this, such as the trimming of candles, which necessitated formal act breaks) had a visceral and practical effect on the plays that were staged here.[25] We will return to some particularly vivid examples of what the indoor theatre spaces made possible in the discussion of revenge drama in Chapter 2 and in Case study E on the second Blackfriars indoor playhouse.

One of the best ways to think about how the different theatre venues and the different make-up of the companies that played there affected the writing and the staging of drama is to think in terms of repertoire. Rosalyn Lander Knutson has done much to alter our way of thinking about early modern drama to seeing it as company-led rather than dominated by individual playwrights like a Shakespeare or a Jonson.[26] Companies built up reputations for certain kinds of plays and their repertoires might reflect this. They also became popular because of particular star players like Alleyn or Burbage (explored in more detail in Chapter 1) and this too would influence both what plays were revived in the repertoire and the terms on which new plays were commissioned. We know that some plays were added to or altered to respond to what had worked or not worked with early audiences. Marlowe's *Doctor Faustus* (1588?), Kyd's *The Spanish Tragedy* and Marston's *The Malcontent* (1604) are just a few well-known examples of where there is recorded evidence of other dramatists than the attributed authors being paid to make additions. In the case of *The Spanish Tragedy* and *The Malcontent* it may even be the hands of Jonson and Webster that we are seeing at work in the adaptations. This is yet further evidence of the largely collaborative context in which early modern drama was produced but also written and a point to which I will return both in this Introduction and in Case study J.

Henslowe's papers are once again a wonderful resource when thinking about repertoire and this ongoing creative approach to playtexts which were in the main held in the company's ownership, as opposed to that of individual playwrights. Audiences might well have understood plays in part through the lens and experience of other plays they had seen in the same season, and possibly understood actors' performances by thinking about them in similar roles. In August and September 1595, for example, we can see playing alongside each other Marlowe's 'docter fostes' and 'tamberlen' (*Doctor Faustus* and *Tamburlaine the Great*) but also plays now lost to us, including 'cracke me this nutte'.[27] In November 1595, we have 'hary the v' (presumably a companion play to Shakespeare's *Henry V*) but 'cracke me this nutte' is obviously still doing well and being given additional performances. These accounts suggest a generic blend of tragedy, history and comedy in the programming for the Rose, whereas, as Case study L will consider, for other companies such as the all-children troupes a reputation for certain kinds of genre may well have weighted their programmes rather differently. Henslowe, of course, lists plays alongside the ticket receipts they had taken and we should not underestimate the extent to which brute economics fed the repertoire: if something worked it was likely to work again. Actors who were successful in certain types of role could expect to be typecast in future productions. Carol Rutter suggests that, in a theatre where there was a need to stage a play almost every day of the week in the summer months, some decisions about what to put in the programme might have been taken on the day of the performance itself.[28] Whatever the exact truth, actors certainly had to perform an impressive feat of memorisation, holding several parts simultaneously in their memories.[29] Andrew Gurr also makes the point that audience members became as potentially familiar as those performing onstage, suggesting that when the actor playing Prince Hal in *Henry IV, Part 1* (1596–7) looked out at the audience and spoke the first line of his Act 1 soliloquy, 'I know you all' (1.2.192), it could have had a resonance both within and without the stage world of the history play in which it was delivered.[30] One way of organising an account of early modern commercial theatre could then concentrate on a linear history that stretched from the building of the first playhouses to their closure with the advent of civil war in 1642. In the months following, the Globe would be dismantled by Oliver Cromwell's men in a reverse of the entrepreneurial spirit James Burbage had shown in 1597 when building the theatre in its first incarnation (the Globe famously burned down in 1613 following a misfiring of cannon in a production of Shakespeare and Fletcher's collaborative history play, *Henry VIII, or All is True*, 1613). That story does appear in these pages but there is also a desire to read across neatly defined chronologies in thinking about how theatre practice and playwriting developed during this time; how works came into and out of the repertoire and had different moments of meaning at different times. Nevertheless, there remains a virtue in thinking about the labels that often attach to plays from certain decades with reference to the particular monarch on the throne at the time and the particular attitudes and tastes that were associated with their reigns.

Elizabeth I acceded to the English throne in 1558 and she had already been on the throne some considerable time when the playhouse history we are interested in here came to the fore. For that reason, perhaps, the age into which commercial London theatre so resolutely inserted itself was strongly stamped as 'Elizabethan'. Elizabeth was a masterful deployer of public relations; the iconography of her court and her reign as the so-called 'Virgin Queen', as she wished it to be understood, was carefully promulgated through portraiture and public performance in the shape of royal ceremonial, accession day tilts, country progresses and the like.[31] We might go so far as to say that it was a highly theatrical age. The commercial theatre could not but help to pick up on and benefit from this self-conscious aesthetic at large in the wider political culture, even though it was expressly forbidden from representing the Queen herself on the stage. The Elizabethan era has become associated with a time of global expansion – an age of discovery and colonisation (the first English colony in Virginia dates from 1585) and of trade that also found its way not only onto the wharves of London's Thameside spaces in the form of the goods and people that entered the capital from ships anchored there but into the plays on the commercial stages.[32] Within ten years of the Theatre opening, Elizabeth's great triumph in quashing the Spanish Armada, with the help of her navy and the charismatic figure of Sir Francis Drake, had taken place and the strong sense of nationalism and national identity that followed in its wake has been traced in the repertoire of theatres like the Rose where the history play became the predominant genre by the 1590s.[33]

Elizabeth died in 1603 and James VI of Scotland, son of the ill-fated Mary Queen of Scots whom Elizabeth had executed in 1587, travelled down from his court in Edinburgh along with a considerable entourage of Scottish courtiers, to become James I of England. A change of tone necessarily accompanied the accession of a new monarch, not least a Scottish monarch but also one who brought with him a very visible royal family: his Danish wife Anna (who would herself prove to be a not inconsiderable patron of theatrical performances)[34] and their children, Princes Henry and Charles and the Princess Elizabeth. The theatres and the playwrights can be seen jockeying for position in the new regime. Several plays in the early years of the reign seem to debate ideas of good government as if almost presenting the new king with a manifesto; Jonson's Roman tragedy *Sejanus, His Fall* (1603), Shakespeare's *Measure for Measure* (1603–4) and Marston's *The Malcontent* (1604) can all be seen through this particular signifying lens. The particular crisis of the so-called Gunpowder Plot conspiracy to blow up the Houses of Parliament in 1605 added to a febrile atmosphere of religious expectation and suspicion that the commercial theatres could not possibly resist as subject matter for their stages (see Case study K for a more detailed analysis of this particular phenomenon and moment), as did the unexpected death of Henry, the heir to the throne, in 1612.[35] Plays inevitably capture something of the times in which they are written and there is considerable value in reading plays against the times in which they were conceived or, indeed, in which they are revisited and remade. Rather than create overly deterministic understandings of what it was to be an 'Elizabethan', a 'Jacobean' or indeed a 'Caroline' play, then, I am interested in the different dynamics of those reigns as they emerged from time to time, at particular moments and from year to year. A Jacobean play in 1604, full of the anxieties but also the expectations of a new reign, is a very different beast to one written and performed in 1624 when the successor to James was being closely watched and when the particular personalities and interests of James himself had become far better known to the general public.[36] Nevertheless, the arrival of a little Scotland into London in 1603 is a phenomenon in itself worth thinking about in relation to the stage. Andrew Gurr has quite rightly asked us to think about how plays might have sounded on the commercial stages right down to the dominant accent that would have been deployed by performers. Citing contemporary observations on the preference for southern pronunciations in works such as George Puttenham's *The Art of English Poesy*, he suggests that we 'must assume that the [companies] normally used speech-forms that came close to Puttenham's prescription of upper-class London speech' but he does also note the number of plays requiring knowledge and mastery of a northern dialect that appear post-1603, including *Macbeth* (1605–6) and several controversial plays such as *The Isle of Gulls* (1606).[37] Exposure to provincial dialects would have been common for actors used to travelling with performances to the regions of England and we should also remember that London itself would have been a veritable melting pot of languages and pronunciations, but there is something in this that captures the ways in which even at the level of speech patterns London plays did respond to changes in the monarchy and in the identity of the court located at nearby Whitehall Palace.

In 1625 the personality of the court changed again with the accession of Charles I and his new wife, the French Queen consort, Henrietta Maria. Both were strongly interested in the arts, as purchasers and patrons but also as practitioners. Charles had danced in court masques and Henrietta brought to the English court a strong French court tradition of ballets and spoken performances by women that challenged the all-male atmosphere of the London commercial theatres. Several critics and commentators have seen this step-change as having a profound effect on the plays that were staged not only at the court (at Whitehall and at satellite palaces such as Somerset House and Greenwich) but also at the commercial theatres, and several of the Caroline plays discussed in this volume will be seen to be picking up on theatrical innovations at court in their new response to issues such as female agency and the depiction of marriage and sexual relations.[38] One way of understanding this increased register of the court's influence on the commercial theatre is to see the form becoming increasingly elite in this period, with the geographical focus moving away from the so-called citizen theatres in the north or on Bankside to the indoor theatres in the City itself: the Blackfriars, of course, but also the Salisbury Court and the Phoenix. Change is, though, effected by a complex combination of factors; different playwrights and their interests rise to the fore in this period, with John Fletcher's pioneering of tragicomic form having a particularly profound effect. Nevertheless the work of Richard Brome, James Shirley and others remains deeply conscious of the plays that were in repertory in previous decades and when we remember that the Caroline theatre not only commissioned new plays but was able to draw on a deep body of existent drama we can begin to see that neat periodisation, while informative to a point, also needs to take account of overlap and the distinctly porous boundaries of commercial theatre programming.

The year 1642 was, however, an end-stop in some obvious respects, with the theatres prohibited from performance. Just seven years later the King himself would be executed on a purpose-built scaffold outside the Banqueting House where some of his most elaborate court masques, collaborations between architect-designer Inigo Jones and sometimes commercial playwright Jonson, had been performed. Theatre does not end there, of course, but there is a necessary hiatus in the kind of dynamic commercial theatre of the previous decades with which this study concerns itself.

Civil war is, however, a highly exceptional event in any country's history and it is perhaps necessary for the purposes of this study, which is interested in the quotidian practices of commercial theatre as they played themselves out on the wooden boards of the Rose and the Globe, the Fortune and the Hope, the Blackfriars and the Salisbury Court, to return us back for now safely to the everyday streets and neighbourhoods of London in our focus period. It is the aim and objective of this study in some respects to imagine ourselves in those self-same streets, to perform a kind of historical ethnography and to think about what it would have been like to be an early modern playgoer. London was, as Darryll Grantley has recently noted, highly 'walkable', and in the case of the Bankside for those approaching from the City or the Blackfriars for Southwark residents, easily accessible either by London Bridge or by the boats of the watermen who cried for business at the water's edge.[39] We will witness at various points in the study the competitive as well as collaborative environment in which early modern playwrights and performers worked. Considerable critical energy has been spent on the particularly heated exchanges of the so-called 'War of the Theatres' when playwrights openly quarrelled with each other through their plays.[40] That sense of a competitive environment can be usefully extended to the experience of spectators too; on a single day, plays of various genres, new and old, would have been showing simultaneously at different venues. Audiences had choices – they might be drawn by a particular player's skills in certain parts, by the reputation of a certain playwright, by a taste for a particular genre, by a wish to see something novel or new. The peripatetic experience of London on a given day when the playhouses were in business would have been a series of signs competing for attention: flyers posted by companies and publishers alike on posts around the city, actors and musicians passing through advertising their wares and announcing the play for that afternoon, gossipy word of mouth exchanges on what had been seen recently and what might be worth seeing: choices.[41]

We know that they did go in their droves to see these plays – our evidence comes not only from extant documentary traces such as Henslowe's receipts but from the vocal opposition of contemporaries who were unseated by the popularity of the new commercial theatre and the implicit threat it posed. Philip Stubbes was an Anglican pamphleteer in the 1570s and 1580s, who disliked the competition that the newly operational commercial theatres posed to the church: he warned, 'you shall have them flock thither, thick and threefold, when the church of God shall be bare and empty'.[42] Ironically his anti-theatrical tract now becomes a way for us to measure the pleasure and popularity for large numbers of people of the early modern theatres. A sense of pleasure, a sense of genuine excitement, about this relatively new phenomenon is what can also be registered in the remarkable quotation from Alfred Harbage which forms the epigraph to this volume:

> They came in wherries, on horseback and on foot, from Cheapside and White Chapel, Westminster and Newington, Clerkenwell and Shoreditch, deserting for an interval their workbenches, their accounts, their studies, their sports, their suits at law, and their suits at court. They preferred the pleasures of the Globe to the pleasures of Brentford and Ware, and if they did not pass coldly by the ale-house door, at least they preserved enough pennies to pay the gatherers.[43]

This is from one angle a rather fanciful reconstruction of events but from another it captures something of just what it might have been like to attend a play at the Rose Theatre one sunny afternoon in June 1595. Brian Walsh observes: 'stage plays take place under the pressure of time before a live audience. This creates an emphasis on the *eventness* of the performance.'[44] Categorisation of generic convention as outlined in the Preface, and the telling of as accurate as possible a history of the evolution and development of early modern theatre as gestured at in this Introduction, are also important aims and objectives in this study but a sense of *eventness* perhaps matters most. What I hope comes across in what follows is an overriding sense of a live art form finding its feet, finding its voice, and reaching a veritable peak of achievement in a relatively short time period; a live art form and a series of events that produced huge excitement and huge pleasure in those who chose to pay their money and enter in.

Richard III at the Globe

London has been almost uncomfortably hot and humid this Saturday morning. The market at Spitalfields was buzzing with activity and there had been just enough time to grab a bite to eat within the sound of the Shoreditch church bells before making her way south across the river, over London Bridge and towards the theatre for an afternoon performance. Shoreditch has, of course, its own important theatre culture but today she is headed for Bankside. The riverside views are, as usual, of a busy river, thronged with people and activity, and as she walks the sun still shines, but the lowering clouds on the skyline behind St Paul's seem ominous harbingers of a change in the weather.

As the performance beginning is sounded, the spectators, with the usual happy crush of bodies, chat and expectation, their food and drink in hand, press their way into the theatre yard. The musicians in the gallery sound their horns as the first drops of rain begin to fall...

Richard of Gloucester is, naturally enough, first onto the stage (for this is a production of William Shakespeare's *Richard III*) and his gripping, challenging delivery of the play's opening soliloquy, sometimes almost knowingly offhand, playing with the edges of the genres with which this play abuts – tragedy, history, comedy – is enough to get the focus of those gathered slightly distractedly in the rain this Saturday afternoon. This is a star actor in the role and many people in the crowd have presumably come to see him as much as the play; for others, it is perhaps the star turn of that opening soliloquy that they have been thinking about beforehand, gearing up to, building their expectations of. Already some of the particular metaphors and tropes of that opening speech are taking on some very local and particular resonances this afternoon as the rain beats ever more steadily down on the groundlings: 'Now is the winter of our discontent / Made glorious summer by this son of York; / And all the clouds that loured upon our house...' and so on (*Richard III*, 1.1.1–3). Those in the galleries take some pleasure in knowing they are at least somewhat protected from the elements.

It is an afternoon when she finds herself deeply conscious, at a sensory as much as at an intellectual level, of the place in which she stands – as characters on the stage allude to gruesome deaths in the Tower of London, it is impossible to forget the proximity of that building complex just downriver. The Duke of Clarence dreams that he has escaped his incarceration in that same tower: 'Methoughts that I had broken from the Tower, / And was embarked to cross to Burgundy . . . ' only to drown on the high seas (1.4.9–10); when he describes his dream of drowning – 'What dreadful noise of waters in my ears' (1.4.22) – just as the afternoon storm gathers pace there is a double recognition of these lines on the part of the now soaked audience (an observation the actor playing Clarence knowingly shares, offering out towards the crowd a palpable sympathy for those watching, already almost wet to the skin).

And then the thunder and the lightning decide to join in. This provides a difficult backdrop over which the actors find themselves frequently shouting to be heard (sore throats may well be the physical reminder of that particular afternoon's playing) but it also adds something fresh, new, specific, and particular to this performance of *Richard III* this August afternoon. This play of prodigious events and cursing, of appeals to the elements to take political and moral sides in the civil wars wracking the stage communities apart, is somehow transformed, altered, enhanced by the uncontrollable and yet sometimes seemingly perfectly timed cracks of lightning that light up the thatched roof of the Globe Theatre in Southwark or the terrifying cracks of thunder that follow only seconds after and often as Richard makes his most shocking pronouncements. As the yard floor floods with the sheer weight of rain that has fallen, and spectators try to retain concentration despite their ever cooling and stiffening muscles, the actors seem to sense a portent in the weatherscape. Eyes cast heavenwards, lines frequently paused by cracks of thunder, they find a special meaning in the afternoon; Richard III seems to speak a certain truth to us before the Battle of Bosworth when he observes: 'The sun will not be seen today. / The sky doth frown and lour upon our army . . . Not shine today –' (5.6.12–15). He comforts himself with the thought that the weather is just as dismal for his enemy in the field, the Duke of Richmond: 'why, what is that to me / More than to Richmond? For the selfsame heaven / That frowns on me looks sadly upon him' (5.6.15–17) but, in fact, in perhaps the most remarkable moment of all that rain-plashed afternoon, when Richmond wins the day, Richard is defeated and the new King Henry VII steps forward to address the crowd, the rain suddenly stops and sunlight glints around the Globe's columns and decorations. The actor speaking these lines of Tudor propaganda is almost rocked back on his heels by the potency of the moment, by being in the moment in this way: 'We will unite the white rose and the red. / Smile, heaven, upon this fair conjunction . . . Enrich the time to come with smooth-faced peace, / With smiling plenty, and fair, prosperous days' (5.8.19–20, 33–4).

The particulars of any afternoon's playgoing affect the way in which we as spectators make meaning. Where we come from, the mood we are in, the company we keep, what we do en route, what we pass by on the way into the theatre, whether we travel on foot, by bridge or boat, whether we watch sitting or standing, our knowledge or expectation of play, genre or, indeed, company or specific 'star' performer. A performance such as this in which all the women's parts are played by male actors will make meaning in particular ways; the doubling of actors in certain roles (here for example the Duchess of York is also the Duke of Richmond and that asks us as spectators to make particular kinds of connection back to the earlier curses and prophecies of the play) and the resonances of those aforementioned spatial proximities and the frisson they give to certain lines as characters head down the Thames to the Tower towards their certain death . . .

But in this instance the afternoon was made as much by the weatherscape in dialogue with the play in performance as anything else; a one-off event not to be repeated as the actors themselves increasingly recognised and made play of that stormy afternoon.

Everything I have described here could have happened in the 1590s when *The Tragedy of Richard III* was performed, as we believe it to have been, outside London or *c.* 1600 at the Globe Theatre on Bankside with star actor Richard Burbage in the title role. The cultural geography of Shoreditch was resonant then as the place where commercial theatre had begun, with the opening of the Theatre and the Curtain in the 1570s, but the centre of gravity in performance terms was by then shifting south of the river as companies like the King's Men dominated the stages at the Globe, the Rose and the Swan, performing in plays by the emergent playwrights of the day – Ben Jonson, Thomas Kyd, Christopher Marlowe, John Marston and William Shakespeare. There would be other transitions over the next few decades as the phenomenon of the children's companies flared and burned itself out and as the indoor playhouses of the city emerged with full force: the Blackfriars, the Whitefriars and eventually the Phoenix and Salisbury Court. Other writers would join the collaborative writing circles of London's burgeoning theatrical scene – John Webster, Thomas Middleton, Philip Massinger and Richard Brome among them. Other kinds of theatre would inform and interact with the commercial theatre scene – the plays read, staged and sometimes written in regional households, the civic pageantry and the court

3. Performing monarchy and performing gender in a Shakespeare's Globe 'original practices' production of an Elizabethan History play.

masques that many of the playwrights I have named were also engaged in the writing of – and a remarkable fifty years would ensue until the particular punctuation point of the closure of the commercial theatres by Oliver Cromwell's Puritan government in the 1640s. But that is a story that will have to unfold in its own time across the pages of this study. I have offered here a first person account; in fact, not some imagined 'reconstructed' experience of early modern theatregoing but a very real, documentable experience of my own in the late summer of 2012. The star actor then was not Richard Burbage but Mark Rylance in a production that was part of a summer-long celebration of Shakespeare, itself part of London's Cultural Olympiad programme of events surrounding the hosting of the Olympic and Paralympic Games that year (see Figure 3, which depicts Rylance as Richard of Gloucester with singer-actor Johnny Flynn as Lady Anne). There are stories enough to tell about the making of meaning on the Bankside that year, that summer, that day; but for me it is the physical act of the journey from the resonant site of Shoreditch in whose church Burbage and several other Elizabethan actors are buried or commemorated to the reconstructed Shakespeare's Globe (by the very modern means of transport that are the so-called 'Boris Bikes', the free bike scheme of London named after the then

Mayor of London Boris Johnson) and the rain that make my highly particularised and personalised experiences of theatre and of *Richard III* that wet, wet afternoon.

This study seeks in turn to capture the historical circumstances and contingencies of early modern theatre, to consider the differences and strangenesses in comparison to our own time and practices and yet simultaneously to argue for the potential of these plays and their lines to speak to us across time in remarkable ways through the reactivations and reanimations that lie at the heart of the theatrical genre and experience. It is my fervent hope that in reading the accounts, arguments and case studies collected here you will be inspired to want to make this history for yourself, through study, interrogation and through the seeing and doing of theatre.

An outdoor theatre repertoire: the Rose on Bankside

Because of the survival of the Rose Theatre manager Philip Henslowe's accounts and inventories, better known as Henslowe's *Diary*, we can gain a wonderful insight into a working theatre in the early modern period and in particular into one outdoor amphitheatre playhouse's repertoire in the last decade of the sixteenth century.[1] The plays that were staged at this time both belonged to and accorded a particular playing identity to the Admiral's Company and they were inevitably strongly influenced by the skill and reputation of their chief actor, Edward Alleyn.[2]

The level of productivity on the part of the Admiral's Company during their residency at both the Rose and subsequently the Fortune Theatres was quite remarkable. Between 1594 and 1597 alone, Andrew Gurr has calculated that they staged eighty-three plays at the Rose, fifty-four of them marked as being 'ne' or new by Henslowe in his *Diary*. In practice this meant that the actors were learning a fresh play every fortnight and that as many as six plays were in repertory in a single week at any given time.[3]

The Rose staged shows on six afternoons every week. What this kind of constant creativity suggests is that audiences would have over time grown very familiar with a particular body of actors, and that in due course the repertoire could begin to exploit this fact, not only through the repetition and restaging of popular plays but through the remaking of popular characters in the context of other plays with ostensibly different plotlines and through the active commissioning of sequels, as well as a rich pattern of knowing allusions and cross-references. In this way the company made a positive virtue out of its practical limitations – a small group of actors appearing on the same fixed stage day after day to spectators who saw as many as twenty plays in a single year.[4]

The Rose Theatre, built on the site of a former rose garden, close to the Thames in the Bankside region of Southwark, clearly enjoyed a highly inventive repertory and pioneered a number of genres, subgenres and theatrical practices that would dominate the early modern stage for some years after.[5] Admiral's Company plays made the most of what an open-air theatre made possible; many of these texts not only include strong visual and aural effects and spectacle presumably intended to grab the attention of large and often noisy crowds and to be heard over the competing noises of the weather and the nearby city, but capitalise on the presence of the groundlings standing in the pit area, close to the stage, by enabling regular opportunities for actors to engage directly with spectators through asides and soliloquy (see Figure 2). Alleyn, in virtuoso roles like Faustus and Barabas, appears to have been a particular master of this art of conversation with audiences.

Andrew Gurr has suggested that the audience familiarity with players like Alleyn also led to a proliferation of quick-change disguise plotlines and self-consciously metatheatrical plays in the programme. 'Star' parts like that of Barabas in *The Jew of Malta* would be knowingly reworked in other plays, even at the level of costume. The tropes and conventions of what came to be known as revenge drama (see fuller discussion in Chapter 2) were worked out at the Rose in regular performances of Thomas Kyd's *The Spanish Tragedy* (1585–6), referred to in Henslowe's papers as 'Jeronimo'. Bloody spectacle and the particular triumph of the use of the play-within-a-play motif in the final act of *The Spanish Tragedy* rippled out in their influence and impact across other plays in the genre: 'The archetypal revenge tragedy, imitated in *Hamlet, Antonio's Revenge, The Revenger's Tragedy* and other plays that often supplied explicit visual reminders of the Admiral's original, its finale was the model catastrophe lodging in every London spectator's mind.'[6] Spectacle was definitely a keynote of the Admiral's Company style, from the devils and explosions of Marlowe's *Doctor Faustus* to the extravagant onstage deaths in Kyd's revenge drama and George Peele's *The Battle of Alcazar*, which was first performed at the Rose in the early 1590s.[7] Other plays of this ilk also found their place in the repertoire, including Shakespeare's *Titus Andronicus* (c. 1593), probably co-authored with Peele.

Tragedy was not the only speciality of the Rose repertoire though, despite the strong presence of Marlowe in their programming. 'Humours' comedy, which focused on character traits linked to contemporary medical theory about bodily humours and disposition, and which would become closely associated with playwrights such as Ben Jonson, had an early outing on the Rose stage in the shape of George Chapman's comedy *An Humorous Day's Mirth* (1597). The playhouse also commissioned an early experiment with city comedy (a form explored in more detail in Chapter 5) with William Haughton's *Englishmen for My Money, or A Woman Will Have Her Will* (1598), whose action takes place entirely within the contemporary city of London. *Englishmen for My Money* included as part of its action some wonderful comic business with the stage posts that were a feature of the physical architecture of open-air amphitheatres. In scene 7, characters groping around in ostensible darkness bump their head against the posts only to be told they are in completely different parts of the capital, creating a wonderfully vivid sense of the disorientating effects of the city on newcomers to its streets and alleyways.[8]

Many of the 'ne' plays in the Admiral's Company repertoire were written specifically for the Rose in the decade of the 1590s and therefore, like Haughton's *Englishmen for My Money*, might be expected to make capital from the particular quirks of the playing space of the theatre itself as well as the tastes and particular behaviours of its audiences. Similarly, plays already circulating seem to map onto the repertoire's interest in spectacle and contemporary realism.

Other significant plays in the Rose repertoire include Thomas Dekker's *The Shoemaker's Holiday* (1599) which pioneered a certain kind of English and London-based chronicle history to complement the emergent form of city comedy and more formal history plays, including a now lost 'Harry V' play seemingly intended to complement and counterpoint Shakespeare's play *Henry V*, written for the rival company of outdoor theatre players at the Globe, and indeed *Sir John Oldcastle* which directly rivalled Shakespeare's two parts of *Henry IV*. There are many other tantalising titles for plays that are now apparently lost: what gems might have been contained in *The Tinker of Totnes* (1596), *The Witch of Islington* (1596), *The Cobbler of Queenhithe* (1597) or *Crack Me This Nutt* (1595)? The first three titles indicate an interest in plays of place, which the concerns of Haughton's *Englishmen for My Money* and *The Shoemaker's Holiday* would seem to confirm.

Fashions come and fashions go in the commercial theatre and in later decades Ben Jonson would openly mock the old-fashioned repertory associated with the Rose and the Fortune and its company of players. But Jonson also wrote humours plays himself (*Every Man In His Humour* and *Every Man Out of His Humour*, 1598 and 1599), and city comedies which themselves allude to and knowingly rework not only costumes but lines from *The Spanish Tragedy* (*The Alchemist*, 1610). The opening scene of his satirical comedy *Volpone* (1605–6) self-consciously reworks that of Marlowe's *The Jew of Malta* (see Case study C) and Alleyn's famous performance as Barabas in ways that suggest the Rose repertoire had influence far beyond the edges of its own stage.

Chapter 1

Tragedy

As the bells toll midnight, an ambitious scholar struggles with his impending demise, fearing he may be torn limb from limb by hellish devils; a young prince stands in a working graveyard, a skull in his hand, and ruminates on mortality and the levelling effects of death; a Jewish merchant falls into his own trap, a burning cauldron intended to catch his enemies, thereby becoming the engine of his end; two young lovers lie dead in a tomb, having committed suicide in a fateful pact, testimony to the bitter enmity of their feuding families; a mother-in-law plays a strategic game of chess while her daughter-in-law is knowingly prostituted to the Duke of Florence in an upstairs gallery; a beautiful young widowed Duchess watches a dance of madmen in a prison, a grotesque piece of theatre that prefigures her violent murder; a Moorish general stabs himself to death before Venetian senators in Cyprus having smothered his beautiful young wife in the marital bed; a brother who has committed incest with his sister brings in her heart on a sword as a grim finale to an exotic banquet; an old man accompanied by his Fool and exposed to the elements following the savage rejection of his own family howls in madness as a fierce storm rages . . . all of these 'moments' and more contribute to the making of what we now understand as the remarkable portfolio of early modern tragedy. Their very difference as moments and their startling innovations can tell us much about the richness and sheer inventiveness of the form on the early commercial stages. What my brief descriptions here also indicate is the extent to which these deeply affecting and effective stage 'moments' depend on the creation of meaningful stage pictures, icons by which spectators and characters alike make sense of the tragic events unfolding before them.[1]

These moments begin to tell us how dependent tragic drama is on powerful central protagonists. Another way of telling this story might have been to offer a litany of the titles these plays were afforded both in performance and in print and which would therefore have announced their core content to prospective spectators and readers (see example title pages in Figures 4, 5 and 7): *The Tragicall History of the Life and Death of Doctor Faustus*; *The Tragedy of Hamlet, Prince of Denmark*; *The Jew of Malta*; *The Most Excellent and Lamentable*

4. Devil arising from a trapdoor in the woodcut image that
accompanied published versions of Marlowe's *Doctor Faustus*: visual
evidence of a performance tradition?

Tragedy of Romeo and Juliet; *The Duchess of Malfi*; *The Tragedy of Othello, the
Moor of Venice*; *'Tis Pity She's a Whore*; *The True Chronicle History of King Lear*
(more on the particular challenges and generic complexities of some of those
titles later) . . . The only exception to the easy rule that many of these plays
concentrate on a single, central individual is Thomas Middleton's play, *Women
Beware Women*, with its ensnaring chess game and staged seduction, and that
shift in approach itself begins to chart Middleton's developments of the genre
in the 1620s as he moved ever increasingly towards a form of multiple plotting
that anatomised societies and particular communities, rather than allowing a
single character or even a fatefully intertwined couple to dominate the action.

Full of character

Character studies can sometimes be regarded as the bad child of literary and
theatrical criticism, especially when looking at early modern drama which is

deemed by some to be a form developed at a time when the notion of the individual was embryonic and when dramatic form lent itself more readily to radical discontinuities of characterisation from scene to scene.[2] The whipping boy in this context has been the early twentieth-century critic A. C. Bradley, who wrote some very powerful and popular character studies of key Shakespearean roles that went so far as to consider those characters' inner psychology and what film screenplay writers might today call 'back story'. Bradley wrote that 'we may . . . speak of the tragic story as being concerned with one person' and with his detailed analyses of characters like Hamlet, Lear and Othello he bore that view out in his critical method throughout his influential 1904 collection *Shakespearean Tragedy*: 'Lear follows an old man's whim, half generous, half selfish; and in a moment it looses all the powers of darkness upon him. Othello agonizes over an empty fiction, and, meaning to execute solemn justice, butchers innocence and strangles love.'[3] Bradley's approach was infamously parodied by a fellow critic, L. C. Knights, in a talk to the Shakespeare Association in 1932: 'How Many Children had Lady Macbeth?'[4] As Carol Chillington Rutter has written, Knights (encouraged in this by a fellow critic, F. R. Leavis) aimed to cause something of a revolution in practice, tired as he was of the 'Bradley-ite' focus on character psychology and notions of audience or reader empathy, and there were certainly flaws with the way Bradley's work was adopted and interpreted in the decades immediately following its publication.[5]

But the time is perhaps ripe to reclaim early modern character studies from this particular negative association and a number of critics are beginning that important work by revisiting characters as 'types' and typologies or simply by authoring rich and suggestive studies of individual parts or roles.[6] In this kind of extended study – one that looks at character from a range of angles rather than simply advancing a singular notion of psychology partly derived from the realist novel – we begin to comprehend the ways in which individual dramatic creations are a means for early modern playwrights to explore cultural and political concerns and to develop and sometimes (often) to manipulate and exploit a relationship with the audience. This in turn provides insight into these playwrights' personalised and often collaborative approach to dramaturgy and aesthetics. Through individual character studies we can make sense of the particular metaphorical associations they conjure, their control of stage space (and by extension other characters), their use of language and direct address, and the ways in which contemporary actors such as Edward Alleyn, who made his name as a series of Marlovian (anti)heroes, or Richard Burbage, a renowned Hamlet and Richard III, interpreted these roles. Marlowe's Barabas, Shakespeare's Hamlet or Iago (hero and villain thereby included in the sample) and Webster's prime malcontent Bosola all lend themselves to this kind of careful attention.

If Bradley loomed large over the critical landscape at the start of the twentieth century, in its latter decades it was a critical approach known as New Historicism that dominated practice, and the key scholar in that movement was Stephen Greenblatt. His 1980 study *Renaissance Self-Fashioning* drew our attention in fresh ways to the making of individualism both in early modern culture and in its stage representations. His work was drawn to the energy and 'will to self-fashioning' of Marlowe's protagonists like Faustus, Tamburlaine and Barabas. Greenblatt's approach was informed by an attention to the 'poetics of culture' which invoked political and theological contexts, deploying pamphlets, political speeches, sermons and the like as evidential data by which to understand literary and stage creations; nevertheless, his 'self-fashioning' constituted an extended series of character studies in a new mode.[7]

As the above references to Alleyn's and Burbage's performances in particular roles indicate, character studies can also provide insight into the practical activities and pragmatics of theatre companies and theatre repertoires which, as the Introduction and Case study B established, are essential to the version of early modern theatre around which I am constructing my surveys of genre in this book and to the ways in which we appreciate the theatrical practice that shaped the writing of the plays themselves. Alleyn's 'moment' was in the 1580s and 1590s when he dominated the stage in Marlowe's plays. He was Tamburlaine and Doctor Faustus in those plays that shared their protagonists' name and Barabas in *The Jew of Malta*. Said to have been strikingly tall, he had a resonant voice that stayed long in spectators' memories.[8] Audience memory is a really significant factor in thinking about the way in which early modern theatre and individual characterisation functioned. People saw many plays, often in quick succession, and in the same week might see Alleyn or Burbage perform different tragedies or roles stretching across genres.[9] These knowledgeable spectators transported their experiences from show to show, across theatrical occasions in ways that lent new and enhanced meaning to their response to any one play or indeed part. It mattered that on seeing Burbage enter the stage as Volpone worshipping at his golden shrine in 1606 many spectators might recall and indeed make comparisons with Alleyn's performance as Barabas who opened his respective play in his counting house worshipping his financial gains. The kinships between these characters and the self-referential performances involved could be easily referenced by audiences, a kind of dramatic shorthand for playwright and performer alike (for a more detailed analysis of these particular opening scenes, see Case study C).

It is sometimes said that we lack much contemporary audience response to early modern drama and it is true that spectatorial insight is often fleeting and frequently made by visitors to the capital from the European mainland, which slightly masks our access to the mindset of an average London theatregoer. Often, though, what is explicitly recalled are spectacular moments and effects – the devils of *Doctor Faustus* get several outings in contemporary notebooks and diaries[10] – or specific characters and often, beyond that, specific characters as played by Alleyn, Burbage and the like. Alleyn's second marriage after the death of his beloved first wife Joan Woodward (as already noted, Henslowe's stepdaughter – this was a very theatrical dynasty) was to the daughter of the poet and theologian John Donne, who was by then Dean of St Paul's. Donne himself had been an avid theatregoer in his youth and the memories of the same – possibly of seeing Alleyn himself in roles like Tamburlaine – surface in theatrically informed poems such as *The Calm* where Donne remembers: 'Bajazet, encag'd, the shepherd's scoff' (33).[11] We should, then, never underestimate the politics of the social and cultural circulation of theatre in terms of its cultural agency and effect, and 'star actors' were part of this circulating discourse.

Richard Burbage came from a theatrical family; you could say it was in his DNA. He was just eight years old when his father was involved in the opening of the Theatre just outside the City of London walls in 1576 and he was actively involved in attempts to open an indoor theatre in the parish of St Anne's, Blackfriars, as well as the building of the Globe on Bankside from the dismantled timbers of the Theatre, which had been forced to close when the landlord who controlled the ground rent refused to renew the Burbages' lease. But more importantly for our purposes he was an actor, starting his career in a touring context, and he was particularly renowned for the parts he took in tragedies by Shakespeare: *Hamlet, Othello, King Lear* and *Richard III* (the latter a hybrid of tragedy and history that we will consider further in Chapter 3), taking the title role in each.[12] We also know that he played Sejanus in Jonson's eponymous Roman tragedy (1603) and Ferdinand, the Duchess of Malfi's vindictive and violent twin in Webster's 1612–13 drama. He was a star actor, so much so that knowing jokes could be made of this fact in other theatre productions. In Jonson's 1614 comedy *Bartholomew Fair* a puppet play apes the styles and celebrities of the London stage in a very knowing way. Audience member Bartholomew Cokes, looking in the basket belonging to puppet master Lantern Leatherhead, asks: 'Which is your Burbage now?' (5.3.64–5). As already noted, Burbage's Rose Theatre counterpart and rival, Alleyn, was similarly associated with tragic leads and this might suggest to us that tragedy as a genre was particularly linked to star roles and dominant central characterisations in just the way we have been describing because of, or in ways that lead to, a focus on particular star actors and their individual performance styles.

Spectators were, then, drawn to plays partly in order to see what actors like Burbage and Alleyn would make of them (there are obvious parallels with the film stars of today); their back catalogue became a point of entry too, a means of understanding, and indeed reading into, the new work of drama. Fans of Alleyn's style may have come to the Rose expecting, indeed hoping, to see him repeat previous feats as a variety of Marlovian overreachers who, Icarus-like, are destined for a fall, an image and idea suggestively contained within the opening Chorus of *Doctor Faustus*:

> So soon he profits in divinity,
> The fruitful plot of scholarism graced,
> That shortly he was graced with doctor's name,
> Excelling all whose sweet delight disputes
> In heavenly matters of theology;
> Till, swoll'n with cunning of a self-conceit,
> His waxen wings did mount above his reach,
> And melting heavens conspired his overthrow.
>
> (Prologue, 15–22)

The operations of Marlowe's renowned 'mighty line' are brilliantly evident here as the lines of blank verse, with careful combinations of iambic and trochaic feet, stressed and unstressed beginnings to lines, and conscious alliteration, perform the rising and falling motions, the swelling and the inevitable piercing of that self-conceit which the Chorus describes.[13] The language itself is highly performative of meaning.

In the same way, Alleyn's (presumably) memorable and striking interpretation of Barabas could have provided the allusive scaffold for later roles that Burbage would inhabit for Shakespeare and the King's Men, not least Richard III (a comic actor in a dark tragedy like Barabas), and, as already noted, Ben Jonson's own riff on the Marlovian 'overreacher', Volpone the Fox, in his 1606 satiric beast fable on urban acquisitiveness and moral duplicity.[14] The tradition of invoking and reanimating the Marlovian overreacher would persist into drama of the Caroline period, though by this point the character type seems to have fully transitioned into the comic genre or mode. Philip Massinger's 1625 comedy *A New Way to Pay Old Debts* features the gargantuan stage presence of monopolist and 'cormorant' (1.1.131) Sir Giles Overreach who in the final act is witnessed being quite literally weighed down by his own conscience: 'Some undone widow sits upon mine arm / And takes away the use of 't' (5.1.362–3). Overreach comes at the end of a decades-long dramatic tradition, and writing in 1625 Massinger could therefore rely on his audiences being skilled enough to recognise the intertheatrical history of this character from something as straightforward as his name. Audiences were able to read across the repertoire and across time in ways that fed into the creativity and schemas of playwrights.[15]

The very pragmatic need for doubling of characters within plays by professional companies that had to depend on a maximum of twelve to sixteen actors for a single performance also trained audiences to read across a single production. If, having been slain by the ambitious Macbeth, the actor playing King Duncan 'reappears' after Act 1 in Shakespeare's Scottish play as the drunken Porter of 2.3, not only are comments about social rank being made but the audience memory of the recent regicide is stirred in acute ways. 'Remember me' implores the ghost of Old Hamlet (*Hamlet*, 1.5.90); tragedy was, it seems, a genre that sought to mobilise memory, cultural and theatrical, to deep effect.

Tragic discourse

It was through language that many of the great and memorable characters of early modern tragedy were shaped and through one particular mode of 'tragic discourse' that enabled a peculiarly intimate relationship with the all-important audiences who shared in the making of meaning at any performance: the soliloquy. It is Shakespeare who is regarded as the master of this form. Expository or revelatory soliloquy is intimately linked to his particular brand of tragic drama:

> To be or not to be, that is the question.
>
> (*Hamlet*, 3.1.58)

> Thus do I ever make my fool my purse –
>
> (*Othello*, 1.3.375)

> If it were done when 'tis done, then 'twere well
> It were done quickly.
>
> (*Macbeth*, 1.7.1–2)

> To be thus is nothing
> But to be safely thus.
>
> (*Macbeth*, 3.1.49–50)

But it would be wrong to describe tragic soliloquy as only or purely Shakespearean; Shakespeare offered a particular kind of psychologising perhaps, and Emma Smith has recently suggested as much by contrasting his approach with that of John Webster in plays like *The Duchess of Malfi*, but we have already hinted at the power of Marlovian blank verse and it is worth therefore returning in some detail to the final moments of *Doctor Faustus* (final moments for both play and character, which gives the moment onstage a particular depth-charge and resonance) and spending some time with that play's astonishing final scene.[16]

We have already broached the topic of the Marlovian overreacher, a particular type of tragic protagonist who undergoes a spectacular rise and then seems destined for a spectacular fall, all within the confines of a five-act play. The Icarus myth invoked in the Prologue to *Faustus* and quoted above trains us as audience members to look for other rhythms and tropes of rise and fall and in the process to attend to a certain kind of providentialist discourse. Much critical ink has been spilt on the complicated relationship between theatre and religion at this time.[17] Certainly the challenge that the stage posed to the pulpit as a source of people's moral, ethical and spiritual education and edification led to a series of outspoken sermons and publications against the theatre. Marlowe seems to deliberately court this kind of attention by bringing the topic of heaven and hell, sin and damnation, so overtly onto the stage in this play, although, as Thomas Healy notes, his actual position on his protagonist remains ambiguous: is Faustus an abject sinner or a tragic hero?[18] Certainly in this play we witness a tragic fall – 'Faustus is gone. Regard his hellish fall' (Epilogue, A-Text, 4) – as indeed we do in other Marlowe plays: in *The Jew of Malta*, Barabas falls quite literally into a burning cauldron of his own devising: 'know you cannot help me now' (5.5.76). But a simple stance of negative judgement on the part of the watching audience ('he deserved what he got') is complicated: Barabas and Faustus have built up an intimacy with the spectators that makes a monolithic moral response difficult to sustain. The form of tragic drama, and the engagement, complicity even, of an audience with the process of watching a play that it encourages and provokes, changes the stakes irrevocably.

Marlowe's use of good and bad angels, and his placing of the concept of the mouth of hell centrestage in his play, do not come out of nowhere, of course, and have a strong theatrical precedent in medieval morality drama, an art form and experience many of these London audiences would have had a working memory of. The extent, though, to which we think Marlowe refers to or makes a radical break from this theatrical past depends in part on the theatrical experience on any given night of performance and indeed on which textual survival of *Doctor Faustus* that we (or an acting company) are working with. As signalled in the Introduction, in many cases in the study of early modern theatre we have to remain alert to the multiple textual forms in which plays survive or indeed circulated in their own time, not just the differences between manuscript and print but also different printed versions which may or may not give us a point of access to variations that were performed on the stages of the day. Some critics speculate that we may be witnessing touring versions of commercial London plays in the shape of pared down or condensed versions. Certainly, some scripts show evidence of adaptation for the different playing spaces that were available – especially when the indoor playhouses became a regular resource for playing companies in the early seventeenth century. Sometimes we have versions that were deliberately added to by the playing companies which held the rights to these plays in performance and in print. We know from archival records, for example, that Jonson was paid by Henslowe to make certain additions to the hugely popular revenge drama *The Spanish Tragedy* in 1602, some eight years after the death of its author Thomas Kyd. Similarly in the case of *The Tragicall History of Doctor Faustus*, first performed we think *c.* 1588 by the Lord Admiral's Company and then revived at the Rose Theatre in 1594 and 1597, we have the so-called A and B texts which give a very different flavour to certain scenes depending on the framing material they do or do not include.[19]

But whether, as in the A-text of *Doctor Faustus*, we are subjected to an intense final scene with Faustus himself, followed by a framing Choric Prologue, or as in the B-text, an extra scene (5.3) with scholars who provide a moral as well as descriptive commentary on what has unfolded on the stage ('See here are Faustus' limbs, / All torn asunder by the hand of death' (B-Text, 5.3.6–7), what remains most in the theatrical memory are those remarkably charged moments alone with Faustus onstage as he delivers a soliloquy on his own impending death. As Healy notes: 'Faustus' rhetorically charged final speech . . . is a wonderful piece of theatre that builds to a crescendo of fear and dramatic expectation.'[20] Partway through 5.2 of *Doctor Faustus* (A-Text), a clock strikes eleven and the scholars who have until this point been keeping Faustus company exit the stage. Our central character is now alone except for us and it is therefore only to us and his own conscience that he can unburden his soul. The impending stroke of midnight is what is on Faustus's mind. With the tolling of that particular bell will come his reckoning, the time he must yield up the body and the soul he pawned for the hedonistic and extreme experiences (including an encounter with the Pope and indeed with Helen of Troy) we have been witnessing in the preceding scenes:

> Ah Faustus,
> Now hast thou but one bare hour to live,
> And then thou must be damned perpetually.
>
> (5.2.57–9)

This preoccupation with passing time gives the scene a particular form of urgency on the stage as the cliché that time runs ever more quickly when you try to hold it back is played out as we witness an hour pass seemingly in the matter of some sixty or so lines. The attempt to slow time is partly played out in the insistent use of monosyllables in the first part of the quotation above. Monosyllables require a kind of concentrated stressing that means the line is more often than not slowed down. Shakespeare often turns to monosyllables at key moments in comic speeches for this reason, for increased emphasis and effect (witness Rosalind's 'Men have died from time to time, and worms have eaten them, but not for love' in *As You Like It*, 4.1.99–101). In the case of *Doctor Faustus*, however, polysyllables intervene in the very next line: the word 'damned' drawing in that chilling end-term 'perpetually', which says it all to Faustus even as he mouths it. Lines such as these perform aurally the effect of a tolling bell or clock, the passing of time which the speech ironically wants to resist:

> Stand still, you ever-moving spheres of heaven,
> That time may cease and midnight never come!
> (5.2.60–1)

Faustus wants to stretch time:

> let this hour be but
> A year, a month, a week, a natural day,
> That Faustus may repent and save his soul!
> (5.2.63–5)

But in dramatic terms the scene performs the opposite effect and with that comes Faustus's understanding that his fate is indeed unavoidable and his return to those chilling, steadily stressed monosyllables and some deliberately ponderous alliteration:

> The stars move still; time runs; the clock will strike;
> The devil will come, and Faustus must be damned.
> (5.2.67–8)

Within the space of twenty lines, half an hour is already past:

> *The watch strikes.*
> Ah, half the hour is past!
> 'Twill all be past anon.
> (5.2.88–9)

All of this is deeply intimate; we are alone with this man in the final minutes of his life and we witness every desperate effort to avoid the inevitable. It is in a sense a celebration of the human love for life, its desperate wish to cling to it and its energies against the odds. This is a very intense and painful journey that we are asked to go on with this character until the very end and the particular form of soliloquy only heightens its impact on our emotions – the 'pity and terror' that Aristotle's *Poetics* referred to as the condition of tragic drama.[21] We experience this scene along with Faustus and like him we see Lucifer and Mephistopheles enter and we know what this means – the end is indeed nigh:

> Adders and serpents let me breathe a while!
> Ugly hell, gape not. Come not, Lucifer!
> I'll burn my books. Ah, Mephistopheles!
> [*The Devils*] *exeunt with him*
> (5.2.113–15)

There remains of course a welter of performative possibilities in these lines and the typically sparse stage directions that accompany the scene. I have seen the moment screamed out as if Faustus is in deep pain, I have seen Faustus dragged offstage into a strongly suggested hell-mouth space, but I have also observed Faustus and Mephistopheles exit quietly, arm in arm, as if to a quiet evening by a household fire rather than to the burning shades of hell. The effects are equally chilling in all three examples but in acutely different ways. In all of them what is to the fore is the question of audience engagement through shared experience of the scene, through their sharing of the moment so intensely and intimately with Faustus. The verse form that Marlowe opted for, the soliloquy, is central to that achievement.

Of course, the use of soliloquy to such great effect in tragic drama was not something invented by early modern dramatists; it, like the suggested hell mouth and good and bad angels of *Doctor Faustus*, has a direct line of relationship with medieval drama and with one character in particular, the Vice. Many of Shakespeare's great soliloquisers have been linked to the Vice and his challenging, intimate and often frame-breaking relationship to audiences: Richard III, Iago, Falstaff, all have their Vice-like qualities, and even Hamlet's close dance with comic madness plays on these theatrical inheritances. The Marlowe character who most obviously and effectively channels the legacy of the Vice is Barabas. He, too, is accorded the power of soliloquy, though his great moments come rather at the start than at the end of 'his' play. Case study C will unpack the opening scene of *The Jew of Malta* in greater detail but suffice to evidence in this context the complicity that the use of soliloquy establishes between Barabas and his audiences. This is an effect that Richard III, Volpone, Iago and characters from early modern tragedy and comedy alike strive to emulate. As Greenblatt notes: 'the audience becomes Barabas's accomplice . . . Barabas first wins the audience to him by means of the incantatory prose of his language' and, as a result of this, we share his energy and excitement, his anger and his determination to seek revenge at various turns.[22] The ending of the first scene (noticeably framed by Barabas's soliloquising as if to drive that association home) is a case in point as he reveals his thinking, the inner working of his mind, to us:

> And, Barabas, now search this secret out.
> Summon thy senses; call thy wits together...
> Howe'er the world go, I'll make sure for one,
> And seek in time to intercept the worst,
> Warily guarding that which I ha' got.
> Ego mihimet sum simper proximus.
> Why, let 'em enter, let 'em take the town.
>
> (1.1.175–6, 184–8)

There is a particular effect that we can start to recognise here in the act of self-naming; Marlowe has both Faustus and Barabas do it at the start of their soliloquising ('Ah Faustus'; 'And, Barabas...'). This emphasises their heightened sense of individuality as does the Latin that Barabas knowingly quotes, which is from Terence's *Andria* and translates loosely as 'no man is nearer friend to myself than I am'. All this emphasises the uniqueness and solipsism of these characters and yet the dramatic irony of soliloquy is that they are never truly alone; we, the audience, are with them every step of the way and in this way theatre starts to weave its particular magic. Soliloquy sees a character *solus*, alone on the stage, and yet in the heady atmosphere of early modern theatre simultaneously working the crowds to great effect (see Figure 2: an image of a 2011 Shakespeare's Globe 'original practices' production of *Doctor Faustus*).

There is, of course, a subset to the soliloquy, the aside, which is an equally potent means of manipulating the audience and talking across the gap between stage world and audience in the early modern theatre, but it seems sensible to reserve detailed discussion of this to the next chapter where we will encounter a particular sub-branch of tragic character, the malcontent in revenge drama. Vindice, Bosola and De Flores are themselves kin to the medieval Vice but they take their bitter reflections to a new pitch in the context of the macabre events of their peculiar play-worlds. What the attention I have been encouraging here to language and the particular stage grammar of tragic protagonists enables is a sense that tragedy requires at all times complicated modes of participation from its audiences. As Muriel Bradbrook has declared, 'tragedy implies engagement'.[23] This engagement can be achieved through linguistic effect, as we have seen, but this is always, in the theatrical context, language performed in very particular spaces and places: the new purpose-built commercial play-houses but also the places and spaces they in turn conjured through the act of invocation and representation. It is therefore to tragic space that we now turn for the next section of this chapter.

Tragic space

Where do ghosts come from? This might seem a highly abstract and immaterial philosophical question but in some respects it is a genuine question that haunts the thinking in a number of early modern tragedies: Hamlet asks of the ghost that appears to resemble his late father in armour, 'Be thou a spirit of health or goblin damned, / Bring with thee airs from heaven or blasts from hell'? (*Hamlet*, 1.4.21–2); Macbeth on seeing a vision at a banquet of the former friend, Banquo, whom he has had murdered by hired henchmen, talks of 'charnel-houses and our graves' sending 'Those that we bury back' (*Macbeth*, 3.4.70–1); Richard III on the eve of the Battle of Bosworth tries to reassure himself that the ghosts he has encountered in his tent were but a dream: 'What do I fear? Myself? There's none else by' (*Richard III*, 5.5.136). Of course the very fact that audience members have shared these 'visions' even when, as in *Hamlet* and *Macbeth*, onstage characters seem to question what is visible to the tragic protagonists, complicates the understanding of their reality and their provenance, but on the very material wooden stages of both the outdoor and indoor playhouses of the London commercial theatre scene the staging of ghosts was also a deeply practical question of stage blocking and choreography. The messages and meaning an audience might take from the way or place from which a ghost enters could vary accordingly.

The supernatural more generally was associated with the space below the early modern stage. The devils of *Doctor Faustus* probably entered from here as did the ghosts of Shakespearean and other Jacobean drama. This association casts further interesting light on how the aforementioned fifth-act damnation scene of *Faustus* might be staged. If Faustus is pulled down into the understage through a trapdoor, that action sends one very particular message about the tragic fall staged by this play. But if, as many critics have suggested, Marlowe's play challenges conventional Christian perspectives on sin and damnation, heaven and hell, this kind of subversive questioning could persist right to the protagonist's end.[24] If Faustus simply exits offstage with Mephistopheles (an alternative posited in the close reading of the scene in the previous section) the effect is tangibly different and takes us back to various points in the play where hell has been suggested as a state of mind.[25] As spectators we might also recall at this very moment Mephistopheles's earlier chilling response to Faustus's brash assertion that 'hell's a fable': 'Ay think so still till experience change thy mind' (1.5.131). There are numerous observations that could be made about this remarkable momentary exchange between two characters. There is comic timing in Mephistopheles's sardonic undercutting reply that asks us to begin to understand this pairing through the prism of the comic double act which Marlowe plays with elsewhere in an equally hybrid tragic context through the partnership of Barabas and the slave Ithamore in *The Jew of Malta*. This comic turn influenced Jonsonian double acts such as Volpone and Mosca and Subtle and Face (see his 1605–6 and 1610 plays, *Volpone* and *The Alchemist*). There is also in this moment, yet again, the brilliant focusing of audience attention that comes through the move to an almost wholly monosyllabic vocabulary; the polysyllabic 'experience' stands out and jars all the more with the mood of the scene. But it is this emphasis on experience, and audience experience in particular, that yet again seems central to the effect of this particular moment as it is to those visible ghosts of *Hamlet* and *Macbeth*.

There is another way in which audience 'experience' might be brought to bear on these moments in tragic drama which I am singling out for attention. As already suggested, some spectators would have a personal, or at least through family members a collective, memory of medieval dramatic traditions, not least of communally performed pageant cycles, where the staging of damnation was common and often featured a scaffold depiction of hell mouth. These active, or reactivated, memories of medieval 'harrowing of hell' scenes could have provided a direct line of cognitive and sensory connection to the Porter's knowing allusions to hell-gate in Shakespeare's *Macbeth* in 2.3 or to Hamlet's observation of the ghost seen by the Elsinore soldiers: 'If it assume my noble father's person / I'll speak to it though hell itself should gape' (*Hamlet*, 1.3.244–5). At the beginning of *The Jew of Malta*, Machevil, a deliberately stagey combination of real knowledges about Catholic Italian political theorist Niccolò Machiavelli and his almost demonic popular reputation in Protestant England, delivers a prologue that acts as a frame for the action that follows and in particular for Barabas's almost conscienceless activities. Some productions have played with the possibilities of doubling by having the same actor who will play the equally cynical and self-serving Governor of Malta, Ferneze, speak Machevil's lines, thereby drawing a direct analogy between the parts, but the analogies can also operate spatially.[26] If Machevil arrives onto and indeed exits the stage through the (as we now see) charged signifier of the trapdoor, it draws another line of connection to the very end of the play where we will witness Barabas 'hoist by his own petard' (to borrow a phrase from *Hamlet*) when he tumbles to his gruesome death through the trapdoor.

The Porter scene in *Macbeth* is a remarkable interpolation into a plot otherwise largely derived from Holinshed's *Chronicles* and, though sometimes cut in modern performances seeking a purity of tragic atmosphere and tone (the scene is resolutely comic), it is, I would argue, essential to the way in which the Scottish tragedy unfolds in performance. The Porter enters to the self-same knocking that disturbed Macbeth's conscience at the end of the previous scene. (It is worth noting at this point that scenes quite readily flowed into one another in this way on the fluid early modern stage; act breaks were only formally marked when the move to the indoor playhouses occurred after 1600, and the effect of that on dramaturgy will be explored in Case study E.) The line of connection to the 'harrowing of hell' scenes of medieval drama is made immediately, albeit only by inference:

> Here's a knocking indeed! If a man were porter of hell-gate he should have old turning the key.   *Knocking within.*
>
> Knock, knock, knock. Who's there, i'th name of Beelzebub? . . .
> *Knock within.*
>
> Knock, knock. Who's there, in th'other devil's name? . . .
>
> But this place is too cold for hell. I'll devil-porter it no further. I had thought to let in some of all professions that go the primrose way to th'everlasting bonfire.
>
> (2.3.1–4, 6–7, 15–18)

The Porter exits on the telling line: 'I pray you remember the porter' (2.3.20), and the reason I think it is important that audiences of *Macbeth* activate their collective memory in this way is because the scene, for all that on the surface it seems like an anomaly, a piece of cheap comic relief, to allow for an actor's break or the passage of time, in fact takes us to the heart of the play's concerns with the supernatural and with humanity's capacity to do hellish things. The scene asks audiences to bring a theatrical experience, memory or knowledge to bear in understanding the hellish associations of this scene and in linking back to what they have seen already on the stage of *Macbeth* and thinking forward in a very engaged and active manner to what might follow. We see audiences making ideas on the hoof as it were, improvising just as much as the onstage actor in this vivid example of theatrical self-fashioning.

I have already mentioned the possible powerful effect of stage doubling if the Porter is played by the actor that we have only moments earlier seen play the now murdered King Duncan. This would bring the regicidal act that the Macbeths have committed even more to the forefront of our minds; the king is bodied forth as it were before our very eyes, albeit at one stage removed, and this proves Macbeth's false bravado at the end of the final scene all too predictive in its trope of ghostly resurrection. This in turn paves the way for the resurrection of the murdered Banquo as the ghost at the feast in 3.4 and this is further underlined if the Porter has entered through the trapdoor and then Banquo's ghost echoes that mode of stage entry later. There is, of course, a logic to a Porter, a liveried household servant in the Macbeths' castle, coming up from below the stage; stage directions (implicit or explicit) in comic dramas set in inns and taverns, including Shakespeare's *Henry IV, Parts 1* and *2* and Jonson's *The New Inn*, indicate that this use of the trap was a useful way of indicating a 'downstairs' community of servants in spaces of public encounter such as these:

Enter a Drawer
DRAWER Sir, Ensign Pistol's below, and would speak with you.

(*2 Henry IV*, 2.4.65–6)

[*Music heard from within.*]
JORDAN The dinner is gone up.

(*The New Inn*, 3.1.104)

But the link to Banquo gives it a different depth-charge, one that might also have been prepared for at the very start of the play if the 'three Witches' enter in this same way onto the main stage to deliver their opening rhymed chants:

FIRST WITCH When shall we three meet again?
In thunder, lightning, or in rain?
SECOND WITCH When the hurly-burly's done,
When the battle's lost and won.
THIRD WITCH That will be ere set of sun.

(*Macbeth*, 1.1.1–5)

These spatial analogies and cross-readings not only mobilised a medieval vocabulary of performance; as Andrew Power has indicated, there is also a strong through-line of classical theatrical allusions to the underworld and in turn to Senecan traditions in these particular moments of early modern drama.[27] Kyd's *The Spanish Tragedy*, one of the most influential early forays into tragic drama on the early modern commercial stage, and which will be discussed in greater detail in the next chapter, features a scene in which the protagonist Hieronimo, a grieving father whose search for justice forms the backbone of the play, literally rips at the ground with his dagger in an attempt to summon the ghost of his dead son Horatio:[28]

> I'll rip the bowels of the earth,
>> *He diggeth with his dagger.*
> And ferry over to th'Elysian plains,
> And bring my son to show his deadly wounds . . .
> I'll go marshal up the fiends in hell,
> To be avenged on you all for this.
>
> (3.12.71–3, 77–8)

There *is* a ghost in *The Spanish Tragedy* but he proves oddly ineffectual within the context of revenge drama traditions: Andrea sits *above* the stage rather than emerging from beneath it and comments on the action in quasi-choric fashion along with his partner, Revenge. Hieronimo's desperate actions seem to draw attention to a failure or indeed a gap in the main action. The gap, Power suggests, is that no furies have appeared from below the stage to spur on the action of revenge.

It is just such a scene that had taken place in a play often described as the prototype English tragedy, one written in a consciously Senecan tradition: Thomas Norton and Thomas Sackville's 1561–2 *Gorboduc*. In that Inns of Court play – Senecan-influenced drama in English found its first flush in the theatre staged by trainee Inns lawyers and by students and scholars at the two universities, Oxford and Cambridge – a dumb show takes place just prior to the fourth act (for a more general discussion of this device, see Case study M) in which 'three furies' come up through a trapdoor:

> forth from under the stage, as though out of hell, three furies, Alecto, Megaera, and Tisphone, clad in black garments sprinkled with blood and flames, their bodies girt with snakes, their heads spread with serpents instead of hair . . .
>
> (*Gorboduc*, 'The Dumb Show Before the Fourth Act', 2–5)[29]

It is this kind of theatrical moment that Hieronimo searches for in *The Spanish Tragedy* but this is also the type of scene directly recalled in the motions and appearance of the 'three witches' at the beginning of *Macbeth* and perhaps even later by the 'harpies' who appear onstage as part of Ariel's supernatural banquet in Shakespeare's 1610–11 play *The Tempest*. Tiffany Stern has noted how the trapdoor could evoke meaning in this pluralistic, recollective way:

> Even when not as obviously the lipped and toothed mouth of hell . . . the stage trap-door retained hellish or bad associations; it is the bloody hole in which Lavinia is raped in *Titus Andronicus*, the grave in *Hamlet*, the place from which the apparitions in *Macbeth* come and go. So whenever

the hole gaped open on the stage, the audience knew that something evil or with deathlike connotations was happening, or about to happen.[30]

Each of these scenes and moments gains meaning and strength, then, from reference to each other and to a longer theatrical tradition, medieval and classical, in ways that will be a recurring theme throughout this volume. So if we consider the spatial semiotics of *Hamlet*, we can begin to comprehend the way in which this play self-consciously evokes different stage 'regions'. This blends together medieval morality traditions with those of classical Senecan revenge, evoking the 'harrowing of hell' scenes already alluded to not just in medieval cycle plays but in Marlowe's great tragedies, and specifically in the downfalls of Faustus and Barabas (and presumably the performance of their demise by Alleyn).

Added to the mix were the Senecan theatrical idioms that underscore Hamlet's status as a revenge drama.[31] *Hamlet* makes much of its meaning through a very careful invocation of the three regions of heaven, earth and hell in its use of the over-stage canopy at the Globe Theatre where we believe the play to have been first performed *c.* 1601 (the 'above'), the main stage and the understage. It is often remarked on by editors and students of the play that Hamlet (and by extension Burbage in the role) alludes to the painted canopy of the Globe in his agonised soliloquy following his first encounter with the Ghost: 'Remember thee? / Ay, thou poor ghost, while memory holds a seat / In this distracted globe' (1.5.95–7). Presumably Burbage might have looked upwards at this point bringing the audience's attention to the potential of heaven as a region. But it is equally notable that this is a region which characters in this play endlessly aspire to but never attain; Claudius's failed attempt at prayer and atonement (at 3.3.36 onwards) is one obvious example, Ophelia's 'maimèd rites' (5.1.214) following her dubious death (suicide was against Christian law) another. It is not as if Shakespeare always avoided the use of the 'above' in his drama; the balcony scene of *Romeo and Juliet* alone (2.1) informs us that he could make pertinent use of those higher levels when it suited him. Therefore it is significant when Shakespeare avoids such a space. If, as Gertrude's poetic narrative of her death suggests, Ophelia is literally 'dragged' down to her watery end – 'her garments, heavy with their drink, / Pulled the poor wretch from her melodious lay / To muddy death' (4.7.153–5) – then her grave is figured as a space where Hamlet and her grieving brother Laertes battle for the role of her avenger. Her grave and the spatial semiotics of the play's fifth act rework all the thoughts of hell and underworlds that were conjured by the Ghost's appearance in the first. From this space below the stage, a space the character of the gravedigger has drawn such detailed and material attention to in the scene with Yorick's skull, Hamlet emerges as a more reconciled Senecan hero. From this point onwards the play seems more certain of its genre and where it is headed. Through space, then, meaning is made and generic outcome asserted.

Changing dynamics in stage tragedy and not least a greater propensity to bring spectacular horrors onstage in Jacobean exponents of the form have been accredited to changing patterns in playhouse space. *The Spanish Tragedy*, *Doctor Faustus* and *Hamlet* all saw their initial performance on the stages of the larger open-air amphitheatres of the Bankside, but the work of Webster, Middleton and others is more readily associated with the macabre horrors of Jacobean tragedy that was written for the new, smaller and candlelit space of indoor theatres like the Blackfriars inside the City walls. Martin White has done much to inform us about the new theatrical possibilities of these indoor theatres through his reconstructed performances which have found special resonance in the sparkle of costume in candlelight. This renders some of the central metaphors of these brittle but brilliant plays all too real:[32] Beatrice-Joanna's observation in *The Changeling* that 'A true deserver like a diamond sparkles' (2.1.15) would seem to place some faith in precious gems to hold their value in a confused world but contrasts sharply with the Duchess of Malfi's chilling resolution in the face of the psychological torture she is subjected to in her prison cell:

> What would it pleasure me to have my throat cut
> With diamonds, or to be smothered
> With cassia, or to be shot to death with pearls?
> (*The Duchess of Malfi*, 4.2.208–10)

Hers is a rejection of the material world that the play has made so visible to us in its candlelit splendour and its rich fabrics and surfaces.

Certain scenes or moments from plays like *The Duchess of Malfi* and *The Changeling* seem to have been specifically designed to exploit these new playhouse possibilities: the Duchess is handed a severed hand in pitch darkness by her own brother (*The Duchess of Malfi*, 4.1.43) and shown a tableau of the 'bodies' of her dead husband and children by Bosola (4.1.54 s.d.); De Flores hands over to Beatrice-Joanna a severed finger complete with sparking jewel (*The Changeling*, 3.4.29 s.d.); these 'moments', intimate yet shocking, compelling and yet repulsive, offer a form of chamber horror palpably different to the overt spectacles of the outdoor amphitheatres. We do need to be careful not to close down too many of the inbuilt flexibilities of early modern plays that actually allowed them in all probability to move quite regularly between open-air and indoor performances, between public theatre and the exclusive environs of the court at Whitehall and at Greenwich, but alongside an inbuilt propensity to portability we also need to recognise that these were plays by dramatists keen to exploit the latest new invention in the staging and generic experimentations of their plays.

If in *Hamlet* Ophelia dies ambiguously offstage, Webster's Duchess of Malfi dies resolutely and horrifically before our eyes, albeit in the newly suggestive shadowy darkness of the indoors Blackfriars playhouse. What I would argue is a novel interest in the staging of violence on the part of Jacobean theatre practitioners is explored in detail in Case study D but it is worth adding to that analysis with an acknowledgement that Jacobean tragedy appears to have brought a new focus on private and intimate space. That seems by association to bring into sharper relief the fate of women in these plays and in society at large. It is, then, to feminised space and the specific spatial politics and poetics of the household and not least the bedchamber that we turn for the final part of this discussion.

The Aristotelian demand that tragic setting be of a certain magnitude encouraged the elite courtly settings of much early modern drama. Hamlet's Elsinore and the corrupted, lecherous European courts of revenge drama will be a subject for discussion in the next chapter but the particular notion of the court as simultaneously castle and prison certainly plays itself out in a series of Jacobean tragedies that focus on women in deep emotional and moral dilemmas. Webster's stoic Duchess of Malfi is a young vibrant widow whose right to remarry is controlled by her tyrannical and psychotic twin brother Ferdinand. She laments her fate in these spatially inflected terms:

> Why should only I,
> Of all the other princes of the world,
> Be cased up like a holy relic?
> (*The Duchess of Malfi*, 3.2.135–7)

When she opts to subvert this situation by marrying her steward Antonio in private (that the marriage is staged as a version of handfast – a ceremony made legal by the act of witness – underscores that this is a behind-doors ceremony, witnessed only by a single maidservant, Cariola), Ferdinand performs the ultimate action of asserting his right to control her private actions when he invades her bedchamber bearing a knife (3.2.67 s.d.). Beatrice-Joanna in Middleton and Rowley's *The Changeling* (1622), for all that she is depicted as a 'changeling' subject to 'giddy turning'(1.1.159) and changes of opinion, is similarly entrapped by a series of customary practices that empower her father to arrange her marriage; her sense of physical and personal claustrophobia leads her into an even more extreme partnership with the household servant

De Flores, a figure for whom she previously professed scorn and utter repulsion on account of his disfigured appearance – 'This ominous ill-fac'd fellow more disturbs me / Than all my other passions' (2.1.53–4) – but to whom she now finds herself beholden financially and sexually as a result of hiring him as her henchman to kill the fiancé assigned her by her father:

> Murder, I see, is followed by more sins.
> Was my creation in the womb so cursed,
> It must engender with a viper first?
>
> (3.4.167–9)

Kim Solga has astutely demonstrated the ways in which the sites and spaces of the castle as they are realised in *The Changeling* lead us as spectators through a physical and sensory experience of Beatrice-Joanna's condition.[33] The play is rife with the language of locks and doors, casements, closets and secret passageways and this lexicon gives a physical shape to the moral space or vacuum in which characters increasingly find themselves: as Beatrice-Joanna herself observes when De Flores comes to claim his sexual recompense from her: 'I'm in a labyrinth; What will content him? I would fain be rid of him' (3.4.71–2). Her gruesome end in the fifth act, incarcerated in a confined space with the object of her hate, follows the earlier grim comedy of the 'closet' scene in which her husband's keeping of a medicinal cabinet with which to test, among other things, female virginity leads to a bed-swap scene involving her maidservant which is itself gruesomely reconfigured from the plotlines of romantic comedies like Shakespeare's *All's Well That Ends Well* (*c.* 1604–5). This all feeds into an atmosphere of heightened enclosure and entrapment that characterises the play-world of the Alicante in which the events take place and end anything but well.

Both *The Duchess of Malfi* and *The Changeling* make much of household and bedchamber spaces, and these also feature in a subgenre of tragic drama that is resolutely set away from the glamorous and glittering courts and castles of the tragedies we have heretofore been discussing. Domestic tragedy as a category focuses on provincial and suburban households and on 'real-life' examples more recognisable to early modern audiences. Several of them – such as George Chapman's *The Old Joiner of Aldgate* (1603), which dealt with a real-life story that was actually *sub judice* at the time of first performances, and Webster and Ford's collaborative 1624 effort, *Keep the Widow Waking or The Late Murder of the Sone upon the Mother*, which drew its inspiration from a local scandal in the neighbourhood where Webster lived and his family ran their carting business – used as the raw material for their plotlines real-life murders and events which had circulated previously in the form of oral gossip or in 'news' pamphlets relating the latest scandal. Muriel Bradbrook has written of the topicality of these plays rendering them 'forerunners of modern journalism' and notes 'their quick power to extemporize news flashes from the countryside'.[34] The impulse to reportage would resurface in comic drama later in the seventeenth century when Richard Brome and Thomas Heywood collaborated on *The Late Lancashire Witches* (1634).[35] This play was staged while the witchcraft hearings it referred to were still taking place in Lancaster. Neither *The Old Joiner* nor *Keep the Widow Waking* are extant as full playscripts but we can see in examples of the form that have survived, the anonymously authored *Arden of Faversham* (1592), *A Yorkshire Tragedy* (1600), now ascribed by many to Middleton, and Heywood's earlier foray into documentary drama, *A Woman Killed with Kindness* (1603), the ways in which the material detail of household lives and practices (scenes of eating and local hospitality in *A Yorkshire Tragedy* and Heywood's play, a carefully contrived plotline of business travel and postal correspondence in *Arden*) help to create a scene of verisimilitude which only serves to heighten the shock of the acts of murder and violence they portray.

Conclusion: movements and patterns

We have begun to register the rich diversity of forms and approaches to theatre that plays categorised under the heading of 'tragedy' came to effect in the commercial playhouses and how the change in the architecture and practices of those playhouses affected the development of the form yet further. Tragedy quickly shaded into companion modes like the history play (witness *Richard III*) and the subgenre of revenge drama, both of which will be discussed in more detail in the next two chapters. In turn, the satirical edge of hybrid comic tragedies like Marlowe's *The Jew of Malta* would affect the development of comic drama as well. Jacobean sex tragedies shade in turn into domestic drama and household plays; and characters inform other characters and other actors' performances of them: the bitter satire of Barabas carries him closer to comic protagonists such as Volpone than tragic counterparts such as Faustus. Revenge drama fashions the malcontent into a radical new version of the Vice figure that we have already seen Marlowe adapting and appropriating and hands it back to audiences in the multi-faceted shape of Bosola.

Genres change across space and across time; in the deeply referential and intertheatrical context of early modern commercial theatre, the story becomes one of influence and interplay as much as it does a rigid story of rules and conventions. Genres are also impacted by real-life events, political, social and cultural, and by the practicalities of working theatres, their playwrights, performers, properties and audiences. That is the complex landscape we have entered in this study and to appreciate it fully it serves us well to remain open-minded and to think of our categories as being as flexible and portable as the plays themselves.

Opening scenes

> Busie old foole, unruly Sunne,
> Why dost thou thus . . .
>
> I wonder by my troth, what thou, and I
> Did till we lov'd?
>
> For Godsake hold your tongue, and let me love . . . [1]

The so-called 'metaphysical' poet John Donne is renowned for the vivacity and sheer affront of some of the opening lines of his poems, not least those in his *Songs and Sonnets* which were first published in 1633 but which were written and circulated in manuscript at the same time that Jonson and Shakespeare were writing some of their most successful commercial theatre plays. The above opening lines of the poems now known as 'The Sunne Rising', 'The Good Morrow' and 'The Canonization' could be openings to plays by Shakespeare and Jonson; they have the same confidence about beginning a scene *in medias res*, mid-conversation, as Shakespeare does in *Othello* for example, and with direct address. It is no coincidence that (before he became Dean of St Paul's at least) Donne was an avid theatregoer and that the influences of the dramatic form spread across his work, even (perhaps most) into the *Holy Sonnets* where Donne seems almost to be conducting a series of doubting and often angry soliloquies with himself and by extension with his only other audience, his God. Donne's daughter married the star actor Edward Alleyn, further cementing the opportunities for cross-fertilisation between theatre, poetry and the pulpit in the early modern period.[2]

Donne's remarkable show-stopping poems direct us then to think carefully about theatrical beginnings and the ways in which their force is created and the expectations they raise.[3] Marlowe was a brilliant creator of opening scenes (and as we have seen already in looking at his tragedies, also of endings). One of the great examples, and one whose influence can be seen playing out over the decades of professional theatre that followed, is the commencement to *The Jew of Malta*, when what an audience sees onstage is Barabas alone in his counting house, revelling in his success as he adumbrates his spoils:

> *Enter Barabas in his counting-house, with heaps of gold before him.*
> So that of thus much that return was made,
> And, of the third part of the Persian ships,
> There was the venture summed and satisfied.   (1.1.1–3)

The scene can in some sense be encapsulated in that alliterative phrase 'summed and satisfied'; Barabas's smugness and self-satisfaction as he calculates his riches is excessive and yet so energetic that it seems to simultaneously repel and draw us in as audiences. This effect is only heightened by the intimacy of the scene; there is only Barabas here at this moment with us for these precious few minutes in the theatre and the closeness, the proximity, of this relationship colours the complexity of our responses to the play and its morally suspect protagonist.

It is undeniable that Marlowe has framed his play so as to warn us to be wary of Barabas from the beginning. What we actually see first on the stage of *The Jew of Malta* is a prologue delivered by a figure called 'Machevil'. The name is meant to evoke the controversial (and indeed censored) political texts of Italian theorist Niccolò Machiavelli but also the stage stereotype that had grown up in his wake: the 'machiavel' whom we will meet in various guises, not least in the shape of the many malcontents of revenge drama. We are meant, I think, by this juxtaposition to associate Machiavelli's promulgation that 'the end justifies the means' with Barabas's life-philosophy, but even in this framing device Marlowe is typically ambiguous: for if the actor playing Machevil is also the actor we see reappear later in the play as Governor Ferneze, ruler of Malta, the play's island centre, then the fact that Barabas is just one of many Machiavellians in this play is made overtly clear.[4] Faith and profession are not reliable indicators in this respect and what seems on the surface a blithely racist play in which the Jewish protagonist is painted as excessive villain becomes both more layered and more interesting as a result.

Our reading of Ferneze and his fellow Christians is also framed by the relationship these opening moments to the play proper create for us with Barabas and his comic wit and impressive control of the possibilities of language. His boredom with the sheer weight of his own trading wealth is almost palpable in the expression of lines such as: 'Here have I pursued their paltry silverlings' (1.1.6) and 'Fie, what a trouble 'tis to count this trash' (1.1.7). Something in the throwaway alliteration invites us to laugh; only later when the more brutal consequences of this moral ennui become visible do we question our earlier complicity with a villain.

This twisting and testing of the audience is a trick repeated by several other dramatists in the wake of Marlowe's early experimentation. There is a direct through-line, for example, not only to the aforementioned Iago (who begins the tragedy of *Othello* with a comparable comic energy and punning drive) but also to Richard of Gloucester and that all too quotable opening soliloquy: 'Now is the winter of our discontent / Made glorious summer by this son of York' (*Richard III*, 1.1.1–2). That speech with its linguistic dexterity and its show-off humour performs a similar act of inveigling the audience into Richard's life in ways that will come to trouble them but from which they can never quite extricate themselves as the play and its full tragic horrors unfold. It is notable that all of these plays with their seductive talkative villains flirt with hybrid generic mixes rather than adhering strictly to one particular genre or set of conventions; Iago, for example, drags comic structures, not least the role of witty servant which Shakespeare has appropriated from Roman comedy, into the domestic tragedy of *Othello*; and, though we will discuss *Richard III* in detail in a chapter ostensibly on history plays, this is an experimental and edgy drama that brings history, tragedy and comedy into vibrant interplay with one another.

Another play that we will explore in greater detail elsewhere (Chapter 6) is Jonson's 1605–6 *Volpone, the Fox*. If we think about how that play opens on the stage we immediately register the theatrical legacy of Marlowe's play and the conscious homage that Jonson performs as well as the understandings and energies this kind of intertheatricality mobilises for the playwright in those striking opening moments:

> [*Enter*] VOLPONE [*and*] MOSCA.
> Good morning to the day; and next my gold!
> Open the shrine that I may see my saint.
> [*Mosca reveals the treasure.*]
> (1.1.1–2)

There are important differences as well as similarities to note; this is adaptation in action, repetition with a twist. Unlike Barabas, Volpone is not alone onstage at the start of his eponymous play; he enters with his witty servant, Mosca. This though is already an important signal to the audience; Volpone's plots and schemes are the product of a remarkable double act (Jonson was fond of comic double acts and would create an equally tetchy version in Subtle and Face in *The Alchemist* just a few years later). When that double act starts to eat itself, as it does when Mosca becomes ambitious for himself – brilliantly signalled by his assumption of control of the stage space in the shape of a lively and shockingly confident soliloquy at the start of the central act – Volpone's power and confidence start to unravel. Volpone may dominate the opening scene but in this way Mosca inserts himself at the heart of the play. Dramaturgy and placement can then tell us a great deal about both character and action. There is an architecture to staging that we do well to reward with deep attention.

The opening scenes of both *The Jew of Malta* and *Volpone* are framed by the controlling personalities of the central protagonists. Both Barabas and Volpone end their scene with a soliloquy, Volpone's being a particularly striking assertion of his individuality and ego that seems almost to test the audience with its rhetorical questioning and relentless use of the first person:

> What should I do
> But cocker up my genius and live free
> To all delights fortune calls me to?
> I have no wife, no parent, child, ally,
> To give my substance to; but whom I make
> Must be my heir; and this makes men observe me.
>
>   (*Volpone*, 1.1.70–5)

We as spectators are also being invited to observe Volpone at close range. By contrast, Barabas's monologue is rather more outward looking; having conjured up the world's oceans and its trading routes and networks in the intimate locale of his counting house ('Infinite riches in a little room' as he himself puts it, *The Jew of Malta*, 1.1.37) he now seems to look quite literally outwards and to bring the weatherscapes and uncertainties of the seas and the world of global finance to which they were so intimately connected at this time (Shakespeare's *The Merchant of Venice*, 1596–7, conjures a similar environment at its beginning) onto the stage and into our thoughts:

> But now, how stands the wind?
> Into what corner peers my halcyon's bill?
> Ha, to the east? Yes. See, how stands the vanes?
> East and by south.   (1.1.38–41)

At this point, a stage direction informs us '*Enter a merchant*'. Merchants and messengers invariably bring news and with news the plot is moved forward. Barabas and Volpone both react to the entrances of others into their strictly controlled interior spaces and in the process onto the stage. This is also part of the important practical work that a beginning must do: making us as spectators eager for more, be it the news of the trading successes or governmental policy as in *The Jew of Malta* or *The Merchant of Venice* or the knock on the door as in *Volpone* – or indeed *knocks* on the door, since there are so many in this beast fable, as in *The Alchemist*, that the action reaches almost farcical heights. It is this basic operation of action that will push the experience onwards for the characters onstage, and also for us, and come to define at least in part the generic frameworks and conventions in which we are moving. Openings create expectations and relationships and they create the opportunity to move the plot forward. It is interesting to note that both Barabas and Volpone are restless in their drive for new experiences and it is this compulsion to the new that in the end proves their downfall. Neither is happy to rest with his successes: Barabas has grown tired of 'Wearying his fingers' ends with telling' of his wealth (*The Jew of Malta*, 1.1.16) and Volpone lets slip:

> Yet I glory
> More in the cunning purchase of my wealth
> Than in the glad possession, since I gain
> No common way.   (*Volpone*, 1.1.30–3)

In theatrical terms at least that is a very good thing since there would have been no play at all had either simply decided that they had made enough, done enough, seen enough, at the start of these scenes. Of course, this drive to action also links them back to the rise and fall of tragic protagonists such as Faustus and there too we are given a certain set of expectations as to how these plots might play out. In these beginnings there is indeed a suggestion of the endings. If John Donne's poems and their astonishing opening lines grab us by the hand (or even by the throat) and demand that we read on, we might, then, begin to suspect that he had learned how to make this work in a poetic context from the simple act of sitting (or standing) in the playhouses of London's Bankside.

Staging violence and the space of the stage

Early modern tragic drama is inextricably bound up with violence. We can register this in the description of it, performed in earlier Elizabethan forays into the form by messenger characters lifted directly from classical Greek dramatic precedents, a technique which kept the most gruesome scenes defiantly offstage and out of sight, and in the later visceral materialities of Jacobean tragedy and its close counterpart, revenge drama, which took a certain delight in the effects of putting acts of extreme cruelty and suffering onstage for the audience to witness and endure.

Andreas Höfele has described the blinding of the Earl of Gloucester in Shakespeare's *c.* 1605 play *King Lear* (it was first published in 1608) as 'arguably the most horrendous scene of violence in English Renaissance drama', but perhaps we need to ask why this scene is so unsettling and what the feelings and responses are it seeks to mobilise.[1] This in turn may start to tell us something interesting about the act of spectating and the particular act of spectating tragedy in an early modern theatre.

Gloucester's blinding takes place in scene 14 of the play but has been prepared for two scenes earlier when in scene 12 the Duke of Cornwall declares 'I will have my revenge ere I depart the house' (1). The house he refers to is Gloucester's own property and, as in plays like *Macbeth* and *The Duchess of Malfi*, we see the supposed sanctity of the domestic space invaded, corrupted and transgressed through tragic plot and action. Cornwall has discovered that Gloucester is working in alliance both with King Lear and with the French army, acting as an intelligencer on their behalf (12.8–11). Edmund, Gloucester's illegitimate son, is all too keen to persuade Cornwall in these views since it smoothes his way towards the earldom and political legitimacy he so craves. Even in this brief example of linguistic action, we can see revenge drama elements (a form and aesthetic we will unpack in greater detail in the next chapter, but one which is closely allied to tragic drama) being incorporated into the ostensible pastoral tragedy that is *King Lear*.

Scene 14, then, sees Cornwall ordering Gloucester's arraignment in his own home. That this is a play predicated on trials, real and staged, is worth mentioning here since it connects us back to the origins of the form in Inns of Court drama such as Sackville and Norton's 1561–2 verse drama *Gorboduc.* Cornwall's discourse is predicated on notions of revenge at all costs and outside judicial process for the Earl's perceived treachery:

> (*To Servants*) Go seek the traitor Gloucester.
> Pinion him like a thief; bring him before us.
> Though we may not pass upon his life
> Without the form of justice, yet our power
> Shall do a curtsy to our wrath, which men
> May blame, but not control.   (14.21–6)

Cornwall's instructions here perform various transgressions of law, rank and decorum; he will see Gloucester manhandled like a petty criminal at Newgate and Tyburn, real-life sites of incarceration and punishment in early modern London, and the signifying spaces inevitably conjured for watching members of the audience. In turn we have to ask to what extent such spectators, their attention drawn to these transgressions, will so readily set aside the moral judgement of Cornwall's actions that he assumes in this speech.

The bloodlust with which Goneril and Regan, Lear's two eldest daughters, urge Cornwall on in his vengeful actions is equally disturbing:

> **REGAN** Hang him instantly.
> **GONERIL** Pluck out his eyes.
> (3–4)

The immediacy and visceral nature of the language in this scene is deeply unsettling; modern comparisons might be found in the cinematic oeuvre of an auteur-director such as Quentin Tarantino who in a series of films in the 1990s tested audience capacity for and response to extreme violence. The torture scenes of films like *Reservoir Dogs* (1992) are perhaps the most visible contemporary artistic legacy of Gloucester's stage blinding in *King Lear.*

'Bind fast his corky arms' (27) Cornwall instructs the servants, thereby making them complicit in his crimes. 'Corky' refers here to the withered arms of Gloucester (the age of both Gloucester and Lear makes much of the central meaning of the play's reflections on mortality) and in this way the audience's attention is drawn to the presence not just of a nobleman, but also an old man on the stage. In the process attention is drawn to the vulnerable physical body as when we see Lear struggling with the elements of the storm on the heath. These are subtle juxtapositions, revealing the echoing, prefiguring and knowing underscoring that Shakespearean dramaturgy participates in when constructing tragedy and tragic impact. Bound to a chair, Gloucester finds his torturers plucking at his beard, a consciously performed insult to his rank and status, more usually performed as a prelude to a duel: as Gloucester notes, 'By the kind gods, 'tis most ignobly done, / To pluck me by the beard' (32–3). He confesses under their sharp interrogation that he has dispatched the King to Dover for his own safety and seems almost to write the script of his own torture in this address to Regan:

> Because I would not see thy cruel nails
> Pluck out his poor old eyes, nor thy fierce sister
> In his anointed flesh rash boarish fangs. (54–6)

Within moments, the Duke of Cornwall has those servants present holding firm the chair in which Gloucester is bound and threatening that 'Upon those eyes of thine I'll set my foot' (65). Within seconds he has put out one of Gloucester's eyes and stamped on it with his foot in the full view of the presumably horrified audience.

Adding to the atmosphere of transgression, the women readily participate in these actions; Regan goads her husband on in shockingly direct terms: 'One side will mock another; t'other, too' (68). It is one of the servants who questions the action and begs for mercy at this point:

> Hold your hand, my lord.
> I have served you ever since I was a child,
> But better service have I never done you
> Than now to bid you hold.   (69–72)

The role of the unnamed servant characters in this scene gives us access to the tragic form and its effects. Shakespeare's conscious framing of the extreme violence with the basic humanity of these men is worth reflecting on, as is the difference between this moment and the narration of offstage horrors that, as we have seen, early Elizabethan tragedies observed in deference to classical Greek tragic form. There is something of an irony, however, that it is in the textual version of the play known as the *History of King Lear* rather than the 'Tragedy' that the framing effect of the servants is contained.[2] The merciful servant is slain for these words by Regan herself and Gloucester's other eye is taken out by Cornwall as that servant lies bleeding to death on the stage: 'Lest it see more, prevent it. Out, vile jelly! / Where is thy lustre now?' (80–1).

Along with the servants, it is important to note, however, that the audience itself is bearing witness to these deplorable and immoral actions. The spectators see all too clearly Gloucester stumbling from the stage 'All dark and comfortless' (82) and perhaps feel the need for advocacy of the kind offered by the murdered servant or his colleague who, once Cornwall, Goneril and Regan have left the scene of their crimes, offers to fetch help and succour: 'I'll fetch some flax and whites of eggs / To apply to his bleeding face. Now heavens help him!' (104–5). This final statement in the scene (as it appears in *The History*) is ostensibly an appeal to the gods but is also in part addressed outwards from the stage to the auditorium to ask the spectators as a collective to understand and to judge the violence they have witnessed.

The particular linguistic means by which Gloucester describes his helpless and tormented position in this scene also speaks directly to the spectatorial gaze and experience and for modern audiences is a direct line to the actual space of the early modern theatre in which this violent scene first played itself out: 'I am tied to th'stake, and I must stand the course' (52). Gloucester represents himself here as the baited bear of Elizabethan popular entertainment but even more specifically as the blinded bear used in particular manifestations of this cultural spectacle, which involved human participants who whipped the poor sightless bear tied to the stake and therefore unable to fight back. This is not the only time in early modern drama that characters ask audiences to make a direct link to this other kind of theatre that took place, sometimes just at different times in the same auditoriums, or at the very least in Bankside amphitheatres and nearby spaces. In the fifth and final act of *Macbeth*, the beleaguered Scottish protagonist also compares his fate to that of the baited bear in an interesting statement of helplessness, but also in what might be seen as an overt plea for audience sympathy at the end of a long line of performed horrors: 'They have tied me to a stake. I cannot fly, / But bear-like I must fight the course' (5.7.1–2). Watching audiences would very swiftly have computed these metaphorical connections being effected between the work of theatre they were watching at this particular moment in time and the weekly theatre many of them also enjoyed that involved captive black and polar bears on the Bankside. Höfele has examined the semantic and semiotic exchange between theatre, bear garden and site of public execution at this time.[3] Case study K considers the inspiration that the discovering of the Gunpowder Plot provided for topical drama but it is worth stating here that the gruesome details of what was done to the conspirators' bodies, much of it while they were still alive, and images of the same, were circulating in 1605 when *King Lear* is assumed to have been written. This and other kinds of public torture along with the cruelties visited on bears and bulls in baiting rings all shaded into an understanding of the Gloucester blinding scene when it was staged, these kinds of proximity provoking the intellectual and emotional 'spillover' that Höfele so usefully explores.[4]

Edward Alleyn, one of the biggest celebrity actors of the day (there were very good reasons why Ben Affleck was cast in the role in the film *Shakespeare in Love*, directed by John Madden, 1996, when he was at the height of his celebrity status in the Hollywood cinematic community), purchased the Paris Bear Garden on Bankside in 1594 and remained active in the baiting business until his death in 1626. From 1604 to 1616 Alleyn and Henslowe, entrepreneur-owner of the Rose, jointly held the official court office of Master and Keeper of the Bears, Bulls and Mastiff Dogs.[5] The dogs were used to bait the bears and the bulls and it is why this particular triad of creatures features in the names Captain Thomas Otter gives his drinking cups in Jonson's *Epicene* (see, for example, 3.3.89–101). The association immediately links Otter back to lower-rank, popular cultural spaces such as the Bankside baiting rings and drinking houses, however much his aspirational city wife might seek to occlude their origins in her move through London and specifically West End society. Such references also served as a reminder to Jonson's more well-to-do spectators in indoor city theatres like the Blackfriars, or the Whitefriars where *Epicene* was performed, that these things lived brutally cheek by jowl in the metropolitan experience and that human and animal could never be neatly divided from each other as a result. As Höfele notes: 'Not only did theatres and bear-baiting share the same locations and audiences, they were also branches of the same business enterprise.'[6]

In a telling archaeological find, a bear skull was found during excavations of the Rose Theatre site in 1989, offering a direct line back to these entertainment practices and the complex issue of reaction and response to violence and cruelty in an early modern theatre context.[7] Höfele observes: 'The spectacle of execution and the spectacle of bull- and bear-baiting share the same basic type of performance space: an area and a scaffold, stake or platform surrounded by spectators.'[8] The Hope Theatre on Bankside actually continued to be known affectionately as the 'Bear Garden' long after it had officially shed that name and Jonson plays on this association in his self-aware Induction to his 1614 play *Bartholomew Fair* with a reference to the 'gathering up [of] the broken apples for the bears within' (Induction, 38–9), presumably a reference to fruit thrown onstage by rowdy spectators. Bankside theatregoers would have passed by bears in their pits or cages en route to parallel forms of entertainment; others would have encountered them on the roads of England as they travelled with their bearwards to perform as hired actors at the homes of significant noblemen and women.[9] Similarly, they would have passed by sites of execution or public punishment and there were then lines of connection between the baited bears and the marked bodies of those branded, tortured or indeed executed in acts of public discipline. Meanings were made through the connections people drew between these quotidian experiences and what they witnessed unfolding on the tragic scaffold of a play like *King Lear* or *Macbeth*.

Mastiff dogs were used to bait bears and bulls; sometimes they were even sent into the Thames after them in water-baiting spectacles. But there was another type of bear-based entertainment that the Gloucester blinding scene in *King Lear* alludes to more specifically: the whipping of deliberately blinded bears for the 'amusement' of audiences. It would be too simplistic a response, however, to assume some moral high ground over our early modern forebears in appreciating or comprehending the cruelties involved or the questionable pleasures of watching others suffer, be they human or animal, real or performed character. A cluster of contemporary descriptions bearing witness to the treatment of blind bears in performance may give us useful access to at least one type of more empathetic early modern spectatorial experience of witnessing the onstage blinding of Gloucester.

Paul Hentzner, a sixteenth-century German traveller, described seeing an Elizabethan bear-baiting. Initially he talks of seeing the kinds of baitings of bears and bulls with dogs that we have previously alluded to but he then goes on to describe the 'entertainment' that 'often follows': 'that of whipping the blind beare, which is performed by five or six men, standing in a circle with a whip, which they exercise upon him without any mercy'.[10] We might almost hear the murdered servant's cry for mercy from *Lear* in this extract. This is no one-off act of empathy with the beleaguered bear. Playwright Thomas Dekker makes some remarkably consistent observations of both a bear-baiting with dogs and the whipping of a blind bear in his 1609 pamphlet *Worke for the Armourer*:

> No sooner was I entred [the Bear-Garden] but the very noyse of the place put me in mind of *Hel*: the beare (dragd to the stake) shewed like a black rugged soule, that was Damned . . . the *Dogges* like so many *Diuels* inflicting torments upon it . . . At length a blinde *Beare* was tyed to the stake, and in stead of baiting him with dogges, a company of creatures that had the shapes of men, and faces of Christians (being either Colliers, Carters or Watermen) tooke the office of Beadles upon them, and whipt monsieur *Hunkes*, till the blood ran downe his old shoulders.[11]

There is so much to unpack in a rich contemporary quotation and act of direct observation such as this: Dekker explicitly compares the Bear Garden to the space and site of hell. In this particular morality play it is the mastiff dogs who play the roles of the devils. There is strange kinship here with *Macbeth*, a play that mobilises metaphors of bear-baiting but which also draws on medieval drama traditions with the Porter's scene at 2.3 which renders the Macbeths' castle as a kind of hell. The closing vision of Dekker's statement, that of the bleeding old bear, both humanises and ages him, and with *King Lear* at the forefront of our minds there would seem to be genuine kinships with the audience responses called into being by the attention paid there to the vulnerable body of an elderly man. Much comes then of juxtaposing these kinds of fictional and non-fictional texts together in that it gives us a point of entry to the possible audience emotional and sensory response to theatre that sometimes seems to be missing from the archival record. Dekker is careful to stress that those who torture the bear are the same people we might encounter in our everyday circulations of the city – watermen and carters and colliers, that is to say, people like ourselves – and we are asked, I think, in the process to imagine ourselves into the shoes of the watcher, wondering if we would be brave enough to stop the torture. The role of the servants in *King Lear* seem very close to this kind of implicit questioning of spectatorial involvement and responsibility.

Dekker goes on to talk in terms directly comparable to Aristotelian theories of tragic response not only about the pity he feels for the whipped bear but also drawing direct comparison with the sympathy he feels for those punished by the early modern judicial system rather than helped. He also refers to 'tragicomedy' in thinking about what is witnessed on a daily basis in places like the Bear Gardens.[12] The plea for a kind of civic duty in all of this gives us access to a different or at least alternative story to the easy one of early modern executions as entertainments akin to bear-baiting in which bloodlust and cruel pleasure were the whole story:

> Yet me thought this whipping of the blinde *Beare* moued as much pittie in my breast towards him, as y(e) leading of poore starued wretches to the whipping posts in *London* (when they had more neede to be releeued with foode) ought to move the hearts of Cittizens, though it be the fashion now to laugh at the punishment.[13]

These are then the kinds of alternative response to laughter or grim pleasure that a Shakespeare or a Webster might seek to mobilise or explore when they stage various forms of violence in their plays, be they tragedies or revenge dramas.

Chapter 2

Revenge drama

If genre is in part, as John Frow has argued, 'a set of conventional and highly organised constraints on the production and interpretation of meaning' as well as something which produces a 'horizon of expectation' for readers and spectators against which their experience in the moment might be understood or tested, then what might we say are the defining characteristics of revenge drama as a theatrical mode that early modern audiences could have expected (and indeed wanted) to engage with as part of the dramatic experience?[1] Thomas Kyd's *The Spanish Tragedy*, generally understood as the prototype Elizabethan revenge drama, and first performed *c.* 1590 at the Rose Theatre, has many of the elements that became firmly associated with the form: bloody spectacle, ghosts (the play is framed in fact by the Ghost of Don Andrea in conversation with the personification of Revenge), madness both feigned and real, corpses piled on corpses by the final act and a thread of self-aware theatricality, not least in the enacting of revenge itself. Revenge is achieved here, for example, by a play within a play performed in '*sundry languages*' (4.4.10 s.d.) and supposedly authored by the grieving protagonist, Hieronimo the Knight Marshal.

Hieronimo is our avenging hero, determined to achieve justice following the brutal murder of his son Horatio, but he also becomes the memorable exponent of what would become yet another recurring feature of revenge drama, the lengthy rhetorical and expository soliloquy which frequently lays bare his grief, despair and sheer mental fragility for the consideration of spectators:

> O eyes, no eyes, but fountains fraught with tears;
> O life, no life, but lively form of death;
> O world, no world, but mass of public wrongs,
> Confused and filled with murder and misdeeds!
> O sacred heavens! if this unhallowed deed,
> If this inhuman and barbarous attempt,
> If this incomparable murder thus
> Of mine, but now no more my son,
> Shall unrevealed and unrevengèd pass,

5. Key moments of the archetypal Elizabethan revenge drama captured in a woodcut image accompanying publication.

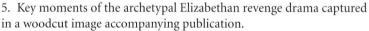

How should we term your dealings to be just,
If you unjustly deal with those that in your justice trust?

(3.2.1–11)

As well as Hieronimo's troubled reasonings with the concept of divine justice in this speech, looking at the words on the page we can clearly register the rhetorical manipulation of the listening audience that takes place simultaneously by means of poetic effects such as repetition and the deployment of balanced figures of speech invoking life/death, right/wrong. The audience is being invited into this conversation and asked at various points to reach its own conclusions about the rights and wrongs of what Hieronimo is debating with himself, and this method of speechmaking will be repeated throughout. This soliloquy is, then, an early foray into the exploration of the relationship with the audience that other revenge heroes (and indeed villains) would expand upon as the tradition advanced.

Theatrically speaking, the heady mix of spectacle and speech in *The Spanish Tragedy* obviously worked; the play was hugely popular with audiences, endlessly quoted and alluded to by subsequent decades, printed on several occasions (see Figure 5, a sample title page from the 1623 edition) and regularly revived in the repertoire right up to the 1640s. What follows in this chapter aims to reflect on what was distinct about revenge drama as a form and experience, and what made theatre audiences come back for more, time and time again.

Tragic resonance

Ticking off the appearance of certain agreed-upon features of a genre as a means of dramatic classification works well as a method up to a point; certainly, many of the key tropes listed above as pioneered by *The Spanish Tragedy* are readily identifiable in a range of playtexts that usually fall comfortably into the revenge drama category: Shakespeare's *Hamlet* (1600), Marston's *The Malcontent* (1604), Middleton's *The Revenger's Tragedy* (1605–6) and Webster's *The White Devil* (*c.* 1612). But, as we are seeing, and as the introduction to this chapter makes clear, if genre is a means of organising knowledge and, in a theatrical context, handling dramatic expectation, it is also notoriously fluid; categories slip, merge or overlap. A play that seems firmly adherent to one set of generic conventions can suddenly shade into a whole other set of practices and signifiers. Neither are genres stable across time; they respond to the moment as much as do actors and spectators. Revenge drama is in this respect the genre that proves the rule perfectly that genre is only one way of thinking about things and that as ever in literature and performance the most exciting energies usually occur at the point of fissure of or challenge to established norms. All of the plays mentioned above exploit tropes and traits from companion genres, not least tragedy and satire, and also, as we shall see in what follows, comedy, albeit in its bleakest, blackest manifestations.

In the previous chapter we began to examine some of the central conventions and attitudes of tragic drama on the early modern stage and it will already be clear that there are strong links and overlaps between revenge drama and tragedy as forms, a fact signalled not least by the use of the term 'tragedy' in the title of several of the plays under discussion here. This endorses Jacques Derrida's point that texts 'participate' in genres rather than being genres per se.[2] The work of the classical writer Seneca provides an important connecting strand in this respect between the modes of tragedy and revenge, as well as in the early history of commercial theatre in Britain. In 3.13 of Kyd's play, Hieronimo enters carrying a book and declaring '*Vindicta mihi!*' (1) – 'Vengeance is mine'. This admonition from the Bible (the full phrase from Romans 12:19 is 'Vengeance is mine; I will repay, saith the Lord') might seem to identify what Hieronimo has in his hands, in terms of a signifying stage property, as the holy book of the Christian faith but from quotations he goes on to read aloud in the same speech it becomes clear that he holds instead a copy of Seneca. There are a number of meanings audiences might take from this moment in the play, not least that Hieronimo is losing his faith under the pressure of circumstances, but what Kyd is also doing is cleverly signalling his own sources via this mechanism.

Revenge was a central theme in Seneca's writing and his style and aesthetic influenced early modern drama, especially tragedy, in a number of respects. Kyd's work was no exception. The choric framework to *The Spanish Tragedy*, depicting Andrea and Revenge in the underworld, owes an obvious debt to Senecan drama, as does Kyd's persistent use of stichomythic dialogue, where two characters exchange words line by line with each other in a structured, often carefully paced manner. In terms of early modern drama more generally, the Senecan influence is usually held to have been mediated by a play written and performed for the Inns of Court in 1561. The Inns were where lawyers were trained in their profession and where, as already noted, Sackville and Norton authored *Gorboduc*, the first verse drama in England to use blank verse, for a production at the Inner Temple. That play demonstrates the influence of both medieval morality drama traditions and Senecan tragedy. Kyd responds to this pre-commercial theatre precedent in significant ways and, as with other intertheatrical examples in this study, this demonstrates the continuities with dramatic forms and innovations that existed prior to the establishment of purpose-built playhouses in the 1570s.

Legal frameworks of understanding

The connection to the particular site and environment of the Inns of Court that the tangible influence of *Gorboduc* draws our attention to is hugely significant for understanding the legal framework and contexts in which the revenge drama tradition developed and was shaped. The four Inns or legal societies (Inner and Middle Temple, Gray's and Lincoln's Inns) were, and ostensibly still are, university equivalents, the intellectual and experiential training ground for young lawyers in London. They were also an important geographical region in the City, their complex of buildings providing term-time accommodation, dining facilities, classrooms and libraries and in the case of the Inner and Middle Temples operating as 'liberties', spaces free from the full jurisdiction of City officials.[3] Chapter 6 will explore further the link between the young men of the Inns and the verse satire tradition that fed into dramatic experimentations in the form, not least in the hands of Marston, Webster and others who were themselves direct products of the Inns' cultural environment. But many professional dramatists were linked to Inn circles through networks of patrons and acquaintances, not least Jonson and Middleton (who wrote extensively about Inn culture in his 1604 play *Michaelmas Term*). The influence of this ongoing exposure to the values and customs of the legal fraternity can be registered in the plays that they produced, especially those for the indoor theatres which after 1600 became an increasingly dominant part of the London theatre world, performed in initially by the children's companies (whose repertoires and reputations are explored in greater detail in Case study L) and later by adult companies like the King's Men.

It was no coincidence that Inn lawyers made up a considerable proportion of audiences for indoor theatre plays or that writers inevitably played up to the knowledges and interests of this particular cohort of spectators when designing plays for these venues. Theatre was embedded in the customary practices and rituals of the Inns so an interest in attending live performances on the part of trainee lawyers is perhaps unsurprising.[4] From the staging of actual trial scenes to the performance of debates that would have been part of the professional training of lawyers, there are a number of ways in which the law as both concept and practice made its presence felt on the commercial stage. We might also refer to Quomodo's rather too knowing address at the end of the second act of *Michaelmas Term* to the student lawyers in the audience: 'Admire me, all you students at Inns of Cozenage' (2.3.485–6). Onstage, this moment expects a highly engaged, even feisty audience, ready to see itself and its values mocked or parodied, but also looking for deep engagement, visceral and intellectual, with what is unfolding before them; this connects directly not only with the bloody spectacle that was undoubtedly a memorable aspect of these plays in performance but with the witty confident addresses of the revenge protagonists in our focus plays, from Hamlet's soul-seeking soliloquies to the rather more acerbic dialogue of Malevole in *The Malcontent* and Vindice in *The Revenger's Tragedy*.

The revenge drama tradition was peculiarly well suited to the forms of forensic training and insight that a legal career provided.[5] The genre is at its heart an extended rumination on justice, and revenge plays frequently stage legal hearings as part of their action; *The Revenger's Tragedy* and *The White Devil* both do this, drawing attention to the close relationship between law and performance, albeit in deeply unsatisfactory ways in terms of serving justice, and we might view Hamlet's staging of the play within a play to 'catch the conscience of the King' (*Hamlet*, 2.2.607) as a further variation on the theme. These plays also invite a forensic and ethical analysis of the rights of wronged individuals to take revenge into their own hands as against trusting to the laws and mechanisms of the state. This is the plotline that recurs from *The Spanish Tragedy* through to late Caroline revisitations of the form; Malevole in *The Malcontent* is a disguised duke, the former Duke of Genoa, Altofront, come back to expose the corruption and decadence of the court that deposed him and which now threatens among other things his own wife, Maria;[6] in *The Revenger's Tragedy* Vindice greets us onstage carrying the skull of his poisoned lover and declaring revenge on the perpetrators of this heinous crime;[7] Rosaura in James Shirley's *The Cardinal* (1641) is driven to breaking point by grief for her lost love, the Count D'Alvarez. Grief and the resulting anger of individuals are both the driving forces and the greatest dangers of these plays. What we are watching in essence is the passing of older medieval codes of individual honour and the introduction of the new Tudor legal system which insisted that the state must hold sway in such matters and all of the tensions that this threw up. In his 1625 essay 'On Revenge', Elizabethan courtier Sir Francis Bacon wrote that 'Revenge is a kind of wild justice; which the more man's nature runs to, the more ought law to weed it out'[8] and in *The Spanish Tragedy*, Hieronimo's professional position as the Knight Marshal sees him caught between these two positions – individual impulse and the law – as he seeks justice for Horatio's death: 'Thus must we toil in other men's extremes, / That know not how to remedy our own' (3.6.1–2), he says at one stage. What he also discovers to his cost, however, is that there are different codes of justice according to social rank; the nobility in this play is prepared to cover up for itself and we see that trope repeated in revenge drama by Marston and Middleton. In *The Revenger's Tragedy*, the rape of Antonio's wife is poorly served by the courts as the wronged husband himself observes when asked what justice can be had in this case: 'Faith none, my lord; it cools and is deferred' (1.4.51), adding that 'Judgement in this age is near kin to favour' (55).

The additional tension that plays out across revenge drama is the contest between free will and fate: in *The Spanish Tragedy*, for all that Hieronimo's wife Isabella tries to trust to the 'just' heavens and believe that 'murder cannot be hid' (2.5.57), these plays tend to indicate time and time again that murder can be concealed: as Hamlet observes of King Claudius in Shakespeare's play: 'one may smile and smile and be a villain' (*Hamlet*, 1.5.109). Certainly these plays hint at external forces operating on revengers, often spurring them to action. The whole of *The Spanish Tragedy*, as we have seen, is framed by having the figures of the ghost of Andrea and Revenge seated in the 'above' and commentating on the action, and if Hamlet's 'dull revenge'(Q2, 4.4.24), temporarily stalled as he philosophises on the rights and wrongs of taking justice into one's own hands, is prompted by the figure of the ghost – 'from this time forth / My thoughts be bloody or be nothing worth!' (Q2, 4.4.56–7) – for

Hieronimo it is the significant object that is the bloody napkin he collected from the scene of his son's brutal murder that acts as a tangible reminder of what remains to be done (see 3.13.85 s.d.):[9]

> Revenge on them that murdered my son.
> Then will I rent and tear them thus and thus,
> Shivering their limbs in pieces with my teeth . . .
>   (*The Spanish Tragedy*, 3.13.121–3)

It is a heady theatrical combination, then, this counterpointing of extended ethical debate, often conducted through the linguistic mechanism of the soliloquy, and extravagant staging of crimes. What also connects these plays is that they frequently reach their climax and find their resolution – however provisional – through acts of theatre and metatheatricality. Kyd's play once again establishes the precedent, with Hieronimo acting as playwright and director of a performance of 'The Tragedy of Solomon' that ends in real deaths, including his own (he stabs himself after first biting out his own tongue and then killing the Duke):

> Behoves thee then, Hieronimo to be revenged.
> The plot is laid of dire revenge:
> On then, Hieronimo, pursue revenge,
> For nothing wants but acting of revenge.
>   (*The Spanish Tragedy*, 4.3.27–30)

In subsequent interventions in the genre, we have murderous masques (*The Malcontent, The Revenger's Tragedy*), bloody banquets (*Titus Andronicus*), envenomed fencing matches (*The White Devil, Hamlet*) and plays within plays (*Hamlet*), and what is noticeable is that theatre has recourse to itself in the ultimate working out of justice.

The geographies of revenge

The environment in which revenge drama unfolds is invariably that of a decadent and glittering Renaissance court with all its competing energies of power, ambition and hierarchy. These courts are noticeably never English but instead located in Catholic mainland European communities – Italian principalities or in Spain – as if that somehow explained or gave a context to the brutal extravagances of the action. Only Shakespeare twists that convention with *Hamlet*'s northern European Danish setting, although we might note that the court of King Claudius with its over-propensity to feasting and drinking, its questionable adherence to religious belief, and its atmosphere of ambition and surveillance, in every other respect seems to resemble the spaces and places of its revenge drama companions ('Something is rotten in the state of Denmark', as the soldier Marcellus observes on sighting the ghost in *Hamlet*, 1.4.67). There is a distancing technique at play here; criticism of courtly decadence and corruption was far more easily visited upon foreigners and strangers than aimed directly at the English court of the day, an action which would inevitably have ended in censorship or suppression of the play concerned. There is also a fairly low-level appeal to audience taste taking place in post-Armada, post-Reformation England for plays in which Spanish or Italian counterparts were readily demonised. But it is the way in which these fallen worlds, these corrupt and corrupting courts, are staged which is perhaps the most revealing of the manner in which these plays were shaped by the spaces and places in which they were performed.

The Revenger's Tragedy opens with a stage procession of courtly characters passing '*over the stage with torch-light*' (1.1.0 s.d.) while an embittered Vindice (even his name marks him out from the start as an archetypal revenger – this is a play where many characters bear grossly indicative names, Lussurioso, Spurio, Ambitioso and so on, heightening the masque-like and symbolic nature of the action) characterises them all in negative terms for the watching theatre audience:

> Duke, royal lecher: go, grey haired Adultery
> And thou his son, as impious steeped as he:
> And thou his bastard true-begot in evil:
> And thou his duchess that will do with the devil . . .
>
> (1.1.1–4)

If we recall that all the while he delivers these lines, Vindice is clutching the skull belonging to his dead lover, Gloriana (see Figure 6 and also Case study F), we are left in no doubt as to the kind of world we are witnessing. Vindice's brother Hippolito will describe the court as being all 'in silk and silver' (1.1.114) and certainly in the candlelight of the early performances of this play which took place in the indoor Blackfriars Theatre (see Case study E) the shimmer of the textiles, threads and jewellery that was a major aspect of the means by which early modern theatre created its stage worlds would have stood out to the eye. But we are also surely being trained to distrust this world of 'silk and silver' at the same time; Vindice's cynical discourse throughout the play is steeped in images of sapphires and diamonds – there is sparkle here but it is entirely brittle. This is a place in which everyone seems intent on undoing everyone else. The Duke's sons and stepsons vie to outdo each other with fatal results:

as Ambitioso declares at the close of 3.1, 'upon thy neck, kind brother / The falling off of one head lifts up another' (28–9).

Vindice's powers of description are crucial to a full understanding of the corrupt court but also to how his disaffected character operates throughout this play. Disguised for a large part of the action and ironically employed by the very courtiers he sets out to destroy, his decadent discourse mirrors the immorality of the court under Duke Pietro's rule. In one telling exchange, Vindice (still in disguise) tests his own mother's propensity to be corrupted by the multiple allures of the court:

> O, think upon the pleasure of the palace,
> Securèd ease and state, the stirring meats
> Ready to move out of the dishes, that e'en now
> Quicken when they're eaten;
> Banquets abroad by torchlight, musics, sports...
> Nine coaches waiting – hurry, hurry, hurry!
>
> (2.1.193–7, 200)

The pace of this speech is exhilarating – Vindice gets caught up in the act of description almost to the point of being overwhelmed. If Gratiana all too easily succumbs to this descriptive and rhetorical power, we might argue that so do we.[10] Our relationship to the play is entirely framed through Vindice's bitter observations and, while we enjoy their verbal extravagances, we find ourselves as beholden to corruption as those we watch onstage. Hippolito is only half-joking when he first introduces Vindice in disguise to the court with the phrase: 'This our age swims within him' (1.3.24). By the close, Vindice is completely taken over by his self-assigned role as revenger, as subject to the dog-eat-dog environment of the court as those he seeks to mete out justice to and in danger of enjoying the violent excess a bit too much: 'Here was the sweetest occasion, the fittest hour, to have made my revenge familiar with him, shown him the body of the Duke his father and how quaintly he died – like a politician in hugger-mugger... And – O, I'm mad to lose such a sweet opportunity!' (5.1.16–22). A similarly bitter framing description of the moral and physical geography of the revenge drama in which he features is provided by Marston's Malevole. Really the deposed Duke Altofront, he has by the fifth act been completely taken over by his role as the court malcontent which he had assumed in order to enact his revenge. Like Vindice, the act of disguise takes him into dangerous proximity to the world he professes to reject. We witness Malevole engaged from the start in an odd kind of companionship with Pietro, the duke who deposed him. Pietro gives him licence to criticise and speak his mind in a manner that directly resembles the role of an official court fool or jester. As Malevole notes:

> Well, this disguise doth yet afford me that
> Which kings do seldom hear, or great men use –
> Free speech ...   (*The Malcontent*, 1.3.181–3)

The malcontent figure certainly has a strong link to the outspoken and cynical fools of early modern comedy. As we will see in Chapter 6's discussion of satire, it is only a small leap of the imagination from the dark humour of Bosola in Webster's *The Duchess of Malfi* – a tragedy that hovers on the edge of the revenge drama tradition throughout its five acts and nowhere more so than in scenes involving the disaffected former galley slave – to the cynicism of a Jaques or Feste in Shakespeare's romantic comedies. Marston was all too aware of this when creating *The Malcontent*, which is a play that luxuriates in its own generic elasticity. The play was actually described as a 'tragicomedy' when it was first entered on the Stationers' Register in 1604 and that is itself a nod towards the pastoral and satirical elements that the play readily embraces.[11] The relationships of both Malevole and Vindice with their audiences are pivotal to the success of this ambitious generic fluidity. The unsettling intimacies created by the propensity of revenge drama to soliloquy and aside as modes of interaction with audiences were only exacerbated by the staging of both these plays by children's companies (at least in their earliest formats)[12] whose repertoires demonstrated a heavy leaning towards the sardonic and the satiric that characterises the rich aesthetic of these plays (see Case study L).

Predominantly, though, what is striking about both *The Malcontent* and *The Revenger's Tragedy* is how funny they are, albeit in the most macabre and bleak manifestations of comic form. Pushing at the edge of genre, almost to the point of collapse, some critics have suggested that revenge drama became parodic of its own conventions so quickly that it was destined to burn brightly but briefly on the popular stage. Caroline drama, however, did seek to reanimate the form as late as the 1630s and 1640s so we should not create too rigid a teleology of peak and fall for this genre. Shirley's *The Cardinal* (1641), on a close reading of which our analysis in this chapter will end, is a play that is so obviously allusive to *Hamlet* and to Webster's Jacobean tragedies that it suggests the playwright assumed he could rely on an audience literate in the revenge drama tradition and therefore able to work at speed both with expectation and surprise as generic conventions were invoked and tested.

Feminising revenge drama

The Cardinal is one of those consciously belated incursions into the Jacobean aesthetic that is now recognised as a recurring strategy of Caroline drama. John Ford's tragedy of incest, *'Tis Pity She's a Whore* (1629–32), is one of the best-known examples, perhaps, of this kind of intervention, with its knowing, and often playful, intertextual revisiting of *Romeo and Juliet* and *Othello* among other plays. Sophie Tomlinson's important research has in many respects set the scene for our thinking about Shirley's play alongside Ford's 1633 play *The Lover's Melancholy* as a 'refashioning' of Elizabethan and Jacobean tragedy and their particular emphases on female performance.[13] But I want to close this chapter by focusing in on the highly innovative nature of Shirley's reworking of revenge tragedy through a central figure of female agency and performance: the Duchess Rosaura.

Shirley was, according to editor Elizabeth Yearling, a 'dramatist of echoes';[14] but I want to suggest here that this impulse to intertextuality on Shirley's part, even at the level of genre, is no mere reiterative action but rather a fundamental pillar of his creative approach. The opening of *The Cardinal* is instructive in this regard, where the appearance of Antonio, the Duchess's secretary, in the very first scene consciously invokes Websterian parallels with *The Duchess of Malfi*, but also deliberately thwarts any audience expectations derived from that earlier play in that *this* Antonio will *not* turn out to be the lover of this nevertheless eroticised widowed Duchess.

There are also invocations of revenge drama more widely in *The Cardinal* that help us to begin 'reading' the character of the Duchess Rosaura before we have even encountered her physical presence on the stage. From the very beginning she is described as being somehow against the grain of the court. It is the First Lord's poetic judgement that:

> She moves by the rapture of another wheel,
> That must be obeyed; like some sad passenger,
> That looks upon the coast his wishes fly to,
> But is transported by an adverse wind,
> Sometimes a churlish pilot.   (1.1.45–9)

The Cardinal self-consciously echoes *Hamlet*, not least in terms of the characterisation of Rosaura and her counterfeiting of an 'antic disposition'.[15] Tellingly, in a direct allusion to Hamlet's 'inky cloak' (*Hamlet*, 1.2.77), this echo is achieved at the level of costume. In 1.2, a self-consciously feminocentric scene staged between Rosaura and her ladies-in-waiting, the Duchess reflects on how her new post-mourning attire sits uncomfortably on her melancholic frame:

> even this
> New dress and smiling garment, meant to show
> A peace concluded 'twixt my grief and me
> Is but a sad remembrance.   (1.2.14–17)

Her resistance here to the 'loud and public marriage' intended for her and Columbo (1.1.11) is expressed through particular dramatic strategies which ensure that this is also the scene in which her special relationship with the audience is established. This is in itself a reworking of the dramaturgic tendency of this genre to place the revenger in the confidence of the audience, a tendency that can be witnessed in characterisations from Hamlet to Malevole to Vindice: 'Thus I must counterfeit a peace, when all / Within me is a mutiny' says Rosaura in an aside at 1.2.28–9.

Rosaura is a character whose part is largely delivered to the audience through a series of confiding asides, monologues and soliloquies. Often her delivery of these is placed in a potent position at the end of scenes, as at the end of 1.2 for example:

> My heart is in a mist, some good star smile
> Upon my resolution, and direct
> Two lovers in their chaste embrace to meet;
> Columbo's bed contains my winding sheet.
>   (1.2.239–42)

There are also Websterian linguistic echoes here; *The White Devil* can clearly be heard at line 239 (see 5.5.94 for example in that play) and sounds again in the winding-sheet image of 242 (see 2.1.65–6, 205). As well as noticing these facts of linguistic register we need to consider the impact of intertheatricality of this kind. The audience is placed in a privileged position of knowledge and foresight; it participates in the specifics of the Duchess's tragic condition and in turn it comes to recognise her agency, moral, physical and, indeed, theatrical: '[*Aside*] I have not the skill to contain myself' (1.2.94).[16] Rosaura's authoring of the letter to Columbo that sets the whole tragic plot in motion in Shirley's play is another deliberately stagey move, connecting to what Tomlinson has termed Rosaura's 'self-scripting' and the play's wider investigation into female subjectivity.[17] But there are many other ways in which *The Cardinal* invokes theatricality and spectacle in a manner deeply suggestive of the revenge genre inheritance.

Metatheatricality was a recurring feature of the revenge plot from *The Spanish Tragedy* onwards (and we might note at this point Bel-imperia and her fatal acting as a further significant female precursor to Rosaura). Shirley pays his dues to this canonical legacy but also wittily subverts the expectations and cross-readings that derive from it. In *The Cardinal*, we have the 3.2 dressing of the players by Antonio and the confused whisperings as to who may have authored the household entertainment about to be staged as part of the wedding celebrations for the Duchess and Count D'Alvarez (it will turn out to be a bloody device to enable Columbo to slay D'Alvarez, ensuring that the Duchess's second marriage is also unconsummated). *Hamlet*'s 'Murder of Gonzago' clearly resonates at this moment: 'Here this, ay this will fit your part; you shall wear the slashes, because you are a soldier; here's for the blue mute' (3.2.1–2; the reference is to the part of a liveried but silent servant character). What follows is a surprisingly intimate exchange in which the players confess worries about their casting and the fit of their costume, and discuss prosthetics such as beards and eye-patches. There is a kind of laying bare of the theatrical scene here that was intrinsic to the house-style of the particular playhouse for which Shirley was writing: the Blackfriars Theatre.

The fourth and fifth acts of *The Cardinal* swerve into the recognisable climactic sequencing of Jacobean tragedy and revenge drama. The audience is exposed in these latter stages to a strangely familiar corrupt court society, one that allows murderers like Columbo to go free by dint of privilege and leaves unheard the Duchess's calls for 'justice'. Shirley's drama, though, in invoking these echoes is more wilfully pragmatic than its predecessors. Yearling notes the veritable absence in *The Cardinal* of the extravagant and macabre death scenes more usually expected of the genre: 'Shirley's last tragedy is a revenge play shorn of many of the macabre accretions of the Jacobean imagination: no skulls, no poisoned helmets or pictures, no exulting in horrible deaths.'[18] I would suggest, however, that the Cardinal's poison-antidote-poison stratagem would come perilously close to the macabre in an actual performance.

It is true to say that there are no ghosts as such to prompt Rosaura to revenge. Noticeably it is she herself, the restricted female of the Navarre court, who has become spectral in this context: we learn in 4.2 that the Duchess is coffined up in her chambers 'like a ghost' (15), the spatialities of this description further emphasising her confinement within the strictures of the society in which she moves, grimly confirmed by the private threat Columbo makes to her in these supposedly private rooms:

> Live, but never presume again to marry,
> I'll kill the next at th'altar, and quench all
> The smiling tapers with his blood; if after
> You dare provoke the priest and heaven so much,

To take another in thy bed I'll cut him from
Thy warm embrace, and throw his heart to ravens.

(4.2.68–73)

It is worth adding that *Hamlet* is also recalled at this moment along with *The Duchess of Malfi* by this invasion of private space. The use later in the scene of an arras (behind which Hernando stows himself) underscores the suggestive consonances between the surveillance cultures of all three plays.[19] But we might also suggest that Hernando functions as the equivalent of the ghost of Old Hamlet, spurring Rosaura to revenge for her dead bridegroom:

> it is too much
> That you should keep your heart alive, so long
> After this spectacle, and not revenge it.

(4.2.135–7; see also 120–2)

Already though, one act of revenge (Hernando vows to kill Columbo as punishment for his crime) spurs on another as Rosaura intends herself to have 'some glory in the next revenge' (315) and bring down the hypocrite Cardinal (ambitious uncle to Columbo). It is at this point that she sets the madness plot in train, once again scripting her own performance in significant ways and ones that are directly conveyed to and shared with the audience: 'I will pretend my brain with grief distracted' (4.2.316). This moment is both a conscious reworking and a witty subversion of revenge traditions: to have this role played, spoken indeed, by a female character, albeit one still in the Blackfriars context performed by a boy actor, can be viewed as a conscious feminising of the genre in the late Caroline dramatic moment. It is a subversion which Shirley expects his audiences to comprehend through the activation of their deep theatrical familiarity with the tropes and traditions of this popular theatrical mode; in this sense, theatrical echoing becomes one of the most creative compositional acts of all.

'Here, in the Friars': the second Blackfriars indoor playhouse

The second Blackfriars playhouse[1] (the first had been a venue for the Children of the Chapel Royal in the 1570s and 1580s) was initially the home of the Children of the Chapel from about 1600 onwards until the King's Men took it over around 1608 and staged plays there right up to the outbreak of the English Civil War. This indoor theatre gained a reputation for cutting-edge drama and innovative theatre practice and attracted work from the top playwrights of the day, including Jonson, Middleton, Marston, Shakespeare and Chapman. It is a fascinating exercise to consider how particular plays written with the Blackfriars space in mind as at least one likely site of performance reflect and respond to the challenges and opportunities of the indoor playhouse with its smaller audience and therefore its greater intimacy, and with its candlelit interior and use of music between the acts to enable the trimming of the wax on the aforesaid candles.

The Induction that Webster is believed to have added to the performance script of Marston's *The Malcontent* when it was adapted for playing by the King's Men in an open-air amphitheatre, having initially been a children's company play, suggests that the use of music between the acts in the so-called 'private' or indoor theatres was an innovation that those older outdoor arenas could not match:

> SLY What are your additions?
> BURBAGE Sooth, not greatly needful; only as your salad to your great
>   feast, to entertain a little more time, and to abridge the
>   not-received custom of music in our theatre.
>   (*The Malcontent*, QC additions, Induction, 99–102)[2]

We might ask therefore what impact these musical interludes had on the dramaturgy and design of Blackfriars plays. Certainly we can observe that marking the space between the acts in this way draws attention to the design of a play in five acts so that the dramaturgy of an open-air production might be deemed to be more flowing (see Case study I), but more than that we start to register dramatists using these moments in the plays as creative space in their own right. In *The Malcontent*, for example, in between the first and second acts we have the following activity onstage recorded in a stage direction:

> *Enter* MENDOZA *with a sconce to observe* FERNEZE's *entrance, who, whilst the act is playing, enter unbraced, two Pages before him with lights; is met by* MAQUERELLE *and conveyed in. The Pages are sent away.*   (2.0 s.d.)

And in Middleton and Rowley's *The Changeling* we have this example bridging Acts 2 and 3:

> *Enter Alonzo and De Flores.*
> *(In the Act time, De Flores hides a naked rapier.)*   (3.1.0 s.d.)

This is a remarkable moment. By having De Flores prepare for the grisly murder of Alonzo in the act break by hiding that key stage property, the rapier, the audience is made horribly complicit in the subterfuge by which Alonzo is tempted into a dark back corridor of the castle to be slaughtered. We perhaps find ourselves aligned with Beatrice-Joanna in that we too are now inextricably bound up with De Flores in the action. It has become something of a commonplace to suggest that in theatres like the Blackfriars act breaks were simply opportunities for showing off lavish new clothing purchases in the audience, and certainly plays like Jonson's *The Devil Is an Ass* make mocking reference to this kind of activity (1.6.33), but it is clearly not the whole story and we need to think about entr'acte moments as spaces of dramatic opportunity and meaning-making as well.[3]

The *Malcontent* example draws attention to specific play with the darkness and low light levels that the candlelit Blackfriars could rely on and experiment with. The sconce carried by Mendoza would have served to uplight his face for the benefit of spectators, enhancing the atmosphere of suspense much as lighting effects in horror movies do. Blowing out candles would in contrast have exacerbated the sense of fear instilled in scenes such as that in Webster's own *The Duchess of Malfi* where Bosola hands the Duchess a severed hand in the dark.[4] These moments are all part of the chamber of horrors so carefully orchestrated and conveyed by Jacobean tragedy as a genre.

Similarly suggestive and symbolic use of the candlelight that was a practical necessity in indoor theatres occurs at the very beginning of *The Revenger's*

Tragedy. The opening stage direction tells us what audiences would have seen in the Blackfriars:

> Enter VINDICE [*holding a skull*]. *The Duke, Duchess, Lussurioso his son, Spurio the Bastard, with a train, pass over the stage with torch-light . . .*
>
> (1.1.0 s.d.)

Moments later, prompted by his brother Vindice to provide 'news' of the court, Hippolito describes it as operating 'In silk and silver, brother, never braver' (1.1.52). This brilliantly sums up what spectators would just have seen; those costly textiles and silver threads of the early modern costume department, caught in the light of the handheld candles. In turn this allows us later all too vividly to imagine in our own minds the ambience in which the horrific rape of Lord Antonio's wife took place:

> Last revelling night,
> When torch-light made an artificial noon
> About the court, some courtiers in the masque
> Putting on better faces than their own,
> Being full of fraud and flattery, amongst whom
> The Duchess' youngest son, that moth to honour,
> Filled up a room; and with long lust to eat
> Into my wearing . . .   (1.4.26–33)

The image of the moth and the destruction of Antonio's property (his wife) says much about the status of women in these kinds of parasitic court built on conspicuous consumption and display, but it is the music and masquing element of the description I want to focus on here. In this play and others created for the Blackfriars space, loud and sometimes dissonant music is knowingly deployed to create meaning and sometimes even quite literally to sound out death cries: the dance of death that is performed by the masque of revengers (including Vindice and Hippolito) in this play is a case in point, as is the earlier murder of Duke Pietro:

> **DUKE** I cannot brook –
>   [*Vindice kills him*]
>
> **VINDICE** The brook is turned to blood.
> **HIPPOLITO** Thanks to loud music.
>   (3.5.219–20)

This is further echoed by the thunder that resounds at the end of the murderous masque (5.3.42 s.d.). *The Malcontent* is similarly taken with the possibilities of the meaning that music can make. The play opens with

'*The vilest out-of-tune music being heard*' (1.1.0 s.d.) which immediately establishes a note of dissonance and provides a frame for understanding Malevole's role even before he steps onto the main stage. In the opening section of this play we hear him railing against the decadent and corrupt court, like some malevolent jester figure, from the 'above' or balcony space which supposedly connects to his offstage chamber:[5]

> I'll come among you, you goatish-blooded toderers, as gum into taffeta, to fret, to fret. I'll fall like a sponge into water, to suck up, to suck up. Howl again. I'll go to church and come to you. (1.2.15–19)

The music and the use of space all serve to underscore Malevole's distanced stance from the court.

All three of the plays invoked so far in part make their meaning from the darker, more intimate, candlelit and music-filled space of the second Blackfriars.[6] But the innovative reputation of the theatre rested not only on what its spatial and architectural features made possible; the Blackfriars also exploited novelty at every turn, from the kinds of generic experimentation it engaged in through to the use of the latest fashions as costumes and properties. Jean Howard has written brilliantly of the reason why a monkey is suddenly brought onto the stage of *Eastward Ho!* in 1605 as a marker not only of Gertrude's aspiration to have the latest 'thing' on the London scene but also of the theatre's own skill in registering the cultural zeitgeist.[7]

By the Caroline theatrical period, this urge to novelty and innovation extended to staging several plays that made a strong case for women to be able to play themselves on the professional stage rather than be aped by boy actors. Jonson's romantic comedy *The New Inn* which was staged (albeit without much success) at the Blackfriars in 1629 depicts several women who can play their parts with considerable skill and wit, and this idea is picked up in a different generic context by Shirley's *The Cardinal* through the manner in which Rosaura responds to the theatrical tradition of revengers that precedes her (precedes her even within the playing history of the second Blackfriars Theatre itself).[8] Queen Henrietta Maria was at the vanguard of the agitation for female performance at this time and it seems therefore highly significant that it was to the Blackfriars playhouse that she chose to come on several occasions in the 1630s to watch plays.[9]

The social life of things: skulls on the stage

A man stands in a graveyard. This is a man whom we have previously become accustomed to associating with ruminations on death and suicide. This is a man who when we first encountered him on the stage was dressed all in black ('Tis not alone my inky cloak, cold mother, / Nor customary suits of solemn black...', *Hamlet*, 1.2.77–8), a figure of melancholy and grief, someone deeply associated in our minds with notions of mortality. Hamlet, Prince of Denmark (for the man is he) comes then already laden by the fifth and final act of this play with associations on the part of the audience with ideas of death, but these are undoubtedly heightened, brought to a kind of performative peak, by the fact that at this particular moment he holds a specific stage property: a skull.

The skull has been quite literally thrown up onto and into the stage space by the gravedigger's excavations of a new plot (which we will later realise is for the drowned Ophelia). It is one of several different skulls produced by the gravedigger's labour and all of them provoke the philosophical Danish prince to trenchant observations on the brevity of life and the levelling effects of death:

> That skull had a tongue in it and could sing once...Here's fine
> revolution an we had the trick to see't...Why, may not that be the
> skull of a lawyer? Where be his quiddits now...?
>
> (5.1.75–6, 88–9, 95–6)

But it is when the laconic gravedigger invites Hamlet to reinvest the final skull, the one he now holds in his hands, with a personality, a memory, a history, by dating it to a precise time and place that the stage property takes on further suggestive layers of meaning in the moment of performance:

> **GRAVEDIGGER** Here's a skull now hath lien you i'th' earth three
> and twenty years.
> **HAMLET** Whose was it?

GRAVEDIGGER A whoreson mad fellow's it was. Whose do you think it was?

(5.1.163–7)

The skull turns out to belong to the former Elsinore jester Yorick, who was well known to Hamlet in his childhood:

> He hath bore me on his back a thousand times, and now how abhorred in my imagination it is . . . Here hung those lips that I have kissed I know not how oft. (5.1.175–9)

Through this sequence, then, the abstract property of a nameless, featureless skull is re-embodied by the practices of memory and theatre in striking ways.[1]

So iconic has this particular scenic moment become in the stage history of *Hamlet* that most actors in the role are depicted in this same gestural moment in the photographic stills and publicity material for their particular productions. It is iconic, then, in the deepest sense of that word. But as well as thinking about its resonance as a piece of theatre history, it is useful to think what the particular stage property of the skull mobilised for early modern audiences, in this play and others. Certainly much of the effect was visual, iconographic in the strictest sense of that word, mobilising what Janette Dillon has described as the 'emblematic functioning of props'.[2] The stage direction that cues up the grieving Hieronimo's physical appearance in 3.12 of Kyd's *The Spanish Tragedy* knowingly stages him as a figure of suicidal despair, one that audiences would have instantly recognised and computed for its signification with regard to his state of mind. The handheld stage properties he carries symbolise means of self-harm, stabbing and hanging, both of which feature as modes of death elsewhere in the play (Isabella's suicide at 4.2 and Horatio's murder at 2.4): '*Enter* HIERONIMO, *with a poniard in one hand, and a rope in the other*' (3.12.0 s.d.). The emblematic mindset that early modern spectators brought to productions and specifically to representations of death has been explored in considerable detail by Michael Neill and he relates some of the stagings of death with skulls and emblematic props to specific church paintings and woodcut images that were available at the time and were part of a broader European culture of *memento mori* traditions;[3] these provided lenses or frames through which a play might be 'read'. Elsewhere in this volume, through the study of specific title pages to print editions of plays, we explore the ways in which plays were appreciated, and indeed remembered, visually in analogous ways. But props did not function solely as visual stimuli; they were tangible objects

6. The significance and iconicity of a handheld property in
The Revenger's Tragedy.

with 'histories' and 'careers', to adopt the terminology of theorist Arjun Appadurai.[4] The skull in *Hamlet* can and should be read as exactly that – a physical remain of the human body such as early modern people might have encountered in their own dealings with graveyards and churches. Of course, that observation in itself is not without its complications. Steven Mullaney has brilliantly demonstrated that charnel houses where skulls and bones were traditionally stored were spaces erased along with monasteries themselves with the English Reformation so, though known to the audiences of *Hamlet*, perhaps a world in which skulls were piled high as in this scene would conjure up a recent past in terms of religious memory and experience.[5]

One property and just one stage moment, then; it would be useful to apply the ideas mobilised here around emblem, icon and material culture to other recurrent stage properties, small and large, on the early modern commercial stages: handkerchiefs, beds, joint stools, coins, the list could go on.[6] But we do have one other way of tracing the significance of this particular moment in *Hamlet* for seventeenth-century audiences because the moment gets picked up and reworked by subsequent plays and playwrights, not least in the early modern revenge drama tradition itself and in ways that verged on the parodic. Middleton's *The Revenger's Tragedy*, which we have already accounted for as a remarkable, subversive, even comic intervention in the genre, begins with a scene that is surely meant to recall Hamlet holding Yorick's skull when Vindice appears on a torchlit stage clutching the skull of Gloriana, his poisoned love (see Figure 6). The resonance of the stage picture accumulates potency when we consider that both *Hamlet* and *The Revenger's Tragedy* were King's Men plays and that *Hamlet* was probably in the repertory at the same time as Middleton's play in 1606 and that the lead role in each was probably played by the same star actor, Richard Burbage.[7]

Reading the life of a handheld skull property on the early modern stage provides an especially rich example of how successful plays got picked up, parodied and reworked often within a few years, sometimes even months of their first staging; elsewhere in this volume we see that *The Spanish Tragedy*, *Doctor Faustus*, *Romeo and Juliet* and *Tamburlaine*, to name just a few examples, were all knowingly alluded to and remade on the commercial stage for a spectatorship clearly keen to make connections between their viewing experiences across time. That this kind of mobilisation of theatrical memory was achieved through the very tangible effects of costume and props can tell us much about the fact that things mattered very much on the early modern stage.

Chapter 3

Histories

In the theatrically vibrant decade of the 1590s, there was one genre of play above all that seemed to virtually ensure good box office for the new theatrical entrepreneurs of London's Bankside, and that was the history play. Philip Henslowe's working diary of his Rose Theatre operations reveals to us regular performances for these plays by Marlowe, Shakespeare, Thomas Heywood, Robert Greene and others, and good commercial returns in the form of ticket sales.[1] Once at least some history plays had proved successful on the stage it was perhaps inevitable that businessmen like Henslowe would seek to commission more of the same and that this kind of economic rationale would have its own effect on theatrical history. But it is also worth asking why this kind of play – drama focused ostensibly on English, and occasionally Scottish, history of the recent centuries and in particular on the causes and consequences of the period of civil war known as the 'Wars of the Roses' and the subsequent foundations of the Tudor regime at the tail end of which an ageing Queen Elizabeth I found herself in the 1590s – caught the public imagination so strongly at this particular moment in time? What was it that these plays addressed or staged that so excited audiences that they wanted to see more and why was it the space of the commercial theatre in particular that seems to have made this kind of work not only possible but deeply alluring?

The explosion of creative energy in the London commercial theatres that stands at the heart of this study has often been allied to the new notions of national identity that were forged during the reign of Elizabeth I. The ships whose masts filled the skyline over the River Thames were a very visible signifier of a newly confident country engaged in global exploration and trade, and this sense of England's significance in the world was perhaps at its most heightened following the victory over the Spanish Armada in 1588. Just as the stage was fashioning new words and phrases with which to describe this newly forged sense of self, so the plays it chose to focus on explored the recent past as a means to understand and to a certain extent justify the actions of the present. A flurry of plays examining English and Scottish monarchs played out on the boards of the Globe and the Rose and other theatres: Marlowe's *Edward II*, the two parts of *Edward IV* by Heywood and Robert Greene's *The Scottish History of James IV*, as well as Shakespeare's *Richard II*, his wildly experimental two-parter on the reign of *Henry IV*, the *Henry VI* trilogy and *Richard III*, were all staged in this heady moment and there is considerable value in thinking about these plays and the topics they embrace alongside each other. As we will see in the course of this chapter, if the 1590s was the decade in which the history play phenomenon both exploded and hit its peak, the genre persists, albeit reconfigured, into other parallel theatrical modes: Shakespeare's *Macbeth* and *Cymbeline* (*c.* 1611) are both important extensions of his earlier experimentation in the form and late in his life he collaborates with Fletcher on a play about very recent history in the shape of *Henry VIII, or All is True* (1613). The genre is then reanimated with particular force as late as 1632–4 by Ford in his self-conscious playtext *Perkin Warbeck*, which is about the counterfeit challenge to the throne faced by Henry VII. But it is the particular 'moment' of the 1590s that we need to understand first in order to make sense of these later developments and interventions in the form.

One very straightforward reason for the 1590s interest in history as a subject matter for drama was its fresh availability in printed form through the 1577 and 1587 editions of Raphael Holinshed's collaboratively produced national history *Chronicles of England, Scotland and Ireland*. Holinshed's *Chronicles* provided a wonderful repository for a group of dramatists who were working at relatively high speed to meet the demanding commissions of Henslowe and his ilk. Marlowe, Shakespeare and much later Ford would all find inspiration for their history writing in Holinshed. But it was not simply a story of putting the history found in Holinshed into play form; the stage is a transformative space and what we can see if we read history plays against their ostensible source is the sheer amount of work that the dramatists do to interpolate, add to, provide new angles on and even challenge the stories they were adapting. It is these acts of transformation performed through both the writing and the staging of history plays that I am most interested in here since they provide a clue to the reasons why the history genre was integral to the moment in which early modern English society, and also early modern theatre itself, was developing a sense of identity and purpose.

Majestical matters

The staging of history inevitably invites questions of representation and it is for this reason that the frisson and effect of history plays are inextricably bound up with the reasons why popular theatre was considered to be a potentially dangerous activity by several theologians of the day. Ironically, then, it is by listening to the extremist voices of so-called 'anti-theatricalists' like Stephen Gosson that we can start to unpack the vitality, force and potentially transgressive nature of the messages and ideas being performed by these plays. Gosson's *Schoole of Abuse* was published in 1579 and was an attack on performance and performers of various kinds – '*a pleasant invective against Poets, Pipers, Plaiers, Jesters and such like Caterpillars of the Commonwealth*' as the text's own title would have it. The pamphlet's author charged the theatre with stirring up and encouraging all kinds of moral and social disorder. *Schoole of Abuse* was dedicated to the high-profile Elizabethan courtier poet Sir Philip Sidney, and minor strains of its influence can be registered in Sidney's own *Apology for Poetry* (1579, published 1595), though the latter is a deliberately more reasoned questioning of the offences against decorum and generic adherence which Sidney undoubtedly detected in the hybrid experiments of the commercial London stage in his criticism of plays that 'thrust in clowns by head and shoulders to play a part in majestical matters'.[2]

History plays at their simplest always involve playing the King, staging the monarch in some way, usually through the transformative effects of costumes, properties, movement and music. To an early modern mindset there must always have been something potentially dangerous or at the very least transgressive in this action. It was, for example, illegal to perform the living monarch on the commercial stage, which is why we can witness a flurry of 'fairy queens' appearing in Jacobean satires and comedies in the years immediately following the death of Elizabeth I – Jonson's *The Alchemist* providing one particularly memorable example in 1610. A striking example of this kind of work of monarchical performance in operation on the stage comes at 3.7 of Shakespeare's *Richard III* (1591). The Duke of Buckingham helps Richard of Gloucester to stage a scene in which he feigns lack of interest in being offered the crown of England only to be 'persuaded' by others to accept it. The moment is carefully choreographed and stage-managed by Buckingham:

> Be not you spoke with but by mighty suit;
> And look you get a prayer book in your hand,
> And stand betwixt two churchmen, good my lord.
> For on that ground, I'll build a holy descant.
> Be not so easily won to our request.
> Play the maid's part: say 'no', but take it.

                              (3.7.41–6)

We then see this described scene performed to the utmost of Richard's actorly skills. At 3.7.89 he appears with two bishops in the stage 'above' with the

requisite prayer book in his hand. By the end of the scene he has been successfully proclaimed King. It is an impressive piece of theatre in which the audience
is entirely complicit.[3]

What is it to claim that kingship can be created through the mere material
accoutrements of textiles and objects?[4] Several of our focus history plays seem to
deliberately toy with this subversive potential; attention is drawn relentlessly to
the performative qualities of particular characters such as Richard of Gloucester
who aspires to become King and who, by various foul methods, succeeds in
the course of *Richard III*. The opening of that play is revelatory of this fact; as
one recent editor, John Jowett, tells us: 'At the beginning of *Richard III*, the
audience first sees an actor alone onstage. He is not a formal prologue who
supplies the narrative context, but presents a character who is temporarily
abstracted from a social world that does not yet exist.'[5] This will colour the
way in which we, as spectators, respond to and seek to understand Richard
throughout the rest of the play. We have been given a privileged insight into
his restless and ambitious mind through his remarkable opening soliloquy:

> Now is the winter of our discontent
> Made glorious summer by this son of York,
> And all the clouds that loured upon our house
> In the deep bosom of the ocean buried.
>
> (1.1.1–4)

Thus far the speech is a display of elegant poetry and eloquent rhetoric; Richard
seems to be describing the time of peace that follows war, and that is uncontro-
versial enough, but if we listen really carefully to this poetry we start to register
a different tone, a sardonic, slightly sneering attitude to the very world that
he describes, which adds to our sense that he stands somewhat aloof from the
world of the play proper:

> Grim-visaged war hath smoothed his wrinkled front,
> And now, instead of mounting barbed steeds
> To fright the souls of fearful adversaries,
> He capers nimbly in a lady's chamber
> To the lascivious pleasing of a lute.   (1.1.9–13)

The spectator can almost hear a sneer in the way that the alliteration works
in those last lines quoted above: 'lady's . . . lascivious . . . lute'; Richard is a man
better suited to the masculine bravado of the battlefield than this world of pipes
and peace and almost immediately tells us as much with the spondee 'But I'
that Shakespeare uses so defiantly to twist around the thoughts and registers

of the sonnet sequence that he was composing at much the same time that he was writing his early history plays.

Tellingly Richard's 'But' is followed by a defiant use of the first person pronoun. A distinct individual is being made and articulated before our eyes:

> But I that am not shaped for sportive tricks
> Nor made to court an amorous looking-glass,
> I that am rudely stamped, and want love's majesty . . .
>
> (1.1.14–16)

We are witnessing, then, language in action in this soliloquy in ways that remind us of some of the most striking of Marlowe's tragic creations, and in particular of Barabas, whose remarkable opening scene and the particular kinds of engagement it established with audiences was unpacked in Case study C. Jowett sees a direct line extending from that opening scene of *The Jew of Malta*, a play written and staged just a few years earlier than *Richard III, c.* 1589–90, to this moment in Shakespeare's play: 'What Marlowe set in place so carefully Shakespeare could use to advantage. The isolation, its meaning, the implication that the onstage figure will propel himself into a socio-political world that he will confront with hostility – all these are already implied.'[6] Jowett also registers a further throwback to medieval theatre traditions and in particular to the frame-breaking figure of the Vice.[7] It is a link that Richard himself makes explicit to the audience in yet another moment of shared intimacy, this time through the mechanism of the stage aside:

> PRINCE What say you, uncle?
> RICHARD DUKE OF GLOUCESTER I say, 'Without
>   characters fame lives long'.
> (*Aside*) Thus like the formal Vice Iniquity,
> I moralize two meanings in one word.   (3.1.80–3)

The link that Richard forges with the medieval Vice here is achieved through a celebration of his linguistic dexterity; he is proud of his comparable skills in punning, his arch wit and by extension his ability to command an audience sitting at a play.[8] What we can also start to register in this analogy, however, are fruitful crossovers with the genre of comedy. The Vice, as well as being frame-breaking, straddled different theatrical registers. *Richard III* knowingly flirts (mostly by means of its highly individual and theatrically seductive protagonist) with the conventions of history, tragedy and comedy and in the end refuses to conform to one of these to the exclusion of all others. This in turn enables us to look another few years ahead to Shakespeare's *Henry IV* plays (both texts appear to have been written somewhere between 1596 and 1599) where, as Lawrence Danson has claimed, the 'manipulation of genre is truly revolutionary'.[9]

The two parts of *Henry IV* build on the experimentation clearly begun by Shakespeare in *Richard III* to bring together the generic signifiers of tragedy, history and comedy in challenging ways. It is not a simply dramaturgic act of juxtaposing comic scenes of popular culture with tragic or high political themes, though sometimes those plays' use of alternated courtly and tavern settings has been read in this binary manner. Rather, through the particular creation of Falstaff, of whom more in a later section, we witness a complex melding of these seemingly opposed possibilities. Falstaff too is a figure easily associated with the Vice. In *Part 1*, 2.5, a scene we will explore in greater detail in the final section of this chapter, Falstaff plays at being a monarch through the skilful deployment of a cushion, a dagger and a joint-stool as his props; the dagger was the prop associated with the stage Vice, and audience members with a working memory of medieval theatre practice would have readily made this link.

Falstaff is a fine performer; he 'stages' Hotspur's death in such a way as to claim the credit at the end of *Henry IV, Part 1* and we see him play-acting various roles in the course of the action but he is actually upstaged by a future monarch, Hal, who possesses truly impressive skills of disguise beyond the surface action of dressing up as a robber at Gads Hill to trick Falstaff into one of his moments of arch vanity and pomposity. Hal is the ultimate player king who takes audiences into his confidence through an early soliloquy, albeit to rather different ends from those of Richard of Gloucester in his history play. At the end of 1.2, the various inhabitants of and visitors to the Eastcheap tavern where Falstaff and his cronies like to hang out exit the stage, leaving Hal alone and able to make the ultimate revelation to us through a sharing of his real thoughts and plans:

> I know you all, and will a while uphold
> The unyoked humour of your idleness.
> Yet herein will I imitate the sun,
> Who doth permit the base contagious clouds
> To smother up his beauty from the world,
> That when he please again to be himself,
> Being wanted he may be more wondered at . . .
>
> (1.2.192–8)

If Richard III and Prince Hal are Shakespearean exercises in 'how to play the king', this is a theme that is returned to in the exploration of charisma that lies at the centre of John Ford's late Caroline foray into the history play genre.

Perkin Warbeck has a chief actor whose part is all about performance; by the close of the play, although Warbeck will go to his death claiming an authenticity in the role, his challenge to the rule of Henry VII (a character whom audiences would in turn recall as the avenging Duke of Richmond who slays Richard III at the Battle of Bosworth in the fifth act of Shakespeare's history) will have been proved counterfeit. The theme is established in the opening lines when Henry VII describes how his authority is questioned by association:

> Still to be haunted, still to be pursued,
> Still to be frighted with false apparitions
> Of pageant majesty and new-coined greatness,
> As if we were a mockery king in state . . .
>
> (1.1.1–4)

As the play's editor Marion Lomax has noted, the complexity is heightened further by the fact that this story of a player king is staged in a public theatre: 'how are we, in the theatre, to distinguish between the man who *plays* the king and the man who plays the man who plays the man who plays the king?'[10]

What is significant for our purposes is the extent to which Warbeck's charisma is located in appearance (there are numerous references to his appearance, his youthful handsomeness and how 'like a king 'a looks', 2.3.73) and in sheer rhetorical power and the control of language. The Earl of Crawford describes, with some resentment, the fact that the Scottish King and court are all too readily won over by the power of words and Warbeck's performance when he travels to the northern court to win support for his challenge to Henry VII and the English throne:

> 'Tis more than strange; my reason cannot answer
> Such argument of fine imposture, couched
> In witchcraft of persuasion, that it fashions
> Impossibilities as if appearance
> Could cozen truth itself.   (2.3.1–5)

The very terms of description wage war within Crawford's speech – his sceptical vocabulary is all of 'imposture', 'witchcraft' and cozening and yet at the same time Warbeck's language is undeniably effective, it 'fashions' and persuades and becomes a kind of 'truth' in the process. It is telling that Crawford is depicted by Ford as being something of an anti-theatricalist, distrusting the Scottish court's penchant for dances and masques:

> Is not this fine, I trow, to see the gambols,
> To hear the jigs, observe the frisks, b'enchanted
> With the rare discord of bells, pipes, and tabors,

Hotch-potch of Scotch and Irish twingle-twangles,
Like to so many choristers of Bedlam
Trolling a catch?   (3.2.2–7)

Of course his own daughter Katherine Gordon will prove to be one of those to 'b'enchanted' by Perkin Warbeck and she remains impressively loyal to her by-then husband to the bitter end.

Even at that bitter end, when we see Warbeck and his supporters heavily defeated and Warbeck needing to confess his counterfeit status or face execution, his language is defiantly regal. Though Henry VII, now once again with the upper hand in the relationship, seeks to diminish him by referring to his youth, it is telling that Warbeck appears undiminished and indeed shares the iambic pentameter line with a king in a manner that would seem to assert equality even when the odds are totally stacked against him:

> HENRY   Turn now thine eyes,
> Young man, upon thyself, and thy past actions!
> What revels, in combustion through our kingdom,
> A frenzy of aspiring youth hath danced,
> Till, wanting breath, thy feet of pride have slipped
> To break thy neck.
> WARBECK   But not my heart; my heart
> Will mount till every drop of blood be frozen
> By death's perpetual winter. If the sun
> Of majesty be darkened, let the sun
> Of life be hid from me in an eclipse
> Lasting and universal.   (5.2.48–58)

Warbeck's is the more traditionally, conventionally 'kingly' or regal rhetoric here. He uses all those metaphors of sun and light that we recognised in Hal's soliloquy in *Henry IV, Part 1*, so in the end are the questions the audience is left with less about Warbeck's authenticity than about the authenticity of monarchy itself and where it lies when costumes and scripts can seem to convey it so effectively on a public stage? While Ford's source in Holinshed clearly declares Perkin Warbeck to be a fake, the stage creation never admits to this. The audience is left to keep guessing right to the very end. This starts to seem like a very radical theatrical experience and perhaps explains why Ford wanted in the 1630s (when, after all, the rule of Charles I was coming in for some serious questioning and criticism) to revive an ostensibly outmoded theatrical genre. As his own Prologue acknowledges: 'Studies have, of this nature, been, of late / So out of fashion, so unfollowed' (1–2), but through his own remarkable character study Ford brings all of the genre's radical and challenging potential back into focus.

Historical perspective and pliant kings

We are beginning, then, to make quite a strong case for the genre of the history play as adopting on a regular basis a questioning method. As a literary mode or approach it does not simply seek to reinforce notions of monarchy and power unquestioningly or in the mode of propaganda on behalf of the Tudor regime, a charge which has occasionally been levelled against Shakespeare's histories. Certainly in trawling for their raw material in Holinshed, Marlowe and Shakespeare opt for some decidedly weak kings as their subject matter: Edward II, Richard II and Henry VI all fit this description and Richard III was potentially villainous in much of the Tudor historiography to which Shakespeare was exposed during the writing of his play and which also influenced Thomas Heywood's foray into overlapping territory in the two parts of his *Edward IV*, which features, in the second part, Richard of Gloucester's rapid ascent to power and his execution of Clarence and the young princes in the Tower, as well as his appalling treatment of his predecessor monarch's mistress, the former London goldsmith's wife, Jane Shore. Monarchy both as concept and in practice is subject to considerable scrutiny in the Elizabethan histories.

The full title, though, of the 1594 printed version of Marlowe's *Edward II* is *The Troublesome Reign and Lamentable Death of Edward the Second, King of England, with the Tragical Fall of Proud Mortimer*. There is tragedy here as much as there is critique of weak governance. If the early part of this play seems to weight judgement against a negligent and egotistical Edward, focusing attention on his derogation of duty towards the realm and the notion of a 'Troublesome Reign', the second half of the play flips that response on its head. Tragedy demands as a form that the fall of a great man strike us in some way, and it is fair to say that in the prison scenes in the later stages of this play, in which we witness Edward II incarcerated in a dungeon, thrown meat like a beast, and ultimately violently tortured to death, a large degree of audience sympathy is achieved (parallel effects might be argued for the scenes of the imprisoned monarch 'improvising' his own abdication and death in *Richard II*).[11] As Meg Pearson notes, 'Edward's is not a quick death, nor a silent one'; we know that he screams from the implicit reference to his noisy death by his executioners: 'I fear me that this cry will raise the town' (5.5.114). This theatrical 'spectacular moment' has a very direct, sensory and even transformative effect on watching audiences, shifting the judgement away from Edward and towards Mortimer, the ambitious earl who has ordered his killing.[12] History shades into formal tragedy here and the audience is the key participant in that gear-shift.

As if to ensure an exploratory approach on the part of his audiences from the earliest possible moment, Marlowe commenced his play not with the King himself or indeed with all the trappings of a regal ceremony but in fact with Piers Gaveston, the King's questionable favourite, newly returned from political exile, reading aloud an amorous letter from the recently crowned Edward. Already, then, we are being asked to view a monarch, his role and his responsibilities, from a very unusual angle:

> *Enter Gaveston reading on a letter that was brought him from the King*
> **GAVESTON** [*reads*] 'My father is deceased; come, Gaveston,
> And share the kingdom with me dearest friend.'
>
> (1.1.1–2)

There is no comment made by the King about the immensity of his new responsibilities; the kingdom is, it seems, no more than a luxurious gift to be shared with a lover. This is in striking contrast to the moments of insight we share with Prince Hal in the *Henry IV* plays. That in *Edward II* we immediately witness Gaveston's revelling in his newly achieved significance is doubly unsettling; words like 'surfeit' seem deliberately jarring in what should presumably be a period of national mourning for the late King:

> Ah, words that make me surfeit with delight!
> What greater bliss can hap to Gaveston
> Than live and be the favourite of a king?
>
> (1.1.3–5)

This suspicion is quickly confirmed as Gaveston also imagines how he will now lord it over those to whom he used to be accountable:

> Farewell, base stooping to the lordly peers;
> My knee shall bow to none but to the king.
> As for the multitude, that are but sparks
> Raked up in embers of their poverty,
> *Tanti*; I'll fawn first on the wind
> That glanceth at my lips and flieth away.
>
> (1.1.18–23)

In a later moment of soliloquy in this opening scene, Gaveston's ambitious and manipulative nature is revealed to extend even to his relationship with the

King. He plots how he will seduce and lure Edward away from anyone who questions his swift ascent:

> I must have wanton poets, pleasant wits,
> Musicians that with touching of a string
> May draw the pliant king which way I please.
>
> (1.1.49–51)

Marlowe's brilliance with openings has already been the subject of considerable discussion and focus in this study but what he achieves in this particular instance makes the point that history plays rarely concern themselves with scenes of high ceremony, but tend instead to favour the side angles and side corridors that reveal the way in which power operates and is performed. Shakespeare and Fletcher's *Henry VIII, or All is True* presents similarly suggestive examples of this approach by depicting those who are sometimes shut out or held out from the main action. We witness Thomas Cranmer seeking to gain entry to the rooms of power, dangerously on the edge of court business, 'without' as the Doorkeeper puts it:

> **NORFOLK** *(to the Doorkeeper)* Who waits there?
> **DOORKEEPER** *(coming forward)* Without, my noble lords?
> **GARDINER**   Yes.
> **DOORKEEPER**   My lord Archbishop,
> And has done half an hour, to know your pleasures.
>
> (5.2.38–40)

The side-corridor perspective on power casts monarchy in a new and highly questionable light.

Women in history: the female angle

Another way in which the history genre achieves fresh angles on supposedly conventional scenes of power is through the introduction of women's perspectives into plays otherwise shot through with masculine scenarios of courtly power and the battlefield.[13] Wooing scenes are a particularly common feature of this kind of dramaturgical contrast. *Henry V*, for all its focus on the death and glory of the Agincourt battlefield, ends ostensibly with Henry reduced to a slightly fumbling wooer, attempting to win the French Princess Catherine to him in poor French rather than simply subject her to the diktats of war which have decreed she should be given in marriage to the victor:

> Fair Catherine, and most fair,
> Will you vouchsafe to teach a soldier terms
> Such as will enter at a lady's ear
> And plead his love-suit to her gentle heart?
>
> (5.2.98–101)

In an earlier play in the group of texts referred to as the *Henriad* the model of a good marriage is portrayed by the lively discourse between Kate Percy and Hotspur in a part-comic scene where she strives to keep her restless warlike husband at home. She insists on knowing and sharing in his business – 'Some heavy business hath my lord in hand, / And I must know it, else he loves me not' (*1 Henry IV*, 2.4.63–4) – and her own terms of engagement are suitably feisty and real: 'A weasel hath not such a deal of spleen / As you are tossed with' (2.4.76–7) she says, threatening to break his little finger if he will not tell her the truth. There is a warmth in this scene that has rendered it much loved in the play's performance history across the centuries, but it also instructed contemporary Elizabethan audiences about the real lives and domestic realities behind scenes of high politics and public history. These female parts all appear in the English chronicle sources of Elizabethan and later seventeenth-century history plays but there is something particular about the way they are crafted by individual dramatists or writing teams that deserves comment.

In a manner akin to Kate Percy, Katherine Gordon has been seen to be a distinct voice and presence in Ford's *Perkin Warbeck*, seemingly resistant as she is to the waves of state politics in which she has become a pawn and a victim. King James IV of Scotland may have given her in marriage to Perkin Warbeck against her father's will to shore up a temporary alliance with the pretender to the English throne but she stays loyal beyond those impermanencies and is defiant in her own nobility to the end:

> We are that princess, whom your master king
> Pursues with reaching arms to draw into
> His power. Let him use his tyranny,
> We shall not be his subjects.   (5.1.82–5)

Several critics have seen in Ford's creation of Katherine's rounded character a further sign of Caroline drama's deeper and more extensive interest in women's roles.[14] This has often been attributed to the influence on theatrical culture of Charles I's French wife Henrietta Maria, who commissioned and performed in theatre at the court and who attended plays in the public playhouses, but it would be wrong to create some naïve periodisation of women's roles in history plays since strong characterisations such as Kate Percy do predate the Caroline theatrical moment.

Neither are wooing scenes or depictions of marriage simplistically all of one type in early modern history plays. In yet another moment of brutal parody and realpolitik in *Richard III* there is a wicked undercutting of even this scenario. At the start of 1.2, Lady Anne (whose husband Richard has also murdered) enters mourning with the onstage open coffin of King Henry VI. Richard chooses this odd, deliberately jarring and unsettling moment to start to woo her as his future wife:

> **LADY ANNE** Ill rest betide the chamber where thou liest.
> **RICHARD GLOUCESTER** So will it madam, till I lie with you.
>
> (1.2.113–14)

Aesthetically this is achieved with considerable brilliance. Richard and Anne engage in the kind of quick-fire stichomythic dialogue (line-by-line exchanges, often punning with and interacting with each other) audiences had been trained to associate with comedy and in particular with warring lovers such as Petruchio and Katherina in *The Taming of the Shrew* (1590–2) and later Beatrice and Benedick in *Much Ado About Nothing* (1598–9). Anne seems to become so wrapped up in the theatrical performance of it all that the realities of the open coffin and recent history are forgotten. By the end of the scene, following various performative sleights of hand involving props (a sword, a ring) and striking gestures (she spits on him at one point, 144, in an action which would have been deeply shocking to early modern audiences), she is won (for a contemporary image of this scene, see Figure 3). Richard then crows over his success in a lengthy soliloquy to an equally seduced and morally and emotionally confused audience:

> Was ever woman in this humour wooed?
> Was ever woman in this humour won?
> I'll have her, but I will not keep her long.
>
> (1.2.215–17)

As well as being another devastating example of the Shakespearean use of monosyllables for emphasis and effect, this is a moment which, as Phyllis Rackin and Jean Howard have indicated, aligns the audience with Lady Anne as equally duped by the power of theatre to seduce.[15] Nor are all seduction scenes necessarily conducted at court. As Rackin and Howard also detail in their important reclamation of the history play genre for the attentions of feminist scholarship, Mistress Quickly's tavern in Eastcheap is the beating heart of the *Henry IV* plays and depicts women as 'theatregoers, entrepreneurs, and purveyors of commercial sex' and, in the process, part of the tavern–playhouse interactions that the plays hinge on for their full impact and effect.[16]

Women in an entrepreneurial context provide a fascinating under-storey to the two parts of Heywood's *Edward IV*. In those plays, we see characters such as the ill-fated Jane Shore, the goldsmith's wife who will become mistress to the King after an unprecedented wooing scene in the goldsmith's own workshop cum shop, her erstwhile friend and hostess Mistress Blage who proves all too ready to betray Jane for material gain when she falls from grace under the new regime of Richard III, and the highly capable, and indeed Lichfield-educated, tanner's daughter Nell, who makes bedding and keeps what she can of the household provisions from marauding rats (see for example *Edward IV, Part 1*, 14.15–18, 118–20),[17] and also catch allusions to other working city women such as 'little Pym', 'bouncing Bess and lusty Kate' (*Part 1*, 10.151, 162) through the dying words of Spicing the rebellious commoner:

> Well, commend me to little Pym, and pray her to redeem my pawned hose; they lie at the Blue Boar for eleven pence . . . Commend me to Black Luce, bouncing Bess, and lusty Kate, and all the other pretty morsels of man's flesh. Farewell, pink and pinnace, flyboat and carvel, Turnbull and Spittle. (*Part 1*, 10, 151–3, 162–5)

These are the kinds of fiercely contemporary narrative and storyline, as well as deliberately localised setting (taverns such as the Blue Boar, familiar London streets such as Turnbull, shopfronts) that we will see resurfacing in a different generic context with the rise of city comedy as a form in the early decades of the seventeenth century and to which Chapter 5 will return. The artistic journey from the goldsmith's shop of *Edward IV* to that of Middleton's *A Chaste Maid in Cheapside*, or from Doll Tearsheet in *Henry IV, Part 2* to Dol Common in Jonson's *The Alchemist*, is part of a theatrical continuum that generic categorisation should not be allowed to obscure.

Cross-fertilisation and sequences of plays

Shakespeare's interest in history plays not as stand-alone experiences but as parts of longer cycles, pairings and trilogies further suggests that it was active cross-fertilisation and interaction of ideas among spectators for these plays that most excited his theatrical imagination and creativity. We have already spent some time focusing on the impact of Richard of Gloucester's soliloquy at the start of *Richard III* but the effects of this highly individuated performance would have been further heightened for those spectators who had been witness to an earlier Shakespearean history play featuring the same character. *Henry VI, Part 3* features Richard of Gloucester and, even here, his character engages in extended time periods alone on the stage when he is talking to no one except himself – and the watching audience. The apotheosis of this is reached in 5.7 when he kills King Henry VI onstage, claiming this moment as his destiny or 'fate':

> Die, prophet, in thy speech,
> > *He stabs him*
> For this, amongst the rest, was I ordained.
> > (5.7.57–8)

But it is the lengthy soliloquy that follows which is the most overt moment when an individual character and the arc of the next play in the sequence is radically shaped before our eyes (and in our ears, for it is through language and rhetoric ultimately that Richard fashions his political and stage identity):

> I that have neither pity, love, nor fear . . .
> Then, since the heavens have shaped my body so,
> Let hell make crooked my mind to answer it.
> I had no father, I am like no father;
> I have no brother, I am like no brother;
> And this word 'love', which greybeards call divine,
> Be resident in men like one another
> And not in me – I am myself alone.
> > (5.7.68, 78–84)

If, as many critics have noted, history plays are by their nature concerned with successions and therefore with the familial relations that enable those successions, then Richard is a statement almost against the genre; in his solitary and unique way, he will shape the history play to suit his own ends.

What the act, though, of audiences bringing this earlier experience of Richard to a production of *Richard III* serves as a fine working example of is the role of memory, theatrical and historical, in the production of meaning in the history genre, something Shakespeare capitalised on through the creation of self-referential sequences and groupings of plays and characters. Janette Dillon has written of the plays' reliance on repetition and variation as an essential element of form.[18] All of this meant that audience members' multiple perspectives on plays, perspectives created from their own historical knowledges and theatregoing experiences, were considerable and were necessarily built into the dramaturgy.

The common people

A further way in which the audience was very consciously built into the creation of meaning and the recognition of both nation and community in these plays was through the perspective they offered on events from the common people of England. Both parts of Heywood's *Edward IV* give considerable stage time to the citizenry of London and to the interests and issues of the mercantile classes, not least through the unusually extended characterisation of John Hobs the Tamworth tanner.[19] We first encounter the tanner onstage when he is returning home from Coleshill Market in Warwickshire where he has been investing in the cowhides essential to his trade. He gestures to his offstage servant Dudgeon, whom we are asked to imagine leading Hobs's horse laden with the precious hides down the narrow country roads of the county:

> Dudgeon! Dost thou hear? Look well to Brock, my mare; drive Dun and her fair and softly down the hill, and take heed the thorns tear not the horns of my cowhides as thou goest near the hedges . . . I'll meet thee at the stile and help to set it all straight.   (*Edward IV, Part 1*, 11.1–6)

He is totting up the cost of his investments when he unwittingly encounters in turn the Queen and the King who are hunting in the Warwickshire forests at Drayton Bassett and, mistakenly believing Edward IV to be Ned, the King's butler, embarks on a lengthy discourse which gives both King and watching audiences access to the view of the common working people of England's regions and provinces. Instead of pleading for selfish special treatment and a monopoly on his tanning trade – the King asks him, somewhat astonished: 'Hast thou no suit, touching thy trade? To transport hides or sell leather only in a certain circuit? Or about bark, on such like? To have letters patents?' (13.72–4) – Hobs proves instead to be a good neighbour who offers common hospitality to the stranger, and a touching scene of welcome in his own homestead follows in scene 14.[20]

It is once again the position, participation and engagement of audiences that proves key to the working of specific moments such as these in history plays. The second part of *Edward IV*, in particular, asks spectators to comprehend historical events – King Edward's taking of a citizen mistress, his eventual death and King Richard III's murderous rise to power – through the traumatised eyes of Matthew Shore, the goldsmith whose previously happy existence and marriage were undone by the King's unwarranted attentions towards his wife Jane, an attention which leads in Matthew's case to a spiral of self-imposed exile and near-execution, and in Jane's to banishment and betrayal of various kinds, only to die of a broken heart beyond the city walls. The power of soliloquy is used here to fasten the audience's attention on the tyrannies and weaknesses of various monarchs and leaders in a pair of plays that is fascinating for its emphasis on the London citizen experience. Elsewhere in *Part 1*, we see the rebellion of Falconbridge and his citizen militia and, extending across *Parts 1* and *2*, the encounter between Edward in disguise and the Tamworth tanner. These moments too, which evoked streets and customs and behaviours familiar to 1590s audiences as those of their own city rather than the historical milieu of the plays, effect a particular kind of engagement through the process of recognition.

In Shakespeare's *Henry IV* plays this kind of interest in the wider communities of the nation than purely the ruling classes develops into the depiction less of London society in all its different strata than a complex, multi-angled perspective on the provinces and regions of England and the trades and professions undertaken by people beyond the court – be it as tavern workers or carriers (in *Part 1*, 2.1, we see two carriers transporting their wares from a Rochester inn in the early hours of the morning), or as agricultural labourers (and press-ganged foot soldiers) in the Gloucestershire locale of Justice Shallow in *Part 2*. Their lines bring a common idiom onto the stage as well:[21]

> **FIRST CARRIER** Heigh-ho! An't be not four by the day, I'll be hanged.
> Charles's Wain is over the new chimney, and yet our horse not
> packed. What, ostler!
> **OSTLER** (*within*) Anon, anon!
> **FIRST CARRIER** I prithee, Tom, beat cut's saddle, put a few flocks in
> the point. Poor jade is wrung in the withers, out of all cess.
>
> (*Part 1*, 2.1.1–7)

It is the kind of seemingly inconsequential scene, on which no plotline hinges or huge insight hangs, which modern theatre companies are often keen to cut in an effort to reduce the running time of these plays, but something is irretrievably lost from the play's landscape when this happens. Danson sees moments such as this one as a fundamental feature of the history play genre and not least of the *Henry IV* plays:

> Common soldiers and their distressed wives, traders and farm labourers,
> a gardener, a waiter in a tavern, the groom who curries the king's horse,
> a courtly justice of the peace and his sleepy old cousin, a fat, boozy,
> decayed old aristocrat; the history that happens in these plays happens
> in a world more thickly imagined, more thoroughly populated with
> vividly recognized members of diverse social classes, than in any
> previous dramatic representation of history.[22]

Rackin and Howard extend this observation to suggest that this also changes something about the cultural geography, the spaces and places, of these plays, rendering the *Henry* plays innovative even within a path-breaking body of work in the 1590s that was trying to come to terms with national identity through history. They compare the rambling structure of these plays to the vogue for chorography at the time, a body of work that was seeking to write the English landscape and its regions into being:[23]

> No longer confined to the elevated domain of court and battlefield, the world of *Henry IV* includes a variety of vividly detailed contemporary settings, ranging like a disordered chorographic 'perambulation' from Shallow's bucolic Gloucestershire, to an innyard on the road to London, to Falstaff's bustling urban Eastcheap.[24]

This in turn links chronicle history plays such as *Edward IV* to experiments in comedic drama such as Thomas Dekker's *The Shoemaker's Holiday* and the emergent mode of city comedy which sought in various ways to represent the nation back to itself in all its glorious diversity and variousness.

Janette Dillon has observed that it is these kinds of punctuating, stand-alone scenes – ones which are not plot drivers but rather part of a play's wider landscape and environment – that are frequently cut in contemporary performance.[25] This runs the risk of eradicating crucial patterning and texture in the process. A perfect example of this phenomenon from *Richard III* is 3.6 where we encounter a scrivener, a person who wrote up documents, usually those of a legal nature. True to his trade, this scrivener enters with a paper in his hand. He speaks just fourteen lines (a sonnet, interestingly enough, a form that early modern audiences would have heard immediately through its aural delivery, in particular through its closing couplet, and that adds to the standout nature of this moment[26]) and he will not be seen again in the play. This is his single moment on the stage and yet it tells us so much. The paper he carries is the indictment of Lord Hastings, whom Richard has just had summarily executed:

> Here is the indictment of the good Lord Hastings,
> Which in a set hand fairly is engrossed,
> That it may be today read o'er in Paul's –
> And mark how well the sequel hangs together . . .
>
> (3.6.1–4)

The reference to 'Paul's' is to St Paul's, a major gathering place at this time, where news such as this would be read aloud to gathered crowds. Another spatial story is being told through this moment without it having to be directly shown onstage. But even more striking is the Scrivener's account of the pains he took to write this out and how he stayed up all night to do so. In recounting these details he also reveals how fact gets rewritten, how history gets written and overwritten, and it is a moment of striking insight for both audience and playwright alike:

> Eleven hours I have spent to write it over,
> For yesternight by Catesby was it sent me;
> The precedent was full as long a-doing;
> And yet, within these five hours, Hastings lived,
> Untainted, unexamined, free, at liberty.
> Here's a good world the while! Who is so gross
> That cannot see this palpable device?
> Yet who so bold but says he sees it not?
> Bad is the world, and all will come to naught,
> When such ill dealing must be seen in thought.
>
> (3.6.5–14)

And he leaves the stage, his opportunity in the spotlight, his brief moment of shared insight, over.[27] But, as before, the memory of this moment rests with the audience and in the overall scheme of things it really matters.

The matter of objects: crowns and cushions

The major stage property in the staging of a history play is invariably a crown. A potent symbol, the crown stands in metonymically for the whole nation over which a monarch rules and recalls the key ceremonial of the coronation in which the frail, flawed human body is made itself to stand for something much greater, the so-called 'divine right of kings'. When we first see King Henry IV onstage at the beginning of *Part 1* of Shakespeare's paired plays charting his troubled reign, it is obvious that he does not wear the crown or the responsibilities it represents lightly. His first line is as follows: 'So shaken as we are, so wan with care' (1.1.1), and that sets the tone for his discourse and demeanour through the two parts. As in the earlier discussion of *Richard III*, audience members with either an historical knowledge or a theatrical memory will know why Henry IV is so burdened by his role and the robes and accoutrements that accompany it; for he is the Henry Bolingbroke of Shakespeare's *Richard II*, an historical actor whom Bankside theatregoers could have seen on other nights depriving the appointed monarch quite literally of his crown and his life:

RICHARD Now is this golden crown like a deep well
　　　That owes two buckets filling one another,
　　　The ever emptier dancing in the air,
　　　The other down, unseen, and full of water.
　　　That bucket down and full of tears am I,
　　　Drinking my griefs, whilst you mount up on high.
BOLINGBROKE I thought you had been willing to resign.
RICHARD My crown I am, but still my griefs are mine.
　　　You may my glories, and my state depose,
　　　But not my griefs; still am I king of those.
　　　　　　　　　　　　　　　(*Richard II*, 4.1.174–183)

Bolingbroke's reply hits home if we hear it with the knowledge of that care-ridden opening to *Henry IV, Part 1* in mind: 'Part of your cares you give me with your crown' (184). The crown as object seems to transfer with it a weight of care (and conscience) to Bolingbroke, which he carries onto the stage at the start of the *Henry IV* plays; in this way we can begin to see how plays enhanced and affected comparisons and connections between them by their co-presence in the repertoire.

One of the reasons proffered earlier for the opposition to commercial theatre's staging of kingship was that it reduced the role and its responsibilities to a story about costumes, robes and props, crowns, sceptres and chairs of state. In Case study F we explored the way in which an object might seem to have a whole biography attached to it. The crown as a stage prop, a handheld, portable item that can nevertheless tell multiple narratives of nation and individual, proves crucially important, then, in *Richard II* and the accompanying or related two parts of *Henry IV*. In the case of the latter, we as audiences are already being trained to seek this visual emblem out and to construe meaning from it whenever it (or indeed impersonations of it) appears onstage, from the very opening moments of the drama.

In *Part 2*, 4.3 we see the dying King attended by his wayward son Prince Hal. His crown is at this point in the action resting on a pillow as he sleeps (at 137 the King has directed Clarence his son to 'Set me the crown upon my pillow here'). Dillon has astutely outlined the fact that this stage picture in itself would have recalled state ceremonial for early modern audiences since crowns were carried on ceremonial cushions during state coronations.[28] This act of ceremony is meant to heighten the understanding of watching audiences that this is a sacred object. The shock is therefore considerable when Hal, visiting his sick father and left alone with him in the bedchamber, is drawn to this talismanic object and all that it says about his future:

> Why doth the crown lie there upon his pillow
> Being so troublesome a bedfellow?
> O polished perturbation, golden care,
> That keep'st the ports of slumber open wide...
>
> (4.3.152–5)

Hal cannot resist trying the item of 'polished perturbation' on and with it experiencing a frisson of the 'divine right' it imposes – 'Lo where it sits, / Which God shall guard' (4.3.174–5) – and exits the room still wearing the 'golden rigol' on his head (167). The King awakens from his slumber and is traumatised to find the crown missing. Initially he and his bedchamber attendants read this scene as an indication of Hal's crass ambition. In a painful private exchange with his son, Henry accuses him of wishing him dead:

> What, canst thou not forbear me half an hour?
> Then get thee gone and dig my grave thyself,
> And bid the merry bells ring to thine ear
> That thou art crowned, not that I am dead.
>
> (4.3.238–41)

This is a scene that projects both forwards and backwards in intriguing ways that once again hook the audience's attention. The unseemly tussling over the crown and the position that attaches to it seems to deliberately recall the struggle over the crown that was staged between Richard II and Bolingbroke in 4.1 of *Richard II* but it also looks forward to when we will see Hal crowned for real as King Henry V in the fifth act of this play. That moment not only ushers in yet another play in the Shakespearean history cycle (*Henry V*) but is also the point in the two parts of *Henry IV* when Hal finally performs the act of banishing Falstaff that he first promised as early as that previously cited cold-blooded soliloquy in the first act of *Part 1*: 'I know you all, and will a while uphold / The unyoked humour of your idleness' (1.2.192–3). The 'a while' says it all; Hal has intentions other than spending his entire life in an Eastcheap tavern in the company of Sir John Falstaff: 'I'll so offend to make offence a skill, / Redeeming time when men think least I will' (1.2.213–14).

But both Hal's action of rejecting Falstaff (and the life that he in turn represents) and the wearing of the crown in *Part 2* have also been prefigured by a much earlier scene of intense theatrical brilliance which takes place in the Eastcheap tavern where Hal spends much of his time in the company of Falstaff, Poins *et al.* in the first part of *Henry IV*, much to the despair of his father the King. In 2.5, the decayed old knight and his princely accomplice decide to rehearse an interview that Hal is destined to have at court with his father the King the following day:

> **PRINCE HARRY** Do thou stand for my father, and examine me upon
> the particulars of my life.
>
> (*Henry IV, Part 1*, 2.5.379–80)

The brilliance of this moment rests partly in its use of stage properties to tell the story of playacting and its complicated relationship to monarchy.

> **SIR JOHN** This chair shall be my state, this dagger my sceptre, and this
> cushion my crown.
> **PRINCE HARRY** Thy state is taken for a joint-stool, thy golden sceptre
> for a leaden dagger, and thy precious rich crown for a pitiful bald
> crown.
>
> (*1 Henry IV*, 2.5.381–5)

The significant props of state (chair of state, sceptre and crown, all significant elements in the coronation rituals alluded to previously) are reduced here simultaneously to the objects to hand in an Eastcheap tavern – and all the insults to ceremony that represents – and to the working tools of a commercial theatre. Tavern is made theatre and theatre tavern in a moment of superb transference that seems to equate both with a vibrant improvisatory popular culture. This scene is warm, witty and funny. We see Hal and Falstaff trade banter as each manages to insult the other to a cheering onstage audience in their respective roles. Initially Falstaff plays the King and suggests somewhat outrageously that Henry IV would praise him in Hal's presence as 'A goodly, portly man, i' faith, and a corpulent; of a cheerful look, a pleasing eye' (424–5) and suggests that while Hal might banish the rest of the Eastcheap company he should keep this knight close by (433–4). Hal decides at this point that they should swap roles and determines that he will take the part of the King himself. His 'kingly' version of Falstaff is emphatically more negative: 'There is a devil haunts thee in the likeness of an old, fat man . . . Why dost thou converse with that trunk of humours . . . ?' (452, 454).

All of this is a cue for some witty invective and roleplay between the two men but as that later scene with the 'real' golden crown informs us in hindsight, this is also deadly serious subject matter. Falstaff may play with the notion of banishment –

> Banish not him thy Harry's company,
> Banish not him thy Harry's company.
> Banish plump Jack, and banish all the world.
>
> (2.5.483–5)

– and audiences may also lament any thought of the loss of the energy of Falstaff from the stage, but Hal's response (for the moment in the guise of the King his father) is another of those time-stopping moments of monosyllabic honesty in Shakespeare: 'I do, I will' (486). This is exactly what Hal will do when he finally wears the crown for real in the fifth act of *Part 2*: 'I know thee not, old man' (5.3.47). The lines between theatre and reality are deliberately blurred in each of these significant moments and the pasteboard crown or indeed the cushion made to stand for a crown on the commercial theatre stage as well as the bare boards of the Boar's Head in Eastcheap can serve to tell a very deep story of kingship and responsibility.

Conclusion: historic agency

A comparable potency attaches to the property of the crown on the stages of both *Edward II* and *Richard II*, particularly in their climactic fifth acts. In 5.1 of Marlowe's play, Edward enters with the crown on his head but it is this very object that the barons are insisting he surrenders and in the course of the scene he seems to toy with the possibility of abdication only to take refuge in that sense of being the divinely appointed King and therefore inseparable from the object that represents his role on earth:

> Ah Leicester, weigh how hardly I can brook
> To lose my crown and kingdom without cause,
> To give ambitious Mortimer my right . . .
> [*He takes off the crown*]
> Here, take my crown, the life of Edward too!
> Two kings in England cannot reign at once.
> (*Edward II*, 5.1.51–3, 56 s.d.–58)

He cannot bear to surrender the final vestige of his power – 'But stay a while. Let me be king till night, / That I may gaze upon this glittering crown' (5.1.59–60) – and temporarily restores the crown to his head only to be forced to surrender it yet again (106). By 5.3, he is being shaven with ditch water in the ultimate act of humiliation.

The tussles for the crown on the multiple stages of multiple history plays enact tales of ambition and usurpation, of good and bad governance, and of the collision between national and individual responsibilities, all of which were storylines available in the chronicle histories that formed the source material for Marlowe, Shakespeare, Heywood, Ford and others when writing their plays. But there are also tangible differences to the telling of those stories and the ways in which they are made to bear meaning that are absolutely specific to the genre of theatre in which they are being remade and retold, stories fashioned from props and costumes and made by the labour of actors on the stage. In this way the role of the individual actor as agent in historical narrative is brought to the fore; life is breathed into the lives and deaths of Richard of Gloucester or Edward II or into the eventual triumph of Hal as Henry V at Agincourt in ways that only the stage knows how to achieve. The role of the audience has proven to be central to all of this; through the use of metatheatre, soliloquy and direct address and through the animation of memories, theatrical and everyday, the spectators for history plays are themselves rendered agents in the story and in the process.

Title pages and plays in print

When playtexts were printed their contents were announced to readers by means of a title page. The content of these title pages did vary considerably and as artefacts in their own right they are increasingly becoming a significant source for theatre historians to use in compiling a sense of what spectators took away from or valued in the theatrical experience. Rather than separating print from performance as can sometimes be the tendency in scholarship, by looking at the visual and textual culture of title pages we may gain access to supposedly 'lost' or ephemeral moments of performance as much as to reading and printing-house cultures.

To concentrate initially, though, on the textual information carried by title pages to plays can in itself yield much interesting detail. As Alan Farmer has demonstrated, title pages for plays began increasingly to provide not just the title – sometimes in itself an indicator of genre, though again the fashion for this waxed and waned over time – but often a more explanatory subtitle and then more often than not, particularly as the seventeenth century progressed, information about supposed authorship and performance history.[1] So, whereas the 1616 title page to Marlowe's *The Tragicall History of Doctor Faustus* (see Figure 4) tells us simply that it was by him, and the title and the address of the printers, the 1623 title page to Kyd's *The Spanish Tragedy* (see Figure 5) has become far busier with information: '*The Spanish Tragedy: Or, Hieronimo is mad againe*' already provides us with an indicator of Hieronimo's significance as a protagonist – something the allusions of later plays have also evidenced (see Chapter 2 on revenge drama). But it also notes that the text contains 'the lamentable end of Don Horatio and Belimperia; With the pittifull Death of Hieronimo'. It is as if the 'hot spots' of the plot are being picked out for readers who are wondering which playtext to buy, to tempt them – much as a modern literary endorsement on a book jacket would do – to enter the pages, to go beyond the cover. Certainly, historians of the book are increasingly reading title pages as a form of printing-house publicity or advertisement, and this gains further credence in the early modern period when we learn that many of these pages were also made into loose flyers and pinned up as advertisements around the city, drawing people to the printers' shops, but also perhaps to the originating playhouses.[2] But we might also think about this list of 'hot spots' in another way, as an indicator of the moments of the play in performance that spectators remembered and talked about and which therefore might be rated by a printer as useful to flag in an advertisement of this kind.

Something else that the *Spanish Tragedy* title page gives us is information about what is 'new' about this particular edition of the play: 'Newly Corrected, Amended and Enlarged with new Additions, as it hath of late been diuers times Acted'. Here we have an indication of the kind of collaborative writing and 'updating' of texts that will be explored further in Case study J, as well as of the value placed on a play having enjoyed multiple performances, which in the hothouse environment of the early modern theatre would have been an assurance of its popularity, a marker of success if you like. So there is an attempt at validation of the importance of one play over another in the account given of success on the stage, or, as in the case of the collaboratively authored *The Witch of Edmonton* (see Figure 7), the stamp of achievement that being performed at court and well received represented: 'Acted by the Princes Servants, often at the Cock-Pit in Drury Lane, once at Court, with singular Applause'. Other details of this title page draw our eyes as well: it is authored by 'William Rowley, Thomas Dekker, John Ford, &c'. That '&c' leaves a large space open for speculation about other authorial hands involved in the process and it is a not unusual occurrence on play title pages. This particular title page seems proud of the play's generic status as 'Tragi-comedy', perhaps because by 1658 when this was published that was a well-established genre; the fact that this is being printed some time after the first performances of the play, and indeed in an era when the public playhouses were closed down on account of legislation against commercial playing under the largely Puritan-leaning republican government, is made a virtue of – 'Never printed till now' – and suggests by 1658 at least a hankering for dramatic experience if only at second remove. Equally fascinating is the status of documentary drama that this publication asserts: 'A known true Story. Composed into A Tragi-comedy' is how this is expressed and links *The Witch of Edmonton* to other plays such as Chapman's *The Old Joiner of Aldgate* (1603) and Brome and Heywood's *The Late Lancashire Witches* (1634) that drew their material from real-life contemporary events (see discussion in Chapter 1).

All of this paratextual material to the plays themselves is fascinating and makes title pages rich reading matter in their own right but we have not even begun in this description to account for the visual material that also appears

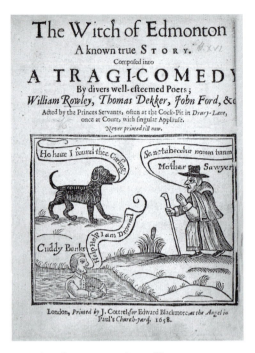

7. Printed representation of key stage moments and dialogue from the collaborative playtext of *The Witch of Edmonton*.

on the three example title pages discussed above. Each of them has an accompanying woodcut image. That in itself was not unusual, although as Thomas Postlewait indicates, in many cases these images were simply lifted from other books and contexts and reapplied in a new context.[3] What is unusual and of especial interest in these examples is that the woodcut images are 'stagings' of a particular moment or a series of conflated moments in the play. Like that list of included moments in the accompanying text on the *The Spanish Tragedy*'s title page, these too become a potential key to what were considered the 'great moments' in these plays, a clue not just to readership but to audience reception.

In the instance of the *Doctor Faustus* title page, we cannot confirm that it is a picture of the play in performance as such but there is a conscious staginess about the way in which the image depicts Faustus himself, book and staff in hand, standing within a conjurer's circle, in an indoor room furnished with a chest and other items, but with a devil clearly appearing upwards through the floor. It is this last element in the picture that for me most suggests the practical operations of the early modern stage – the devil appearing up through the trapdoor, through which, as we have speculated elsewhere (see Chapter 1), characters associated with hellishness or the underworld well might enter onto the stage – but this hunch is underscored by the attention to detail paid to the handheld 'props' that Faustus holds and indeed his costume, which we have stressed on several occasions was a chief means of making meaning on the early modern stage.

The *Spanish Tragedy* example takes us to the next level by juxtaposing three key moments in one image: Horatio's murder in the arbour, the night-time discovery of his corpse by his grief-stricken father Hieronimo (the night-time is signified by the burning torch that Hieronimo appears to grasp in this image, which again maps very readily onto the torches and tapers carried by actors onto the stages of the open-air theatres to signify darkness, even when in reality it was broad daylight, in plays like *Hamlet* or *Macbeth*) and the assault on Bel-imperia by Balthazar and Lorenzo. Once again we seem to have a 'staginess' that draws attention to the way in which certain props might have functioned to tell the story on the stage, not least the arbour in which Hieronimo's body hangs. Philip Henslowe's inventories, as we saw in the introduction, indicate that early modern theatres owned a range of props of different sizes and scales, and we can imagine how such an arbour as drawn here could have been relatively easily transported onto the stage or 'revealed' within a discovery space when this play was performed. Tom Postlewait writes with energy about the way in which the dialogue banners that attach to these scenes make a direct connection between text and image that is also part of how early modern theatre operated with its 'speaking pictures', but it is also a further hint as to what were considered memorable lines or 'moments' on the stage: Bel-imperia crying out 'Murder helpe Horatio' in ways that implicated the watching audience and Hieronimo's grief-stricken soliloquies and speeches: 'Alas it is my son Horatio'.[4]

The Witch of Edmonton performs similar effects, collapsing different moments of that play together to depict, through image and accompanying text, the devil dog, sometimes called 'Tom' in the play, the near drowning of Cuddy Banks in a pond (a moment which is referred to in the play but which actually takes place offstage, so we have the further phenomenon of seen and unseen elements of a play being collapsed together in the representational woodcut) and the central character of Mother (Elizabeth) Sawyer spouting Latin in ways that associate her both with witchcraft and with a set of anti-Catholic representations that were prevalent in woodcut and pamphlet culture at this time (the devil dog is clearly responding to this fact in his line 'Ho haue I found thee Cursing' which occurs in the play at 2.1.121). As with the previous two woodcut examples, there are also clues to costuming and props, with Sawyer's hat and staff. The play proper depicts Sawyer being beaten by her neighbour Old Banks for gathering sticks on his land to make a warming fire for herself (2.1), and in the process of being shunned by the community she sells her soul to the devil, who appears to her rather memorably in the form of Tom the dog. We should not be surprised that the printer thought this was worth placing the emphasis of the title page imagery upon.

When the Beaumont and Fletcher tragicomedy *Philaster* (1610) was published in 1620 it too was accompanied by a woodcut image of an extended grouping of short scenes from the play's fourth act (the dramaturgy of this act is discussed in Case study I). It is a fascinating choice and depicts one of the pastoral scenes that were considered central to this particular genre as it developed, not least under Beaumont and Fletcher. Philaster is seen creeping away into a bush, having wounded his former lover the Princess Arethusa, and she is found by 'A Countrie Gentellman'. In fact that slightly collapses the play's action; Philaster does not creep away until he has fought with the 'Country Fellow' and been wounded in the process. The image is actually an inversion of a stage direction at 4.6 in which '*Philaster creeps out of a bush*' (84 s.d.). The characters are clearly labelled, but it is the greenery into which Philaster seems to be escaping that intrigues me most. Just as the arbour in which Horatio hangs could easily have been recycled for overhearing scenes in romantic comedies like *Twelfth Night* or *Much Ado About Nothing*, so this looks like a stock 'bush' from the props department, approximately the height of an average male actor, and therefore portable enough to be able to manoeuvre on and off the stage as required.

There is a large amount of speculation in the work I am doing here but it is speculation informed by visual and textual artefacts from the period and that seeks to connect these title pages with what we now know about early modern theatrical culture. From this perspective, title pages become rich traces of reception and of the ways in which individual plays were thought about in the early modern period and, for that reason alone, they warrant serious attention.

Chapter 4

Comedy, pastoral and romantic

Comedy covers a very broad spectrum of writing, thinking and playing in the early modern theatre context; it stretches from pastoral and romantic drama, concerned with quasi-idyllic rural settings and the vicissitudes of love, to sharp-witted and frequently foul-mouthed urban drama of the streets, via biting social satire and political commentary. Towards the later part of our focus period comedy ends up as part of the heady generic mix that becomes tragicomedy. If we accept the premise of Jean Howard that dramatic genre is always in process, always 'provisional and productive' in the context of live event-based theatre, is there anything that we can confidently declare defines dramatic comedy or at least defines what aided early modern audiences to bring to bear those all-important frameworks of expectation?[1]

Howard gives us a very useful platform from which to begin: focusing initially on what she terms 'London comedy', by which she means plays based on and representing the life of the capital city itself, she observes: 'These city plays represent a remarkable break from the conventions of the "higher" genres such as tragedy and the national history play. Seldom dealing with monarchs and rarely with aristocrats, they pitch their social register lower.'[2] There are certain useful truths that Howard's definition hits on here; Jonson talks in the Prologue to *Every Man In His Humour* (1616 folio edition) of using 'language such as men do use' (Prologue, 21) in these plays and we might extend that thinking to note that many comedies written in this period reflect a world that was eminently familiar to audiences, representing back to them the streets, taverns and even prisons of the urban centre which they inhabited and where they practised daily, whatever their trade or profession, rank or gender.

Comic drama per se appears, then, to be interested in a more complex and perhaps more everyday 'social register' than many formal tragedies. It treats with sites of far less grandeur than the decadent and violent European courts that we saw populating tragic and revenge drama. There are of course always immediate challenges to any such neat definition. We have already mentioned the specific subgenre of domestic tragedy which would seem to bring the same essence of the everyday and of the local onto the stage in plays such as *Arden of Faversham* or *A Woman Killed with Kindness*. Even in the 'national history play' of which Howard speaks we can think of the challenges to the formal rules for representing monarchs effected by chronicle dramas such as the two parts of Heywood's *Edward IV* or by Dekker's *The Shoemaker's Holiday*, and also of the groundbreaking mix of interests that the two parts of Shakespeare's *Henry IV* evidence in their ranging and rambling from court to tavern to rural road network. No definition will be wholly satisfactory or fully workable, but if we look to the particular precedent of ancient Greek and Roman comedy, from Menander and Aristophanes in Greece to their Roman successor Plautus, with its street scenes and witty servants, we might begin to see early modern comedy's interest in language, spaces and places 'such as men do use' as having a distinctly classical origin.

The comedies of Plautus are particularly instructive in this respect, adopting and adapting Greek models as they themselves did. Plautus presented to his Roman audiences a version of the city streets and households and therefore communities that they themselves inhabited. As a result movements in and out of those households and the spatial organisation of comedy proved to be very important in the unfolding of his dramas, as did certain kinds of recurring archetypal characters, from fathers and sons to the witty servants that we will see as an essential ingredient in some of Jonson's own Plautine experiments in comic satire in Chapter 6. It is exactly this kind of scenario and framework that Shakespeare seeks to reconstruct in his early dramatic experiment *The Comedy of Errors* (1594), which is directly based on a Plautus play, the *Menaechmi*. Ostensibly set in Ephesus, the play makes great dramatic capital of the various house and tavern fronts that it features on the stage and in and out of which characters and action pass.[3] Early Jonsonian ventures into comedy are similarly Plautine in both theme and tone: *The Case is Altered* (1597) with its shoemaker Juniper, and the humours plays *Every Man In His Humour* (1598; and substantially reworked in 1616) and *Every Man Out of his Humour* (1599), with their working characters like Cob the water-carrier, take place in the same environments of inside and outside, household and streets, and share the themes of families and households that are seen as lying at the core of Plautus's canon. This would ultimately lead in Jonson's case to the creation of the whole new subgenre of city comedy, with a cast of characters and set of common scenarios which also featured in the work of Middleton and later inheritors of the Jonsonian mantle like Brome (see Chapter 5). In Shakespeare's case, however, there seems to have been a turn to a rather different mode of comedy, more inflected by Italianate and romantic traditions and still interested in the space of the court albeit now through careful juxtaposition with its rural and bucolic counterpart via the particular mode of pastoral, and it is to these particular strains of comedy that we will turn first in seeking to engage with the genre in its most diverse manifestations and forms.

Practising Petrarchan motifs of love

The writing of love in the Elizabethan period, when early modern commercial theatre was first finding its professional feet, was strongly Italian in flavour. The sonnets of fourteenth-century humanist poet Francesco Petrarch, not least those addressed to his beloved Laura, were widely imitated and led to a series of sonnet sequences authored by English writers, including Shakespeare himself. Shakespeare was working on his own complex collection of sonnets, variously addressed to a young man and a supposed 'Dark Lady', in the 1590s when he was also honing his talents as a professional playwright, and the cross-fertilisation between the two forms is self-evident. The ill-fated and 'star-crossed lovers' Romeo and Juliet first meet, and kiss, on a piece of dialogue that is actually a shared sonnet (1.5.92–105) and *Love's Labour's Lost* (1594–5, first printed 1598) commences with a sonnet from the King of Navarre in which, somewhat ironically perhaps, he swears abstention from the world and in particular from women. The use of the sonnet form, which well-trained early modern ears would have heard and registered, perhaps draws attention to the fact that these are likely to be short-lived vows abjuring of love on the part of this monarch and his small band of male courtiers:

> Let fame, that all hunt after in their lives,
> Live registered upon our brazen tombs,
> And then grace us in the disgrace of death
> When, spite of cormorant devouring time,
> Th'endeavour of this present breath may buy
> That honour which shall bate his scythe's keen edge
> And make us heirs of all eternity.
> Therefore, brave conquerors – for so you are,
> That war against your own affections
> And the huge army of the world's desires –
> Our late edict shall strongly stand in force.
> Navarre shall be the wonder of the world.
> Our court shall be a little academe,
> Still and contemplative in living art.   (1.1.1–14)

The King's sonnet includes a series of images recognisable from Shakespeare's *Sonnets* – devouring time figured as a cormorant, death by means of an agricultural scythe, and a strong blend of military and hunting metaphors to boot. These poetic conceits were all familiar from Petrarch's work and from English translations and imitations of his sonneteering style. The *Love's Labour's Lost* scene actually takes place in formal parkland on the King's estate, which lends itself to quasi-Petrarchan and quasi-pastoral constructions as a space of sanctuary (though conventionally it would also be a site of hunting as a pastime), and it is this space that the Princess of France and her accompanying women very visibly invade during the first act. We can begin to see through the use of the parkland scenario the deft and dextrous ways in which Shakespeare embodies, makes real and at the same time interrogates and tests Petrarchan metaphors of love on the stage;[4] the Navarre courtiers will even woo the women in strained sonnet compositions of their own in the fourth act.

The opening moments of *Twelfth Night* (*c.* 1601) are equally instructive in terms of demonstrating how romantic comedy tests the very premise of its main subject: romantic love. Following Duke Orsino's 'If music be the food of love' speech (1.1.1), which opens the play and concerns itself with the extremes of romantic passion the Duke feels he is enduring in his unrequited feelings for the Countess Olivia, his household servant Curio enters to ask if he intends to go hunting that day (hunting was a fairly standard practice in courtly and elite households at this time):

> **CURIO** Will you go hunt, my lord?
> **ORSINO**   What, Curio?
> **CURIO**   The hart.
>   (1.1.16)

Orsino, drowning in his own melancholia, turns even this practical question into a highly wrought metaphorical conceit, invoking instead the Diana–Actaeon myth in which Actaeon, out on a hunt, was killed by his own hunting hounds after the goddess Diana turned him into a stag as punishment for gazing upon her naked form:

> O, when mine eyes did see Olivia first
> Methought she purged the air of pestilence;
> That instant was I turned into a hart,
> And my desires, like fell and cruel hounds,
> E'er since pursue me.   (1.1.18–22)

As well as invoking the literary precedent of Ovid's influential text *The Metamorphoses* in the retelling of the Actaeon story, there are very obvious puns taking place here on the hart (stag) representing the wounded heart of the rejected lover, familiar from Italian romantic and poetic traditions that were very much in vogue in Elizabethan England, but the play seems to take a questioning stance on all these clichés and commonplace phrases from the off.[5] If what we are witnessing in the early modern stage's engagement with Petrarchan love tropes are metaphors made real, this process also becomes a way of investigating and exploring love as a concept as well as the courtly penchant for love poetry into the bargain.

Shakespeare's *As You Like It* (1600) takes this to the next level and carries the investigation of love across its entire action. While the action opens in the troubled court of Duke Frederick, we soon find ourselves propelled along with the play's protagonists, in a movement of exile and banishment that the next section will explore within the context of pastoral literary conventions, into the forest of Arden where the requisite hunting of the stag and the writing of sonnets duly take place but where discussion and debate about love also dominate the stage. Orlando certainly interprets the space around him from a courtly sonneteer's perspective, carving sub-Petrarchan sonnets of dubious quality into the trees:

> Hang there, my verse, in witness of my love . . .
>   these trees shall be my book
> And in their barks my thoughts I'll character.
>   (3.2.1, 5–6)

As Jane Kingsley-Smith has rightly emphasised, the play assumes a reasonable familiarity with Petrarchan and pastoral discourse on the part of both character and spectators.[6] Shakespeare's source, Thomas Lodge's *Rosalynde* (1590), is rather more explicit at this point in the action: in her temporary disguise as the shepherdess Aliena, Celia finds the tree-poems and remarks:

> No doubt . . . this poesie is the passion of some perplexed shepherd, that being enamoured of some faire and beautifull Shepheardesse, suffered some sharpe repulse, and therefore complained of the crueltie of his Mistris.[7]

The perplexed shepherd and the cruel mistress were character types that the audience of *As You Like It* were able to mobilise relatively quickly as a framework for understanding not only the role that Orlando assumes at this stage but also the relationship between Arden inhabitants Silvius and Phebe. In a play that is fond of pairings, symmetries and parodic juxtapositions (Touchstone and Audrey's relationship is at the extreme end of the spectrum), we are constantly reading different experiences of love against each other. But it is in practice –

and what is important to note is pastoral drama's investment in action, in putting things quite literally into practice – Orlando's encounter with Rosalind in the forest that will test his recourse to romantic cliché and commonplace to breaking point. Albeit in her disguise as the boy Ganymede (the particular significance of this assumed persona we will explore later in the chapter), Rosalind confidently undoes the worst romantic excess through her own plain speaking. To all the Petrarchan figures of love as death, she says: 'The poor world is almost six thousand years old, and in all this time there was not a man died in his own person, videlicet, in a love cause' (4.1.88–91). Recounting the archetypal narratives of doomed couples such as Troilus and Cressida and Hero and Leander, she ends in a wonderfully puncturing descent into the monosyllables that we have seen Shakespeare use to such devastating effect in other plays: 'But these are all lies. Men have died from time to time, and worms have eaten them, but not for love' (4.1.99–101). As well as imitating the marked turn effected by the use of a stressed 'But' in so many counterpart Shakespearean sonnets on the theme of love, Rosalind determinedly uses prose here to resist the fairytale constructions of romance: 'Say a day without the ever' (4.1.138) she urges the hyperbolic Orlando. We can identify a tragic counterpart to Rosalind's educative stance here in Juliet who, following the aforementioned sonnet encounter and first kiss with Romeo, immediately pulls him away from his tendency to empty reiteration of Petrarchan metaphors: 'You kiss by th' book' she says in a moment of striking self-possession (*Romeo and Juliet*, 1.5.109). This is just one small indicator of the ways in which Shakespeare's romantic tragedy adopts and adapts many of the conventions of pastoral and romantic comedy, many of them with Petrarchan origins and associations, not least the central theme of banishment and exile that we are outlining here.[8]

What enables Rosalind's particular act of educational realism in *As You Like It* is, however, a forceful recognition of the pastoral convention by which exile, enforced or otherwise, usually into some sort of greenwood or analogous space, can provide the occasion for self-discovery and the specific empowerment and agency afforded a female character by the act of cross-dressing. The next two sections will explore both of these phenomena of pastoral and romantic comedy as they were interpreted by Shakespeare, among others, on the early modern stage.

Some versions of pastoral[9]

If Petrarch was the Italian godfather of English pastoral literary traditions, the Elizabethan poet-courtier Edmund Spenser was strongly associated with the native interpretation of the genre through hugely popular works such as *The Shepheardes Calender* (1579). Spenser's text, which featured shepherd and shepherdess characters, rural games, songs and festivities, all of which had their effect on the writing of Elizabethan pastoral, was largely structured around the form of the dialogue, with two characters taking opposite positions on various themes, pastoral, political and romantic. *As You Like It* is equally fond of the dialogue form as a means of debating the court–country contrast that lies at the heart of its action and is itself a standard pastoral trope. If all of Rosalind and Orlando's meetings can be understood as being structured through the dialogue form, the most significant pastoral debate in the play comes at 3.2 when the court jester Touchstone exchanges terms with Corin the working shepherd. Even Touchstone's own discourse is carefully constructed via contrapuntal clauses:

> Truly, shepherd, in respect of itself it is a good life; but in respect that it is a shepherd's life, it is naught . . . Now in respect that it is in the fields, it pleaseth me well; but in respect it is not in the court, it is tedious.
>
> (3.2.13–15, 17–19)

In a motion that aligns him in intriguing ways with the down-to-earth statements on love that we have seen Rosalind making in her exchanges with Orlando, Corin is the voice of a practical agricultural realism that in its own quiet way challenges Petrarchan metaphorical extremes of freezing fires, burning love and spiritual darkness that filled the sonneteering traditions of the age:

> I know the more one sickens, the worse at ease he is, and that he that wants money, means, and content is without three good friends; that the property of rain is to wet and fire to burn; that good pasture makes fat sheep; and that a great cause of the night is lack of sun . . .   (3.3.23–8)

Having drawn a somewhat easy distinction between grittier Jonsonian city comedy and Shakespearean pastoral in the opening section to this chapter, we might begin to acknowledge that there is real proximity here between Jonson's interest in comedy representing 'language such as men do use' and the shepherd's discourse in *As You Like It*.

Court versus country

The court–country dualism is effected at large across *As You Like It* by the storyline of the two contrasted dukes: the malign and tyrannical regime of Duke Frederick in the court that casts out both Orlando and Rosalind from its environs and which has previously sent Duke Senior (Rosalind's father) into exile. This is a fundamental version of pastoral, as Jane Kingsley-Smith's helpful working definition makes clear:

> Exile is often the means by which courtiers and shepherds meet in a bucolic landscape... A person of high birth – most often a duke or heir to the kingdom – is banished for some unjust cause or deposed and forced into exile, often with his relatives and supporters... subsequently, by wandering, shipwreck and occasionally by choice, the exile enters a pastoral landscape where shepherds offer succour and a new way of life... the pastoral sojourn ends with the reconciliation of family members and former enemies, often preceding a betrothal. At this point the exiles are enabled to return to society.[10]

This is, in a nutshell, a summary of the plot of *As You Like It*, which ends with the betrothal of Rosalind and Orlando and the restitution of Duke Senior to the court in a classically shaped fifth act of resolution and containment. Rosalind is noticeably returned to her woman's attire and the threat of her agency achieved through cross-dressing, according to some critics at least, defused. Everyone, it is supposed, is changed for the better by their experience. There is even a dance to emphasise the restoration of harmony, although one character noticeably dissents from this action: Duke Senior's man Jaques declares 'I am for other than for dancing measures' (5.4.191), and sounds a striking note of discordance even at the comedy's denouement. The stance of questioning and a conscious desire to push at the edges of literary convention is retained to the close of this play, then, and spills over quite readily into its potentially radical Epilogue, delivered by Rosalind herself, which is the focus of Case study H.

Jaques (as is discussed further in Chapter 6) readily assumes the part of the satirist in the forest of Arden, questioning the pastoral idyll that the Duke and his 'brothers in exile' (2.1.1) seem so keen to construct (see the Duke's lengthy exposition of the joys of his woodland life where he finds 'good in everything' at 2.1.1–17). The hunting of the stag in this context is presented as a brutal necessity and no longer a safe poetic construct:

> **DUKE SENIOR** Come, shall we go and kill us venison!
>   And yet it irks me the poor dappled fools,
>   Being native burghers of this desert city,
>   Should in their own confines with forked heads
>   Have their round haunches gored.
>   **AMIENS**   Indeed, my lord,
>   The melancholy Jaques grieves at that,
>   And in that kind swears you do more usurp
>   Than doth your brother that hath banished you.
>   (2.1.21–8)

The woodland setting that characterises *As You Like It* was a favourite one of Shakespearean romantic comedy. The forest of Arden shares many kinships with the Athenian woodlands of *A Midsummer Night's Dream* into which a group of young lovers banish themselves and through their numerous confused encounters there, aided and hindered by the supernatural forces of the fairies whose dwelling and 'local habitation' (5.1.17) it is, prove true Lysander's observation that 'The course of true love never did run smooth' (1.1.134).

It was not always necessarily a forest or woodland, though, through which Shakespeare sought to test these topics and themes. As already noted, the opening of *Twelfth Night* merely invokes the hunt and never enters a forest per se, but that play's Illyrian island as a setting is in so many ways a space and locale for the same kind of Petrarchan-informed and simultaneously Petrarchan-resistant questioning of what love is that we have seen unfold in *As You Like It*. That this play, through the charming protagonist Viola who disguises herself as the pageboy Cesario after finding herself shipwrecked upon the island, also turns to cross-dressing as the practical dramatic device through which to unpack these concerns, can tell us much about the precedents and practices of romantic comedy on the early modern stage.

The example of John Lyly

Early modern English romantic and pastoral comedy as we now understand it would not exist without the significant precedent of John Lyly who wrote ostensibly for companies of boy actors (largely composed of choristers) who performed for the court and in a schools drama context. Arthur Kinney has recently described Lyly as 'the most neglected, underappreciated and misunderstood Elizabethan playwright' and credits him with establishing 'romantic love as the proper subject for secular comedy'.[11]

It is the pastoral scene of *Galatea* (*c.* 1585) that best exemplifies Lyly's theatrical legacy and takes us in a developmental line to romantic comedies such as *As You Like It*, *Love's Labour's Lost* and *Twelfth Night*. *Galatea* has shepherds who, in a mode inherited from the Italian pastoral literary tradition, share their woodlands with gods, goddesses and nymphs, but it is also a very English pastoral, set as it is on the banks of the Humber. In the opening scene, which consciously reworks Virgil's First Eclogue, Lyly also stamps a claim for the originality and specificity of his drama. Tityrus and his daughter Galatea sit down under a tree in the opening scene: 'The sun doth beat upon the plain fields . . . we may enjoy the fresh air, which softly breathes from Humber floods' (1.1.1–5). Galatea is already dressed as a boy in what we learn is a protective move to prevent her being made a virgin sacrifice to Neptune. Even that fanciful storyline is rooted in the landscape and environment of the Lincolnshire setting where flooding was, and remains, a regular occurrence. The human sacrifice will be tied to a tree to be taken by the swollen tides of the Aegir (a tidal bore).

At 1.3 we encounter a mirror-image of this scene when Melibeus also talks to his daughter Phillida of the need to disguise her 'in man's apparel' (1.3.15) to prevent her being chosen for death. These two self-contained yet artfully contrasted scenes of duologue between a father and a daughter, and the joint disguises of Galatea and Phillida that will lead to much romantic angst and confusion in the play when each falls in love with the other in their persona as a boy, exemplify Lyly's particular creative techniques: his use of carefully balanced dialogues and structural juxtaposition and symmetry. These techniques form an important part of the legacy of theatrical experimentation with the representation of love on the stage and related themes of gender that were inherited by those professional playwrights who followed in Lyly's wake, William Shakespeare not least.

Galatea was performed by the St Paul's Cathedral choirboys before the Elizabethan court at Greenwich Palace in 1585 and the playtext bears the traces of that compositional context. Written in a series of episodic and quite short scenes, it makes considerable but targeted demands on its boy performers and it makes great play of their own liminal, pre-adulthood state and unbroken voices in introducing the plotline of gender confusion that characterises the touching and tormented onstage exchanges between Galatea and Phillida. Phillida's tortured aside on Galatea – 'It is pity that nature framed you not a woman, having a face so fair, so lovely a countenance, so modest a behaviour' (3.2.1–3) – leads directly into the way in which Shakespeare makes his protagonist Viola share her sense of the tangled knot of sexual attraction in *Twelfth Night*.[12] Dressed as the pageboy Cesario and drawn to her employer the Duke Orsino while ostensibly tasked with wooing the Countess Olivia on his behalf, only to find that Olivia has fallen for 'him' in the guise of Cesario, Viola reflects with winning wit:

> I left no ring with her. What means this lady?
> Fortune forbid my outside have not charmed her . . .
> I am the man. If it be so – as 'tis –
> Poor lady, she were better love a dream!
> Disguise, I see thou art a wickedness
> Wherein the pregnant enemy does much . . .
> How will this fadge? My master loves her dearly,
> And I, poor monster, fond as much on him,
> And she, mistaken, seems to dote on me.
> What will become of this? As I am man,

> My state is desperate for my master's love.
> As I am woman, now, alas the day,
> What thriftless sighs shall poor Olivia breathe!
> O, time, though must untangle this, not I.
> It is too hard a knot for me t'untie.
>
> (1.5.17–18, 25–8, 33–41)

It is a remarkable moment on the stage. The closing couplet (which end-stops the scene in a very determined way while also being completely inconclusive in its assertions) and its direct address to Time reconnects us with the sonneteering tradition that we have already seen feeding its way into Shakespeare's aesthetic in his romantic comedies in the 1590s and early 1600s. We might also see the internal philosophising of this speech as an extension of the sonnet tradition, but there is also something that feels entirely fresh and new which is the use of questions thrown out to the audience who are the only people other than Viola who can hear them: 'What means this lady?', 'How will this fadge?', 'What will become of this?' We can begin to unpack how an extended soliloquy engages and lures in its audience, asking them to make sense of situations that the characters themselves cannot (Hamlet's soul-searching in Shakespeare's tragedy is the obvious analogue and it is no coincidence that he was working on these two plays in close proximity to one another). We need to take account here of the sheer stretch of stage time that the boy actor playing Viola/Cesario has to hold the stage, presumably working the forestage to get maximum intimacy with the audience that the speech is designed to connect with. Was eye contact made on delivery of particular questions? Could the dextrous boy actor in the Globe or indeed the Middle Temple at the Inns of Court, where we know the play was staged in 1602, play off particularly empathetic audience members on a particular night of performance?

This is tangibly different from the heightened rhetorical structures of Lyly's play and its cross-dressing themes but we can see the beginnings of what were to develop into full-blown Shakespearean soliloquies in his brilliant use of asides:

> **PHILLIDA** My father had but one daughter, and therefore I could
>   have no sister.
> **GALATEA** [*aside*] Ay me, he is as I am, for his speeches be as mine are.
>
> (*Galatea*, 3.2.42–5)

Kinney describes these as 'foreshortened, truncated soliloquies' and remarks how these dialogues are 'ripe with inhibitions in which spontaneous hypotheses stand in for silenced desires'.[13] Equally striking are the wonderfully ambiguous lines on which Phillida and Galatea jointly exit this same scene:

> **PHILLIDA** Come let us into the grove and make much of one another
> that cannot tell what to think of one another.   (3.2.62–3)

There is much crediting of the theatre audience with the ability to fill in the gaps here and to construct their own meanings and this persists to the very end of the play. If overall the plot of *Galatea* is ostensibly resolved through supernatural intervention – one of the girls will be transformed into a boy, thereby enabling a heterosexual partnership and marriage between them, to an extent reasserting social norms along with comic conventions – the spectators never learn in which direction this leads, in a wonderful extension of the play's default mode of ambiguity, right until the end.

Cross-dressing, identity and disguise

Early modern commercial theatre's penchant for plots involving disguise in general and cross-dressing in particular can be seen as in part a reflection of the complex cultural politics of the plays but also a product of the very practical demands – and therefore opportunities – of working theatre. As the Introduction to this volume stressed, the ostensibly bare stage of the public theatres placed a great deal of emphasis on costume, props and movement for the creation of meaning. A character's identity could be stamped or indeed masked by a change of outfit. In Chapter 3, we looked at the anxieties created by a professional actor's ability to play figures of high rank and even a king simply by the assumption of the clothes and handheld properties associated with that role in ceremonial court culture. This all needs to be understood in the context of an age when sumptuary laws (laws about the clothes that were fitting to be worn by people of certain social ranks) were enforced with some vigour. Related anxieties were inevitably mobilised by the commercial theatre's use of boy actors to play all female roles (for a modern reconstruction of this practice, see Figure 3 depicting a Shakespeare's Globe 'original practices' production of *Richard III*).[14]

While a practical kinship is often stressed between women and boys – 'as boys and women are for the most part cattle of this colour' (3.2.398–9) is how *As You Like It* articulates this assumption – the complicated phenomenon of sexual attraction both on the stage and on the part of engaged members of the audience when you have a boy dressed as a girl (and more often than not in disguise as a boy in the romantic comedies we are currently examining) was a hotly debated issue.[15] So while Lyly's dramas are often described as taking a depoliticised approach to their material in light of their courtly audience, the way in which a text like *Galatea* deploys cross-dressing and the attendant generic confusions of comedy to explore gender ambiguity and sexual allure, all the time making the most of the specific pragmatics of the make-up of working theatre companies, might be seen as highly engaged with contemporary debates about what constituted masculinity and femininity. This form of cultural poetics feeds directly into Shakespeare's experimentations with cross-dressing as a dramatic technique in a whole range of his romantic comedies, from *The Two Gentleman of Verona* (1590–1) through to Portia's performance as a lawyer in *The Merchant of Venice*, and would resurface in his later experiments, influenced by his exposure to the work of sometime collaborator Fletcher, with tragicomedy such as *Cymbeline* (*c.* 1611).

But it is undoubtedly in the roles of Rosalind in *As You Like It* and Viola in *Twelfth Night* that Shakespeare's strongest inheritances from Lyly's oeuvre can be registered. We have already considered the dramatic force of Viola's extended soliloquies in the latter play in terms of the relationship with the audience that they establish. Rosalind's first line in her male disguise as the boy Ganymede – the name is a direct allusion to the pageboy who was loved by and who attended on the god Jupiter in classical mythology – shares a knowing joke with spectators: 'O Jupiter, how weary are my spirits!' (*As You Like It*, 2.4.1). If less overtly inhabited by gods and nymphs than Lyly's forest or indeed the Athenian woods of *A Midsummer Night's Dream* (only with the appearance of Hymen in Act 5 do the two worlds of natural and supernatural coalesce), Arden is still imbued with Ovidian theories of metamorphosis and change, not least when people are under the influence of sexual attraction. Rosalind's shared joke with the audience here establishes both a strong relationship with them (which will ultimately be summed up by the direct address of the Epilogue to spectators of both genders – see Case study H) and a sense of her wit and agency which is fundamental to the way her part operates in the play and on Orlando in particular. Her educative role and her control over language, even to the level of metrics, has already been discussed; it is also worth noting that Rosalind's is by far the largest female role in terms of lines in the Shakespearean canon. This can be understood in part as having a very practical impetus – there must have been a particularly strong boy actor in the King's Men at this point in time to be able to cope with this level of stage time and that amount of line-learning – but it also makes a point about women's capacity for agency in their lives, even if that agency can only sometimes be enacted through the mechanism of male dress. This is the conundrum referred to by Galatea in Lyly's eponymous comedy when she too is forced by circumstance into masculine attire and behaviours: 'I will now use for the distaff the bow, and play at quoits abroad that was wont to sew in my sampler at home' (*Galatea*, 2.1.10–12).[16]

If ambiguity is the keynote of the cross-dressing plotlines of some of the most loved romantic comedies of the day, the play with ambiguity was also worked out brilliantly at the level of the dialogue, and once again it is the figure of Lyly whom we see at the vanguard of this socio-linguistic development and experimentation. George Hunter and David Bevington have written eloquently in their edition of *Galatea* of the dialogue between the cross-dressed hero/ines of that play as operating as a kind of dance of logic:

> the dialogue moves by a series of redefinitions, sharpened and made insistent by phonetic patterning, that at once acknowledge what the interlocutor is saying and change the meaning of dialogue as a kind of dance of logic in which every move by one party is countered by an opposite move on the same spot . . . Our pleasure is created by the neatness of the verbal footwork . . . [17]

This kind of verbal patterning is not solely the product of cross-dressing plotlines; the Corin–Touchstone debate discussed earlier from 3.2 of *As You Like It* stems from the same poetic impulses, but this kind of multi-layered discourse is given particular edge by the confused gendering of scenes facilitated by the cross-dressing device:

> **PHOEBE** (*To Silvius*) Good shepherd, tell this youth what 'tis to love.
> **SILVIUS** It is to be all made of sighs and tears,
>   And so am I for Phoebe.
> **PHOEBE** And I for Ganymede.
> **ORLANDO** And I for Rosalind.
> **ROSALIND** And I for no woman.   (*As You Like It*, 5.3.78–83)

Ultimately these all become methods and means of exploring and interrogating love and bring a witty self-awareness to the subject that audiences can revel in. Not all comedies that involved boys dressed as girls necessarily shared that knowledge with spectators: in Chapter 6, we will examine Jonson's sharp London satire of 1609, *Epicene*, which very deliberately does *not* share the crucial information about the real identity of Morose's 'ideal' wife and, similarly, in their 1610 tragicomedy *Philaster* (examined further in Chapter 7) Beaumont and Fletcher do not openly share the crucial information about Bellario's true identity as the courtier's daughter Euphrasia. Nevertheless on a second viewing of either play it becomes abundantly clear that both planted obvious clues for theatre-literate audience members to pick up and speculate on for themselves (and enjoy in a second viewing) and could in reality depend on the ability of audiences to do this work precisely because spectators were grounded in the witty boy-heroines of the romantic comedies that preceded them.

New and other versions of Caroline pastoral

It remains to ask what developmental courses romantic and pastoral comedy followed in the early seventeenth century other than into the social satire of *Epicene* and comparable plays. In Philip Massinger's *The Guardian*, first performed and published in 1633, a group of forest outlaws appoint an exiled courtier Severino as their king, and in Robin Hood style these 'merry men' also agree to battle against the wealthy elite who operate against the interests of common people, be it through the holding of trade and industry monopolies, through acts of enclosing common lands for personal profit, or through the imposition of punitive rents on tenant farmers on their estates. In the Robin Hood analogy of a group of outlaws banding together in a forest there are obvious links to Duke Senior's forest of Arden exile in *As You Like It*, at least as Charles, Duke Frederick's wrestler, constructs it in the opening scene of the play:

> They say he is already in the forest of Arden, and a many merry men with him; and there they live like the old Robin Hood of England. They say many young gentlemen flock to him every day, and fleet the time carelessly, as they did in the golden world.   (*As You Like It*, 1.1.109–13)

But in Massinger's hands, where there is direct discussion of usurers and enclosers and 'Builders of Iron Mills, that grub up Forests / With Timber Trees for shipping' (*The Guardian*, 2.1, p. 32),[18] dramatic pastoral conventions appear to take on a distinctly political hue, especially when we consider the fact that the real monarch Charles I was in the process of reviving a whole series of so-called Forest Laws that would make life for the common tenant worker much more complicated and costly.

As our earlier attempts to identify the blend of pragmatism and poeticism in *As You Like It*'s treatment of love have hopefully evidenced, it would be wrong to suggest that Shakespeare's version of pastoral in 1598 is simply naïve or innocent. Corin the shepherd hints at situations in Arden that are at least akin to those attacked by Massinger's self-appointed woodland outlaws, a situation of punitive landlords and downtrodden tenant farmers:

> But I am shepherd to another man,
> And do not shear the fleeces that I graze.

> My master is of churlish disposition
> And little recks to find the way to heaven
> By doing deeds of hospitality.
>
> (*As You Like It*, 2.4.77–81)

Richard Wilson and other historicist critics of the 1980s and 1990s were keen to identify in *As You Like It* similar responses to its own political moment.[19] Whatever the truth of references to actual events of popular agricultural protest, the politics of Shakespeare's play seem more embedded, more ambiguous, less overt than Massinger's and this is a view that seems to gain credence when we widen the scope out to consider a whole cluster of politicised forest plays that emerged at around the same time in the 1640s, including Brome's *A Jovial Crew* (1641–2) and Shirley's *The Sisters* (1642). All of these plays re-engage the by now familiar dramaturgic structure of an escape to the greenwoods and the formation of an alternative community there in ways clearly modelled on the Shakespearean template of *As You Like It* but which also deploy that structure to examine new questions; these plays are less worried about Petrarchan love and literary convention than about reflecting new social tensions.[20]

Brome's play opens with a good landlord, someone who is able to demonstrate the hospitality within the neighbourhood that Corin complains his master is incapable of.[21] Oldrents, as his name suggests, is a representative of older patrician values that recognised the duty of a landlord to his tenants, and is loved for it:

> **HEARTY** Are you not th'only rich man lives unenvied?
>   Have you not all the praises of the rich
>   And prayers of the poor? Did ever any
>   Servant or hireling, neighbour, kindred, curse you,
>   Or wish one minute shortened of your life?
>   Have you one grudging tenant? Will they not all
>   Fight for you?   (*A Jovial Crew*, 1.1, speech 12)

The 'escape' of this play is, however, duly effected by Oldrents's daughters, Rachel and Meriel, who feel smothered by their father's over-protective nature and yearn for the excitement of a life on the road. This takes them, and their rather less savvy partners, Vincent and Hilliard, into the 'hedgerow community' of beggars who overwinter in Oldrents's barn at the behest of his steward Springlove, who is keen to join them on their springtime excursion when the play opens, much to Oldrents's disappointment:

> Does not the sun as comfortably shine
> Upon my gardens as the opener fields?

> Or on my fields as others far remote?
> Are not my walks and greens as delectable
> As the highways and commons?
>
> (1.1, speech 47)

We can recognise here a reformulation of older pastoral city–country juxtapositions now newly refracted through contemporary Caroline concerns about vagrants and itinerant workers on the road networks of England.[22] New versions of pastoral in the hands of Caroline playwrights working for the indoor theatres of the Blackfriars, the Phoenix and Salisbury Court, then, transported the form into new geographical, topographical and, indeed, topical domains: encompassing subjects such as gender, rank, property owning and the legal system in the process.

Many of these topics are encapsulated by the play-within-a-play performed by the crew of beggars in the fifth act of Brome's drama but they also take shape in other kinds of experimentation with pastoral by 1630s playwrights. Pastoral is re-envisioned in the light of the new socio-cultural contexts of elite and urban leisure that we will also see impacting on commercial drama in later chapters on satire and city comedy: Shirley's *Hyde Park* (1632), Nabbes's *Tottenham Court* (1633) and Brome's *The Sparagus Garden* (1635) all engaged with a new form of urban pastoral that joined together the Jonsonian and Shakespearean versions of comic register that we were tentatively juxtaposing at the start of this chapter.

Jonson would venture into the woods and into his own unique pastoral domain in the 1630s by reviving the Robin Hood story once again in his unfinished *The Sad Shepherd* (1637).[23] All of the givens of the pastoral genre can be found here, from the Spenserian and Petrarchan conceits of love-perplexed shepherds to a literal hunt for venison that Robin and his feisty partner Marion undertake in Sherwood Forest, and there is even a version of the supernatural pastoral element that hedged around Shakespeare's Athenian woodlands in *A Midsummer Night's Dream*, with a local witch called Maudlin and her master Puck-Hairy, a direct reimagining of the Robin Goodfellow of rural tradition and Shakespeare's drama. The tendrils of Petrarchan pastoralism reach across the decades, then, and re-emerge in comic drama in ever more fascinating and convoluted ways, finding perhaps their final questioning home in the complex hybrid of tragicomedy, of which there is much more yet to come.

The boy actor: body, costume and disguise

As already noted in this study, there were laws against women performing in the professional English theatre and so all female roles were performed by so called 'boy actors', usually adolescent males. The children's companies, which were entirely composed of boy actors and which enjoyed particular success in London theatres at the turn of the seventeenth century and which can be associated with a particular kind of theatre repertoire and acting style, are the subject of Case study L. Here I want to concentrate on the specific phenomenon of the boy actors in the adult companies, the ways in which genre might have inflected their performances, and the significance of costume in their successful performance of the 'woman's part'. To do this, we will perform a close reading of one particularly significantly placed speech: Rosalind's Epilogue to the audience at the end of Shakespeare's *As You Like It* (1600).

Disguise was, as we have seen, a recurring feature of boy actors' roles in early modern comedy: these plays persistently drew attention in their plotlines to boys dressed as girls dressed as boys (and sometimes even then re-performing the female role as in Rosalind's case in the forest 'seminars' on romantic love with Orlando in *As You Like It*). This was a tradition that can, as Chapter 4 evidenced, be traced back to the courtly drama of John Lyly, and strongly inflected Shakespeare's comic experiments as well as the development of later tragicomedy (see Chapter 7). Tragedy and the related genre of the history play demanded a rather different skill-set from boy actors in the female roles. Except for Cleopatra, who, prior to her carefully stage-managed death in Shakespeare's *c.* 1606–7 tragedy *Antony and Cleopatra*, imagines how some 'squeaking Cleopatra will boy my greatness / I'th' posture of a whore' (5.2.216–17), the female protagonists of tragedy tend not to draw attention to the body of the boy actor beneath the stage costume in the same way. In this respect we can see how generic categories made different demands on a performer and on audience response.

Henslowe's inventories for the Rose Theatre and the Admiral's Men are, as noted in the Introduction and Case study B, an important evidence base for a working knowledge of early modern theatre, and the significance of textiles and costumes to a company's resources shine out from a perusal of those documents. In one particular inventory taken on 10 March 1598, Henslowe lists not only what is in the company's wardrobe ('Item v payer of hose for the clowne') but also what is 'Gone and loste', which is an indication of the financial costs involved in these investments and holdings (what is 'loste' includes 'j lyttell doublet for boye' which is a nice indicator in itself of the physical presence of children in the early modern theatre).[1] It also serves as a reminder of the importance of costume for telling particular stories on the predominantly bare stage of early modern public theatres: as Andrew Gurr and Mariko Ichikawa observe, 'The deception of playing was very largely a matter of dress', but that act of deception became further complicated in plotlines and performances that involved a disguise element.[2] As Farah Karim Cooper notes: 'Principally, disguise is constructed through parts. Gowns, petticoats, doublets, hose, stockings, cloaks, beards, wigs and cosmetic ingredients constitute the prosthetics of identity and were easily available to theatre companies.'[3] Boy actors playing cross-dressing women in early modern romantic comedies like *As You Like It* or *Twelfth Night* drew attention to this prosthetic aspect of their role with much wit and verve and we can see a wonderful culmination of the effects of this kind of acting in Rosalind's Epilogue.

An epilogue is of course an important theatrical device in its own right, crossing the threshold as it does from the play back towards the 'real-life' world of the audience to which they are about to return through the theatre's exits. Feste's song draws attention to this particular transaction at the end of *Twelfth Night* when he sings not only of how 'The rain it raineth every day' (5.2.388, and repeated as a refrain at 392, 396, 400), but how the actors themselves 'strive to please you every day' (404). In a notable metatheatrical move, akin to the self-awareness of cross-dressing plots to which we have already alluded, we have our attentions drawn back to the nature of the working theatre at the close of this play as in several others through the epilogue format: the natural resurrections and returns of theatre where 'dead' characters get up to live again, or imprisoned characters like Jonson's Volpone can turn to the audience as court of appeal and request not only supportive applause but also to come back and do it all over again another night (see Chapter 6).[4]

Rosalind's Epilogue at the close of *As You Like It* is striking for the fact that it is given by a woman character (and by extension the boy actor in that role) and direct attention is drawn to the potential subversion this constitutes:

> (*to the audience*) It is not the fashion to see the lady the epilogue; but it is no more unhandsome than to see the lord the prologue. If it be true that good wine needs no bush, 'tis true that a good play needs no epilogue. Yet to good wine they do use good bushes, and good plays prove the better by the help of good epilogues.   (Epilogue, 1–7)

What is also underlined here is the role of costume in terms of convincing the audience that this boy actor *is* a woman (for a modern reconstruction of the boy actor tradition equally dependent on costume, see Figure 3 depicting singer-actor Johnny Flynn as Lady Anne in *Richard III*); Shakespeare and the actor delivering the speech to the audience (presumably working the crowd, not least the nearby groundlings, at this point through eye contact) have great fun with this idea: 'What a case am I in then, that am neither a good epilogue nor cannot insinuate with you in the behalf of a good play! I am not furnished like a beggar, therefore to beg will not become me' (7–10). Attention is drawn here to the idea, enforced in the real world by sumptuary law, that certain kinds of outfit were only appropriate to certain positions in life.

'My way is to conjure you', says Rosalind, 'and I'll begin with the women' (10–11). Once again we are being asked to notice and register this potentially radical charge – it is women in the audience who are addressed first and who are empowered to take from the play what meanings it suits them to take. This is in itself a challenge to those critics who have argued for a conservative reading that sees Rosalind recontained by women's clothing and social expectation by the end,[5] but it also throws a challenge out to the audience sitting or standing in the Globe Theatre:

> I charge you, O women, for the love you bear to men, to like as much of the play as please you. And I charge you, O men, for the love you bear to women – for I perceive by your simpering none of you hates them – that between you and the women the play may please.
>
> (Epilogue, 11–16)

The emphasis here on the co-production of meaning not only between stage and audience but between different members of that audience, depending on rank, age or gender, is striking. And the Epilogue closes by reminding the audience of the questions of gender ambiguity and sexual allure that the play has explored, drawing attention in turn to the social and cultural anxieties that we know the figure of the boy actor provoked in certain sectors of the community:

> If I were a woman I would kiss as many of you as had beards that pleased me, and breaths that I defied not. And I am sure, as many as have good beards, or good faces, or sweet breaths will for my kind offer, when I make curtsy, bid me farewell.   (Epilogue, 16–21)

We can imagine the female costume in which the boy actor is garbed here figuring through gestures as skirts are gathered to perform that farewell curtsy and therefore we can also see all the different aspects of a boy actor's skill – gesture, voice, costume, interaction with the audience – being mobilised in this vivid moment of self-aware performance.

Chapter 5

City comedies

Genre can, as this study has set out to prove, be an immensely insightful tool to work with; it can guide us to the ways in which playwrights worked within established parameters and conventions when creating their work for the commercial stages but also to the ways in which they may have set out deliberately to challenge those conventions or to shape them anew. For this reason then we almost always begin to slip away from a rigid categorisation of any text by genre almost as soon as we have defined it. Bearing all this in mind, there has been a significant body of work on the creation of an entirely new subset or genre of drama that came out of this particular 'moment' in the early modern theatre and that is now known by the general title of 'city comedy'. It is well worth our while paying attention to the ways in which this mode of writing and of dramaturgy was both a reflection of new urban formations at the time – London increased massively both in terms of human population and in terms of national and international activity through acts of trade and diplomacy in the late sixteenth and early seventeenth centuries – and a direct agent in the shaping of those new cultural and economic formations.

In looking at a series of texts that are known as city comedies, and at the playwrights most associated with experimenting and innovating in this context – for example, Middleton, Jonson and later the Caroline dramatist Richard Brome – we will also find ourselves referencing backwards and across to genres we have already begun to analyse and unpack, not least domestic tragedy, chronicle history and indeed comical satire. This kind of slippage is all part and parcel of gauging the sense of experiment and excitement that commercial theatre generated at this time and an understanding of a cluster of writers, often working in collaboration with each other, who were constantly pushing at the edges of the forms that were available to them.

Writing the city

As London grew exponentially, then, so seemingly did the impetus for commercial drama to reflect the city that was growing up around its particular communities, energies and tensions. We have already begun to see how this impacted on genres, including tragedy and history, which began to embrace a more domesticated version of the form as well as a more regional and provincial understanding of national identity. Brian Walsh has noted: 'The commercial stages were wide enough to accommodate visions of the English past in which housewives, merchants and citizen figures dominated.'[1] It is in the city comedies that, perhaps unsurprisingly, these kinds of cast and concern dominate. With population growth came housing shortages and perceptions at least of increased criminal activity, and many plays of the time seek to capture this situation in dramatic form. As the Prologue to Jonson's 1610 play *The Alchemist* states: 'Our scene is London, 'cause we would make known / No country's mirth is better than our own' (Prologue, 5–6), and a brief glance at the *dramatis personae* for key plays in this category – for example, Dekker's pioneering play *The Shoemaker's Holiday* (1599), Middleton's *A Chaste Maid in Cheapside* (1613), Jonson's collaborative drama with Chapman and Marston, the 1605 *Eastward Ho!* or, indeed, later Caroline ventures into the form such as Brome's *The Sparagus Garden* (1635), all of which will be a focus of discussion in this chapter – reveals to us a bustling world of goldsmiths, shoemakers and their apprentices, of lawyers and legal notaries, shopkeepers and innkeepers, constables and prostitutes, sea captains and vagrants, Cheapside seamstresses and Thames watermen. The stages of these plays are accordingly heavily populated; they have large casts (Jonson's *Bartholomew Fair* features thirty-six speaking roles and would have required a considerable amount of doubling from its Hope Theatre cast) and multiple plots.

What we can see then is this body of work that comes to be known as 'city comedy' striving to represent these new urban communities and the new forms of social mobility, elasticity and aspiration that attended them. There is an almost inevitable link to theatricality and performativity in all of this: people aspiring to a different social rank or lifestyle effectively 'act up' in these roles, be it through the mechanisms of clothing or of language, and Jonson's *The Alchemist* memorably captures this phenomenon with its central scenario of the 'house' to which a considerable cross-section of society, from fundamentalist Protestants to overweening aristocrats (the wonderfully named Tribulation Wholesome and Sir Epicure Mammon) and from lawyers to shopkeepers (the equally hapless and hopeless Thomas Dapper and Abel Drugger),[2] is drawn. This scenario is sketched out in printed editions of the play via the mechanism of the acrostic 'argument':

> The Argument
> T he sickness hot, a master quit, for fear,

H is house in town, and left one servant there.
E ase him corrupted, and gave means to know
A cheater and his punk, who, now brought low,
L eaving their narrow practice, were become
C ozeners at large; and, only wanting some
H ouse to set up, with him they here contract,
E ach for a share, and all begin to act.
M uch company they draw, and much abuse,
I n casting figures, telling fortunes, news,
S elling of flies, flat bawdry, with the stone,
T ill it and they and all in fume are gone.

(The Argument, 1–12)

The kinds of topic or theme or subject matter that concern these plays do differ from those of the formal tragedies or revenge drama we have considered previously. We see civic authorities worrying about riotous behaviour in inns, and shoemakers reflecting on their workmanship and seeking political representation for their rights; we witness prostitutes and watermen plying their trade, on the London streets and waterways respectively, and we see ordinary people in china shops and textile shops or in markets browsing and purchasing goods and commodities. In the very 'everyday' nature of these themes, several writers and pamphleteers saw direct challenges to so-called dramatic decorum and the kinds of 'rules' that we saw the likes of Sir Philip Sidney and others defending in the face of what they labelled as hybrid or 'mongrel' tragedies. In *Pierce Pennilesse* (1592), Nashe, for one, appeared to rail against 'lay Chronigraphers [and by extension dramatists], that write of nothing but Mayors and Sheriefs, and the deare yeere, and the great Frost', but in fact these kinds of local particularity of administration and governance or simply of weather events feed into a hugely vibrant body of dramatic activity at this time.[3] The 'great Frost' of 1632 features very visibly in the dialogue of *The Sparagus Garden* when John Brittleware reflects on his wife's tendency to compulsive cravings for the latest fashion such as sedan chairs or riding on one of the camels exotically displayed on the River Thames at festival times: 'Heyday! So last frost she loved to ride on one of the dromedaries over the Thames, when the great men were pleased to go over it afoot' (2.2.567–9). From Dekker's *The Shoemaker's Holiday*, then, which charts the rise of London shoemaker Simon Eyre to Mayor of the city, to Jonson's 1633 *A Tale of a Tub* with its extended interest in the work (and sometimes dysfunctionality) of local authorities, city comedies, and other plays that built on their precedent, engaged with and embraced lives, professions and issues that would have been directly familiar to the watching spectators.

Dekker's play has rightly been categorised within a range of overlapping genres, from chronicle history to city comedy, and in this way it clearly relates to the kind of creative hybridity of texts which, like the two parts of Heywood's *Edward IV* or Shakespeare's *Henry IV*, as already noted in Chapter 3, embrace the conventions and codes of traditional history plays while simultaneously challenging them through an enhanced provincial and regional (and, by extension, everyday) focus in terms of characters, settings and themes. A king does briefly appear in *The Shoemaker's Holiday* but he remains unnamed and unidentified and in many respects tangential to the action. By the time of later Jonson and Brome plays there will be no monarchs at all on the stages of what are resolutely city plays about city people. The seeds of this particular development are sown in typically playful and yet arch fashion by Jonson in *The Alchemist* when the Southwark prostitute Doll Common, temporarily plying her trade in Lovewit's Blackfriars house as part of the alchemical scam headed up by Subtle and Face (Lovewit's butler Jeremy who has seized the opportunity of his master's absence during a particularly virulent bout of the plague), performs the role of the Fairy Queen. This was a role that only a few years earlier had been directly associated with the iconography surrounding the then monarch Elizabeth I (who died in 1603), suggesting a fairly radical journey towards acceptability in stage terms by 1610; the Queen has become a 'quean' (slang for a prostitute) in quick measure, suggesting the transformative nature of the urban in potentially disturbing and deliberately unsettling ways that are modelled by this play as a whole.

The opening bickering scene of *The Alchemist*, soaked as it is in colloquial discourse, is not only another superb example of Jonson's theatrical craftsmanship – we enter in the middle of a full-on argument between Subtle and Face over who is the leader of the gang:

> [*Enter*] FACE [*with his sword drawn*], SUBTLE [*holding a glass*
>   *containing a liquid, and*] DOLL COMMON.
> **FACE** Believe't, I will.
> **SUBTLE**   Thy worst. I fart at thee.
> **DOLL** Ha' you your wits? Why, gentlemen! For love –
> **FACE** Sirrah, I'll strip you –
> **SUBTLE**   What to do? Lick figs
>   Out at my –
> **FACE**   Rogue, rogue, out of all your sleights.
>
>   (1.1.1–4)

– but also a brilliant locating of the play in the dense housing stock of Blackfriars: 'Here, in the Friars' (1.1.17) we are told the play takes place, and this would have resonated with Blackfriars Theatre audiences in very immediate ways. Doll fears the overhearing of prying neighbours – 'Will you have / The neighbours hear you? Will you betray all?' (1.1.7–8) – and the consequences of the local constabulary being summoned to the property. Her images here are of being made to ride in a cart as prostitutes were commonly made to do and of the pillories in which those who had been cut and branded were often placed and subjected to violent public humiliations:

> Rascals
> Would run themselves from breath to see me ride,
> Or you t'have but a hole to thrust your heads in,
> For which you should pay ear-rent?
>
> (1.1.167–70)

This play, like many of its fellow city comedies, is, then, at its heart an exploration of what it is to try and live and make shift in a close community with all its competitive rivalries.

The world of temporary lodgers and people on the make preying on less 'savvy' or cautious rural visitors to the city, as depicted in *The Sparagus Garden*, is tantamount to social commentary. One of the warring couples in that play are two elderly Justices of the Peace, Touchwood and Striker, who have apparently nursed their personal enmity over the course of three decades. In the process they draw in family members, household servants, city business people and the local curate in terms that are as embracing of a complex community as Jonson's play. In simple terms, though, *The Alchemist*'s opening scene is one about two men squabbling over the spoils of their trade, over money, and in that respect through this mechanism Jonson brings into sharp focus one of the main drivers of city comedy: economics.

Urban socio-economics, or, money makes the world go round

The critic Christopher Burlinson's pithy definition of Jonson's 'interest in trust and exchange, honesty and deceit, credit and coining' captures the economic driver that lies at the heart of city comedy as a genre;[4] all of these concerns are figured through the physical and metaphorical presence of money on the early modern stage: money appears as fact, as fantasy and as literal, practical stage property. Burlinson suggests that the sheer frequency of coins as props on the Jonsonian stage should alert us to the 'unprecedented importance that coins had in the lives of the people who would have attended Jonson's plays', so we can also see the aspirations of the audience being imaged in these stagings and plotlines.[5] From Volpone's stage gold in that play's previously analysed opening scene (see Case study C) to the dreams of infinite wealth that spur on the visitors to the alchemists' Blackfriars 'house', Jonson consistently depicts characters trying to get ever more money through plots and projects, schemes and scams, and in the process he is able to depict a varied cross-section of urban society which was supposedly all too recognisable to watching spectators and may have left a few shifting uncomfortably in their seats, whether trickster or tricked.

But money and what it makes possible are also present both on- and offstage in other objects than minted coins per se. In *Eastward Ho!* a goldsmith's daughter, Gertrude, is desperate for the coach that will signify her new social status as the wife of the knight Sir Petronel Flash – 'As I am a lady, I think I am with child already, I long for a coach so' (3.2.27) – and in the first scene in which we encounter Gertrude she is already accompanied by a tailor carrying various high-fashion clothing items which she has clearly purchased at considerable expense. A similar version of the London lady's life as one of conspicuous consumption is painted by Sir Thomas Bornwell's description of his own wife Aretina's extravagant pleasures at the start of Shirley's 1635 *The Lady of Pleasure*:

> Though you weigh
> Me in a partial scale, my heart is honest
> And must take liberty to think you have
> Obeyed no modest counsel to affect,
> Nay study ways of pride and costly ceremony;
> Your change of gaudy furniture, and pictures
> Of this Italian master and that Dutchman's;
> Your mighty looking-glasses, like artillery,
> Brought home on engines; the superfluous plate,
> Antic and novel, vanities of tires,
> Fourscore pound suppers for my lord your kinsman,
> Banquets for t'other lady, aunt, and cousins;
> And perfumes that exceed all train of servants,
> To stifle us at home, and show abroad
> More motley than the French or the Venetian
> About your coach, whose rude postillion
> Must pester every narrow lane, till passengers
> And tradesmen curse your choking up their stalls,
> And common cries pursue your ladyship
> For hindering o' their market.
>
> (1.1.69–88)

As hinted at by this quotation and its reference to Aretina's coach choking up the narrow London streets, this play also starts with intricate discussion of coaches and their expensive fittings in ways that seek to capture the intense materiality of the aspirant culture of London in the early seventeenth century.

Both these women will in certain respects be punished for their respective lusts and cravings by the plays in which they feature. Aretina finds herself shamed by a loveless adulterous encounter with the city gallant Alexander Kickshaw (his association with the new culture of luxury goods is signified onstage by the expensive sweets and 'comfits' his associate John Littleworth carries around); Gertrude learns that not only has she signed away her grandmother's inheritance to her new husband Sir Petronel Flash (the cynical apprentice Francis Quicksilver refers to this landholding as 'Two hundred pounds' worth of wood ready to fell', *Eastward Ho!*, 2.2.113), but his promised castle in the east of the country proves to be 'built with air' (2.3.7). Furthermore, Sir Petronel's ambitions are to desert his new wife and sail to the English colony of Virginia in the Americas. That particular plot is itself thwarted by bad weather and some ferocious Thames tides, which mean that Sir Petronel's ship is cast ashore at Cuckold's Haven and poor Gertrude is sent home with her tail between her legs to the very father she earlier scorned. As Quicksilver observes: 'This is not the first time a lady has rid a false journey in her coach' (3.2.160–1). He alludes here to the association of coaches with illicit sexual encounters in the period – it is in just such a place that Lady Kix is made pregnant in *A Chaste Maid in Cheapside* – but it also captures something of the false dreams of wealth that so many of these plays expose. Sir Epicure Mammon's plaintive exhalation in the fifth act of *The Alchemist* when he realises the seedy reality of the house where a Southwark pimp and his 'punk' or prostitute have colluded with Lovewit's butler to take everyone for a fool – 'What! In a dream?' (5.5.83) – might be taken as an overarching description of the ways in which financial aspiration usually figures in these plays. Furthermore, that a number of the victims of the schemes and dreams of these plays prove to be female leads us to the observation that the financial markets, as in Gertrude's all too telling case, seem deeply bound up with the marriage markets in which daughters of households were invariably offered and pawned.

If *Eastward Ho!* is in part about the dangers of 'marrying up', other plays, like *A Chaste Maid in Cheapside,* are equally concerned with the fiscal and social consequences of marrying or not marrying one's children into certain families. The Allwit marriage is a sham that hides an adulterous relationship between Mistress Allwit and the aptly named Sir Walter Whorehound that has resulted in several children. Allwit himself accepts the situation in return for rent and board in a fine London household. The goldsmith's wife, Mistress

Yellowhammer, craves wealth and social status and is in the process willing to barter her own children's happiness. Tim Yellowhammer is matched with a 'Welsh gentlewoman', supposed niece (though really a prostitute acquaintance) of the lascivious knight Whorehound, whose name is enough to warn us not to trust him at any stage of proceedings, and her daughter Moll is being matched with Sir Walter himself much against her wishes: 'The knight is rich, he shall be my son-in-law' (*A Chaste Maid*, 4.1.267), declares the goldsmith's wife.

There is a moral economy at stake, then, in these plotlines as much as there is a desire to depict the operation and impact of the actual money markets of the City of London at this time. Touchstone suggests as much when he turns to address the audience directly at the close of *Eastward Ho!*: 'Now, London, look about, / And in this moral see thy glass run out' (5.5.181–2). As Jean Howard has evidenced, the commercial and the sexual have become inextricably inter-twined in these plays, such that families prostitute themselves and prostitutes cannot be distinguished from gentlewomen.[6] Whorehound's particular brand of alchemy in *A Chaste Maid in Cheapside* is reliant on this fact; he tells the 'Welsh gentlewoman': 'I bring thee up to turn thee into gold, wench' (1.1.107).

The Virginia colony which Sir Petronel and Captain Seagull fashion as a false paradise or utopia in *Eastward Ho!* as they sit in a Billingsgate inn awaiting embarkation – 'A whole country of English is there . . . gold is more plentiful there than copper is with us' (3.3.13–18) – also figures forth for audiences the particular geographies of global trade and exploration that shaped the late Elizabethan and early Jacobean period.[7] The River Thames, such a potent force in *Eastward Ho!* – in a brilliant moment of creativity, Slitgut delivers a monologue in the fourth act that takes in all of the events as they unfold on the river in the midst of the mighty storm and flood that causes Sir Petronel and others' boats to be wrecked – was a particular focus of these activities. Contemporary engravings and panoramas depicted the Thames as a veritable forest of ship masts and in 1632 Donald Lupton observed that the river 'sends forth ships of Trafficke to most parts of the Earth'.[8]

Migrant workers

People as well as goods were part of the flow in and out of London. Lupton noted astutely of the city that 'there are so many little worlds in Her . . . Shee swarmes foure times in a yeare, with people of al Ages, Natures, Sexes, Callings';[9] and city comedy as a genre reflected this flow of capital within the capital, its broad communities and its micro-societies of incomers and immigrants. In Act 3 of *The Sparagus Garden* audiences are given sight of the Gardener and his Dutch wife Martha (presumably delivering her lines with a recognisable Netherlands accent) working the garden plots that supply the dining and drinking rooms of the pleasure garden, not least with the 'dirty sparagus' (3.1, speech 413), a newly fashionable culinary commodity that is the focus of much double entendre and desire on the part of the paying visitors, though also with other plants associated with the Low Countries at this time including artichokes and tulips. The Gardener draws attention to his wife's immigrant status by drawing a deliberate geographical parallel between the marshlands which they work (it seems likely the play takes place in Lambeth Marshes which was a popular growing area for asparagus in the 1630s) and those from which she derives:[10] 'I had once a hope to have bought this manor of marshland: for the resemblance it has to the Low Country soil you came from – to ha'made you a Bankside Lady' (3.1, speech 414). In turn, of course, he invokes another 'Bankside' place and space, that of the public open-air theatres across the water from the indoor theatres in which the majority of Brome's plays were staged, though also a site of prostitution. These multiple senses of the term appear to be deliberately, simultaneously mobilised for audiences to respond to.

Immigrant Dutch workers such as Martha were a source of genuine anxiety to so-called 'native' Londoners of the day and a number of these tensions arise in the city comedies as well as elsewhere on the stage of early modern drama. Natasha Korda's research has indicated that, due to the strong presence of Dutch workers in the textile and clothing and shoemaking industries, this was a tension that would have been highly noticeable in the immediate environs of the theatre.[11] The Gardener's multiple allusions to the relationship of his wife to the riverside communities of London in *The Sparagus Garden* pick up on these issues in a very immediate way.

An earlier play that engages directly with the Dutch presence in London is Dekker's *The Shoemaker's Holiday*. There Rowland Lacy, whom we learn trained as a shoemaker in Wittenberg after he had frittered away the family money he was entitled to as a gentleman (1.29), assumes a disguise as Hans, a Dutch shoemaker or 'uplandish workman' as Firk the apprentice terms it (4.50), and attempts to gain employment in the 'gentle craft' at Eyre's thriving London workshop. This creates space in the play for much faux-Dutch dialogue – 'ik bin den skomawker' (4.81) – an approach to the learned and hybridised languages of immigrant communities that is reworked in numerous plays including several of Brome's London plays in the 1630s, where he parodies French, Spanish, Dutch, Cornish and Welsh among other modern languages – but in addition to the more obvious comedic elements, this aspect of the plot draws attention to what were very real issues and tensions in the London of Dekker's day, collapsing the historical time of the play into something much more immediate and familiar, and also to the kind of active trade networks that works such as Lupton's attempted to capture in their descriptions. Eyre's rise to prominence as a London mayor hinges on black market dealings in goods from a Dutch cargo boat, 'sugar, civet, almonds, cambric, ed alle dinge [and all things]' (7.3–4), which Hans/Lacy is able to facilitate. In a further wonderful time-collapsing example of the ways in which trade activity shaped the London landscape we also learn about a particular inn, the Swan near Thames Street, which the Dutch community frequented in the late sixteenth and seventeenth centuries and where this kind of business was transacted.[12]

The inclusion of characters such as Martha or assumed personae such as Hans the shoemaker do more cultural work than simply to populate the already busy stages of city comedies with yet more examples of the rich traffic in humanity that London participated in. Through allusion to immigrant communities and specific neighbourhoods of London, a complicated landscape of trade and finance, markets and exchange, is established and that landscape serves a literal and a metaphorical purpose, slipping as it so often does in these plays into even deeper considerations of the alternative exchange rates of the marriage market in which women characters in particular find themselves advertised and sold. When Maudlin Yellowhammer drags in her own daughter Moll by the hair, the poor girl still dripping from a close encounter with the River Thames in her efforts to escape her family's attempts at arranged marriage for her, the audience is being asked not only to register a world of watermen and the labouring landscape of the river, though that certainly adds a potent charge to the scene, but also that aforementioned moral hinterland in which mothers are prepared to sell their daughters to the highest bidder in order to survive in the competitive circumstances of the city.

Working women

London's fecundity as a place, generative as it is of the kinds of complex and often conflictual activities that we have already been outlining in accounting for the multiple plotlines and large casts of city comedies, is further mirrored in the themes of fertility and indeed its impotent opposite that constantly surface in these plays. In *A Chaste Maid in Cheapside* Lady Kix's barren marriage leads her into compromising encounters in a coach in the hope of getting pregnant; in the same play, Allwit's wife has the opposite problem, bearing a succession of children to Whorehound. The china-shop co-owner Rebecca Brittleware in *The Sparagus Garden* shares Lady Kix's problem of a childless marriage and the play makes much fun of her cravings, sexual and otherwise.

Sex and fertility become in these storylines one powerfully suggestive means of describing and representing the aspirational urban world where city men and women yearn for social mobility and the wealth and the status that both enables and accompanies that mobility. One particular butt of jokes on this account is another china-shop owner, Mistress Otter, in Jonson's 1609 play *Epicene*, who burns her own dress, so caught up is she in aspirational daydreaming:

> Yes, sir, anything I do but dream o'the city. It stained me a damask tablecloth, cost me eighteen pound at one time, and burnt me a black satin gown as I stood by the fire at my Lady Centaur's chamber in the college another time.   (3.2.55–8)

The comic examples of women's ambitions in these plays should not however blind us to other remarkable stories that characterisations like Rebecca Brittleware or Mistress Otter also contain. Both are, as already stated, china-women, that is to say they sell in their London shops the china and porcelain ware which like asparagus was a hugely desirable commodity in the materially consumptive early modern London. For all the jokes at their expense, their professionalism tells us much about the global trade networks which we have already described as a driver behind the energies and flows of many of these market-driven and market-determined dramas, but it also give us remarkable and surprising insight into a surprisingly diverse urban community of working women.

Korda's research has been hugely influential in uncovering for us the entrepreneurial traces of these working women both on and off the early modern commercial stage:

> Women's work was not only represented by male actors on the stage, it was woven into the fabric of players' costumes, concealed in the folds of their starched ruffs, set into the curls of their perukes [wigs], arranged in the petticoats of boy actors, calculated on the balance sheets, and inscribed in the terms of their bonds.[13]

As well as shopworkers and saleswomen such as Mistresses Brittleware and Otter (and, notably, the former has a second trade as a landlady renting rooms in her own family home to the dubious gentleman Sir Hugh Moneylacks), we have met already with *The Sparagus Garden*'s Martha, a gardener and hostess of a boarding house and inn, with housekeepers and maidservants, with seamstresses such as Jane in *The Shoemaker's Holiday*. While 'working women' such as *The Alchemist*'s Doll Common are one part of the story, prostitution is not the only career available to women even in the sexually heightened atmosphere of the capital city of these plays.

The Shoemaker's Holiday's comic narrative hedges around darker themes of war and poverty, with Ralph the newlywed apprentice from Eyre's cordwainers' workshop pressed into military service in the wars against France. But our focus as an audience is largely on the fate of the woman he leaves behind, his new wife Jane. Eyre remarks early on in the play about the necessity that Jane undertake manual work to keep herself during her husband's absence (and by implication in case he fails to return):

> Let me see thy hand, Jane. [*He takes her hand*] This fine hand, this white hand, these pretty fingers must spin, must card, must work, work, you bombast-cotton-candle quean, work for your living… (1.217–20)

This is an idea to which the play will notably return when Hammon, having failed in another effort to woo a life-partner, returns his attention to a former amour, Jane, and turns up at the residence where she now works as a seamstress in the Old Exchange building. Jane has been forced to move away from the relative sanctuary of Eyre's workshop, which inevitably leaves her prey to the attentions of her former suitor: 'Yonder's the shop, and there my fair love sits. / She's fair and lovely, but she is not mine' (12.1–2).[14] The focus in this striking scene is on her hands and by extension on the handicraft that is such a central theme to this play. For all of Hammon's sexual acquisitiveness – he will claim to know of the death of Jane's husband in the wars in an effort to secure her hand – there is something intimate in the observations made in this moment onstage:

> How prettily she works! O pretty hand!
> O happy work! It doth me good to stand
> Unseen to see her. Thus I oft have stood
> In frosty evenings, a light burning by her,
> Enduring biting cold only to eye her.
> (12.13–17)

As well as being a memorable moment of stage focus on women's work, the play is all the time drawing our attention to the working world of the city more generally, its guilds and craft companies, its workshops and its points of sale. The dominance and the presentation of this workshop space is something we will return to in a moment but before focusing in on a specific place it is worth accounting for the sustained engagement with the idea of 'place' which these plays perform.

Local attachments

As specific references and allusions in plays such as *The Sparagus Garden* or *The Shoemaker's Holiday* indicate, and as the carefully located action of plays such as Jonson's *The Alchemist* or *Bartholomew Fair* demonstrate, places –

named places, places of political or social significance, familiar places in the watching audience's own experience – were incredibly important to this particular subset of early modern drama. As humanities and social science research has undergone what many refer to as a 'spatial turn' in recent decades, a plethora of studies have sought to engage with the ways in which these plays invoke, create, represent and to a certain extent actively shape place and space.[15]

Play titles can tell us much in this regard. If Jonson, Chapman and Marston wish to indicate directionality, literal and social, in the title of *Eastward Ho!*, other city comedies invoke particular locations and communities in order to raise and sometimes to challenge audience expectations. *A Chaste Maid in Cheapside* makes a wicked joke of the fact that this hugely active neighbourhood of craftspeople and tradespersons and their families and clientele was also understood by many to be a place in which a highly sexual trade took place – through prostitution in its most obvious sense in the daily trade and operation of brothels in the vicinity but also more widely through the operations of the marriage market which, as we have seen, the play depicts with savage sarcasm. In the 1630s Brome and Nabbes consciously set their city plays in newly established or emergent locales, not least the piazza Covent Garden, designed by Inigo Jones, in the fast expanding West End of the city, but also Tottenham Court – a thriving suburban locale at this time where people went for recreation of all kinds, licit and illicit; Nabbes's *Tottenham Court* accordingly features characters such as a dairy maid who sells provisions to these city visitants but also hints at much that is sexual just below the surface. In 1632 James Shirley authored a play called *Hyde Park* which concerned itself with the newly opened green space in London where the elite showed off their fine coaches and bet on horse and footraces (3.1 of this play is a brilliant, economical reconstruction of an athletics race complete with onstage betting; see Case study I). This kind of drama is reflecting the new leisure practices of London's elite and the spatial impact they were having on London's architecture and environment – shopping emporia and pleasure gardens are all part of this emerging landscape.[16] As we have seen, *The Sparagus Garden* deals with exactly this kind of space; the pleasure garden where the Gardener and Martha work their fingers to the bone to make their 'poor piddling doings' (3.1, speech 415) is also a covert brothel for London's wealthier set.

In the majority of these instances, activation of audience recognition of all these spaces and what they signify, practically and ethically, is essential. Spectators' awareness of and associations with specific places and spaces are being self-consciously mobilised. Audiences entering the theatre to watch Brome's *The Weeding of Covent Garden* (1632), for example, the first act of which makes detailed reference to the building works in progress aimed at realising Inigo

Jones's dreams of an Italianate piazza in London, would likely have passed by the real-life equivalent en route to the performance.[17] Similarly, the closing sections of *The Shoemaker's Holiday* make extended reference to Eyre's proposals for a new building (Leadenhall Market, so called because lead uncovered during the digging of the foundations was eventually used as a roofing material) with a special charter to control the sale and purchase of the leather that was essential to his former trade as shoemaker. Eyre asks the King: 'vouchsafe some privilege to my new Leaden Hall that it may be lawful for us to buy and sell leather there two days a week' (21.157–9). This is a depiction of the building's historical provenance but for Dekker's 1590s audiences there was a distinctly contemporary and immediate flavour to what was being described. As one editor suggests: 'The audience are being offered the pleasures of familiarity, a play set in the streets through which they had just walked to the theatre, punctuated by the sounds that measured out their daily lives.'[18] These plays are, then, physically and psychologically mappable by early modern audiences and for these reasons this is a genre that is peculiarly alert to the conditions of its own reception, drawing attention to and hailing its contemporary spectators all the time, and not least through its mobilisations of space and place.[19] It would be wrong, of course, to suggest this is something wholly particular to city comedy as a genre; as discussions of plays such as the two parts of Heywood's *Edward IV* in Chapter 3 has indicated, there was considerable precedent in chronicle history as well as comedy for this kind of conscious urban cartography. In Heywood's play, Falconbridge's rebels imagine (albeit with a fantastic exorbitance more akin to mythical notions of plenty in the Land of Cockaigne) how they will appropriate the City of London through its civic and mercantile spaces, its goldsmiths' shops, its trade markets and its bakers and brewers:

> **FIRK** We will be masters of the Mint ourselves,
>   And set our own stamp on the golden coin.
>   We'll shoe our neighing coursers with no worse
>   Than the purest silver that is sold in Cheap.
>   (*Edward IV, Part 1*, 2.49–52)

> **SPICING** You know Cheapside? There are the mercers' shops,
>   Where we will measure velvet by our pikes,
>   And silks and satins by the street's whole breadth!
>   We'll take tankards from the conduit cocks,
>   To fill with Hippocras, and drink carouse!
>   Where chains of gold and plate shall be as plenty
>   As wooden dishes in the weald of Kent.
>   (*Edward IV, Part 1*, 2.66–72)

In a striking moment at the close of this scene, Spicing describes them standing on a hill gazing at a panorama of the city and all of its sights and sites much as a herd of deer might contemplate the landscape (80). What city comedy does as a genre, though, is to take us down to street level and ask us to enter directly into the shops of merchants and their wives and in the process to share their struggles and their aspirations.

Handwork and window shopping: the site of the workshop

On leaving his new wife Jane for the wars in *The Shoemaker's Holiday*, Ralph's parting gift is not the traditional scarf or ring but instead a handcrafted pair of shoes, a proud and collaborative product of the Simon Eyre workshop:

> Now, gentle wife, my loving, lovely Jane,
> Rich men at parting give their wives rich gifts,
> Jewels, and rings to grace their lily hands.
> Thou know'st our trade makes rings for women's heels.
> Here, take this pair of shoes cut out by Hodge,
> Stitched by my fellow, Firk, seamed by myself,
> Made up and pinked with letters for thy name.
> Wear them, my dear Jane, for thy husband's sake
> And every morning, when thou pull'st them on,
> Remember me, and pray for my return.
> Make much of them for I have made them so
> That I can know them from a thousand moe.
>
> (1.235–46)

There is much to explore here about the allocation of labour and its depiction of collaborative production, but since this is picked up in Case study J, the focus here will be on the very literal and material staging of a workshop space. Sociologist Richard Sennett has written recently in thought-provoking ways of the centrality of atelier or workshop space and activity to the early modern period and it is noticeable how often this kind of space is either invoked or actively staged in city comedies.[20]

One thing to note immediately is that these were hybrid spaces – sites of work, where apprentices and journeymen lived, and with boarded fronts from which wares could be sold directly to passing trade, but also family homes, and this mixed spatiality begins to explain many of the tensions and confusions of city comedy communities. In *The Sparagus Garden* Rebecca Brittleware shares her home not only with visitors to the shop but also with lodgers who help to cover costs, and the most intimate secrets of her childless marriage seem to become public knowledge as a result.[21] In *The Shoemaker's Holiday* we have sight and sound not only of Eyre's productive workshop with exactly the kind of mixed society previously described of apprentices, journeymen, maidservants and direct kin, but also scenes conducted in the mercer's shop where Jane takes up her seamstress's work. Scene 4 takes place in the street outside Eyre's shop; scene 7 is in the workshop; scene 10 deals with comings and goings in or outside the shop; and in scene 12 we get Jane's shop in a different part of London. The opening scene of *Eastward Ho!* is conducted before the goldsmith Touchstone's shop with Golding the apprentice crying their wares in their street: 'What do ye lack, sir? What is't you'll buy, sir?' (1.1.54). In fact, as Golding performs the role of street hawker or crier in this way, a page to Sir Petronel Flash comes to the property to 'buy' not gold chains or rings but rather Gertrude the goldsmith's daughter with his false promises of wealth and castle residences.

All of this raises very practical questions as to how these hybrid workshop spaces and the movements in and out of them were depicted on the commercial theatre stage. Much could have been made of discovery spaces and doors in both the indoor and outdoor auditoria, though there is possibly something even more precise indicated by some of the extant playtexts. Scene 13 of *The Shoemaker's Holiday* opens with 'Hodge at his shop boord etc'. A shopboard was either a hinged counter that covered a window at night or could be let down during the day to form a shelf, or a stall from which to sell goods or sometimes a moveable worktable. References in this play at 4.9 and 17.54 suggest that it is the former that Dekker imagined for Eyre's workshop.[22]

If Dekker's play is for the most part a positive depiction of a working community, its tools and activities, its customs and expectations and indeed aspirations, Brome's workshop stagings are rather more suggestive of the kinds of shading of commerce and prostitution that we have seen alluded to in other city comedies. In his *c.* 1629–32 play *The City Wit*, the courtier Rufflit accuses Crasy of prostituting his own wife Josina in the window of their jewellery shop (Act 4, speech 622). What remains clear in this diverse set of depictions of working London, and not least of its new predilection for shopping, is that the world up on the stage was one deeply familiar and recognisable to the audience, and from that standpoint playwrights could make all kinds of challenges to contemporary culture and practice under the guise of simply depicting 'real life'.

Chronicling the city

In Chapter 3 we began to chart a move away from a pure history of kings and queens towards a more regionally and provincially inflected understanding of the form by the late 1590s. It is in the wake of these developments that Dekker composes *The Shoemaker's Holiday* and we should therefore not be surprised to see this 'chronicle comedy' picking up on some of those evolutions and developments in its own experimentation with form, staging and representation. And from this early foray, the rather more bitter and satirical city comedies of Jonson, Middleton and others emerge as a genuine force in commercial theatre by the early decades of the seventeenth century.

Thomas Blundeville offered up in his 1574 prose text *The True Order and Methode of Wryting and Reading Histories* a statement of purposes that seems oddly pertinent to how to 'write city comedy' in that it opens a space for contrapuntal or dissident action simply by dint of its rigidity of purpose: 'It is meete that the lyues of Princes shoulde be chronicled.'[23] Playwrights from Dekker onwards appear to ask why it is not equally 'meet' that the lives of everyday artisans also be chronicled, and the huge popularity of city comedies, these plays depicting everyday workspaces and living spaces, plays about shoemakers and cobblers, puppeteers and gingerbread sellers, petty criminals and prostitutes, china-shop women and seamstresses, suggests a genuine need to challenge restrictive theories of literary and generic decorum such as Blundeville's. The energy of these plays would change the face of theatre on a permanent basis; the voice of the common person was now being well and truly heard on the English public stage and this was, thankfully, a point of no return.

The dramaturgy of scenes

We are very used to analysing those moments of early modern drama when there is an intimate relationship between the audience and specific characters; in particular, we are drawn to moments of soliloquy when a one-to-one relationship is almost within our grasp with a Hamlet or a Barabas, or indeed an Isabella, who in Shakespeare's *Measure for Measure* looks to the audience in the 'To whom should I complain?' soliloquy (2.4.171–87) as the only people left in the world to whom she can speak, other than the God from whom she is estranged following her journey away from the Viennese convent in a desperate effort to save her brother's life. But what can moments of ensemble, large group scenes, featuring a large degree of movement and flow, tell us about both the architectonics of the stage and the dramatic shape of individual plays in performance?

We have had recourse on several occasions already in this study to the largely bare stage of early modern commercial theatre which could then be significantly populated with bodies, costumes and key props. In this climate, gesture has proved to be a strong maker of meaning, but gesture can be read at the level of an individual hand movement (see for example the discussion of dumb show in Case study M) or the movement of bodies and groups of bodies on the stage. Shakespeare's *As You Like It*, 3.2, which commences with Orlando pinning his sonnets to Rosalind on trees, is worth invoking first as an example. We ostensibly begin the scene in the realm of courtly love poetry and pastoral literature (see more detailed discussion of generic conventions in Chapter 4) but this is immediately juxtaposed with the country versus city debate between Corin the tenant shepherd and Touchstone the court jester, before we flow back to Rosalind and Celia in their respective disguises (Rosalind as the boy Ganymede) and an extended intellectual exchange between Rosalind and Orlando on the theme of love. Love is therefore debated as a theme throughout but juxtaposed with a wider context of the working agricultural world as represented by Corin. If we widen the lens yet further to encompass the entire act, we will see multiple versions of both love and forest existence presented for our consideration, from Duke

Senior's alternative woodland assembly of 'merry men' (1.1.109) to the troubled relationships of Silvius and Phebe and Touchstone and Audrey ('I do not know what "poetical" is', 3.3.14). All of this is further punctuated by the melancholic and cynical observations of Jaques, the forest satirist. The flow of the scene and its various participants creates a very mixed economy within this woodland space.

The Beaumont and Fletcher tragicomedy *Philaster* also has extended pastoral action, this time located in the fourth act where the King's hunting trip becomes an occasion for encounter between a whole grouping of courtiers who are in the woodlands for a variety of different reasons, as well as with those forest workers who make elite hunting rituals possible by their careful preparation of the stag for the kill ('What, have you lodged the deer?... Yes, they are ready for the bow', 4.2.1–2) and a passing country 'fellow' who has come out for a walk that day expressly with the purpose of seeing the monarch whom he has been told is in the vicinity. As we move through different parts of the woodland we are also invited to see different moments and actions through different eyes and from different angles. A multi-perspectival reading on the part of the audience is directly facilitated by both the textual and the stage architecture in this instance.

Brome was something of a master at large ensemble scenes and one of his finest comes in the sweeping third act of *The Sparagus Garden*. This is the point in the play when we finally get to enter the space referred to by the play's title and much discussed by the play's characters up to this moment: the pleasure garden on the Bankside with its outside gardens and arbours and its rooms for rent where the much coveted asparagus is for sale to Londoners conscious of consuming the latest fashion in food. The entire act is one flowing sequence as we move seamlessly around different parts of the locale; sometimes this is notionally signified by certain properties being carried onstage, such as the table and dishes of sugar and asparagus carried on by servants attending to Gilbert, Samuel and Walter, the play's younger city males, but more often than not it is signalled verbally as characters announce what they are doing or what is within their sights.

We begin, interestingly enough, and in a way that echoes the deployment of the woodsmen in *Philaster*, from a workers' perspective as the unnamed Gardener and his wife, the Dutch immigrant Martha, discuss the day's takings and their longer-term aspirations to own their own property. Then visitors to the Asparagus Garden arrive. This is a classic technique of early modern drama: to have a central location that can serve as a meeting point for a cross-section of society. The forest of Arden with its exiled courtiers and working shepherds is one such example but we might also invoke Jonson's fondness for this particular spatial technique in plays such as *Bartholomew Fair* where fair workers and visitors collide throughout Acts 2–5, and *The New Inn* where a Barnet inn becomes the magnetic space in which we witness encounters between inn workers, coachmen and visiting aristocrats and all of the spin-off action and dialogue that this enables.

The visitors to Brome's Asparagus Garden are, indeed, a veritable cross-section. In addition to the aforementioned young male gallants we have courtiers, London men on the make, a Somerset man and his servant who are proving to be victims of a scam perpetrated by the former group, an adulterous couple, and a china-shop owner, John Brittleware, and his wife Rebecca, who have been persuaded to come to the Garden in the hope that consuming asparagus will act as an aphrodisiac for their sexually repressed marriage. In the process the audience is asked to think about all the different corners and areas of the larger space of the Garden and to imagine interior space just offstage, such as the bedroom to which the Brittlewares momentarily retreat only to re-enter with the painful exclamation from John: 'But half pleased, sweetheart?' (3.1, speech 615). This is choreography of the finest order and we can see its effects mirrored in another Caroline play, by James Shirley, which deploys the newly opened London recreational space of Hyde Park to capture the movement and flow of a large range of characters around the very location that the title has asked us to imagine at the heart of this play. Shirley's *Hyde Park* goes so far as to place an athletics race (a common occurrence on this site, along with horseracing, in the 1630s) in the extended scene in the park in 3.1; it takes place just out of sight offstage, of course, but is created in large part for us by the responses and reactions of the betting spectators who are onstage throughout and by the occasional criss-crossing of the stage by the runners (an English and an Irish footman) themselves:

> (*Within:*) A Teague! A Teague! Hey!
> **TRIER** Well run, Irish!
> (3.1, p. 23)[1]

Exactly where in plays ensemble moments and scenes are located is usually equally resonant with meaning. The open-air theatres were more about a fluid movement between acts and scenes and there were no clear demarcators of those moments in terms of the staging. This contrasts with the formal observation of the five acts in indoor theatres, usually through the use of music and sometimes via stage activity taking place between the acts (see Case study E). In spaces like the Globe, the Hope, the Rose and the Swan, then, act breaks were less the keynote than juxtaposition; something about the flow of these performances encourages a reading of scenes and moments against each other. One wonderful example of this in action occurs in Shakespeare's *As You Like It*, with Jaques's 'Seven Ages of Man' speech which begins with that memorable metatheatrical observation that 'All the world's a stage' (2.7.139), thereby inviting spectators to reflect on what they are seeing from a very practical standpoint. The speech reaches a rhetorical climax with the 'Last scene of all' (163), which is old age and death. If we imagine how exits and entrances occurred, with actors starting to enter as cue lines were spoken, Jaques is describing 'second childishness and mere oblivion, / Sans teeth, sans eyes, sans everything' (165–6) just as Orlando arrives onto the stage bearing the body of his exhausted elderly servant Adam.[2]

Peter Holland has suggested that these open-air performances often deployed the sense of a play's heart, midpoint or centre to create emphasis and effect, describing this in terms of a 'central plateau'.[3] Hamlet's prime moment of metatheatre with the performance of 'The Mousetrap' in a play of appearance and reality where 'one may smile and smile and be a villain' (1.5.109) is one example (and this too is a great ensemble scene); a more intimate example would be Mosca's soliloquy of self-assertion at the centre of *Volpone*, 3.1.15–33, the moment where the witty servant announces his intention of outdoing and indeed toppling his master with his own ambition. *Philaster*'s pastoral ensemble scene is not in Act 3 but instead Act 4, its slight off-centre placement perhaps in alignment with the swerves and avoidances more typical of tragicomedy as a genre (see Chapter 7 for further discussion).

Ensemble scenes and scenic connections allow us, then, to think about the architecture and choreography of plays. At a practical level this can be achieved by means of diagrams which map the flow of scenes and/or characters, and indeed by workshopping the blocking of large ensemble scenes so that we can take into account who is *not* speaking as much who is and what kinds of stage picture are being created in the process. Putting any scene or section of a play 'on its feet' gives us access to the practical, pragmatic working theatre in ways that can only help to bring the texts alive.

Collaborative writing or the literary workshop

The genre of urban-located and urban-conscious drama that came to be known as city comedy is fascinated with the particular spatial signifier of the workshop. In plays such Dekker's *The Shoemaker's Holiday* and Middleton's *A Chaste Maid in Cheapside* the hybrid spaces of family workshops provide, as we have seen (see Chapter 5), sites for stage business with props and hands, for cultural reflection on the artisanal population of London, and function as mechanisms for plot as characters of different provenance and rank visit the shoemaker's or the goldsmith's workshop in search of all manner of objects of desire. But the workshop had another very real application in the context of the early modern theatre as both a literal and a conceptual space in which the practice of collaborative authorship took place. As sociologist Richard Sennett has detailed in his wide-ranging study *The Craftsman*, the atelier or workshop was a significant creative space in this period, one that can tell us much about group activity and the collaborative production of art and culture.[1]

Even in the case of Shakespeare, it is now widely accepted that the early modern theatre was a commercially driven, collaborative enterprise, not just between writers and the wider personnel of any theatre company or printshop (players, seamstresses, tirewomen, feathermakers, scribes, book-sellers, to name just a few)[2] – what Ton Hoenselaars has described of late in memorable terms as making the playwright's 'creativity . . . inseparable from his interaction with colleagues on the workfloor'[3] – but also frequently between the writers themselves who produced plays both with and in com-petition with each other in the hothouse environment of the public theatres. The title page of *Eastward Ho!* when it was first issued in print described it as being 'Made by Geo. Chapman, Ben: Iohnson, Iohn Marston'. This 1605 play appears to have been an example of the first category of what James Bednarz describes by the umbrella label of 'literary coactivity', namely 'col-laborative writing', which is to say when a playtext was scripted by more than one dramatist, sometimes with particular sections of the plot (main plot and subplot for example) being parcelled out to particular individuals or perhaps different acts apportioned to different writers to ensure a speedy, efficient and therefore economically favourable production line.[4]

A second category of literary coactivity embraces what Hoenselaars categorises as 'revision', when 'one or more playwrights working on an existent text... make it meet certain requirements, be it for the stage or page'.[5] Printed title pages to plays often acknowledge or indicate that this kind of work has been undertaken by the use of the phrase 'additions' and we have already encountered 'additions' creating new textual variants of plays such as Marlowe's *Doctor Faustus* (the so-called 'A' and 'B' texts), Kyd's *The Spanish Tragedy* (see the declaration of this on the 1623 title page reproduced as Figure 5 and discussed in detail in Case study G; Henslowe's diary suggests these 'additions' to an already popular play may largely have been undertaken by Jonson)[6] and Marston's *The Malcontent*. The latter revenge drama, initially written with the indoor theatre children's companies in mind, was altered and adapted, probably by John Webster, so that the adult King's Men company could perform it at the Globe. All of this gives us a very vibrant, kinetic understanding of writing contexts at the time, with plays being altered and adapted over time, perhaps to suit changing audience tastes, or the practical requirements of new venues; perhaps to enable a commercial play to go on tour in the provinces with a different company and perhaps a particular set of costumes and props for the purpose. It is striking that quite often the additions and revisions appear to be of a theatrical nature, perhaps boosting those aspects of a play that had worked well for audiences (this has certainly been suggested of the work undertaken on *Doctor Faustus*).[7]

The Book of Sir Thomas More is a rich example of a collaborative play *and* a revised play. Written by Anthony Munday and others, possibly Henry Chettle, the play is also revised by several other hands. In all, six hands can be identified in the single manuscript copy of the play that exists in the British Library (Harley MS 7368). Hand A is generally accepted as being Chettle's and he was a known collaborator of Munday's.[8] Hand E is almost certainly Thomas Dekker's and Hand B has been attributed to Thomas Heywood (this hand is involved in the kind of theatrical addition described above, improving scene ends and enhancing the role of the Clown). Hand C gives us sight of a different kind of professional hand, the professional bookkeeper who annotates and smoothes out the text, perhaps for a printer. But it is Hand D in this manuscript that has grabbed most scholarly attention since many critics now believe it to be Shakespeare's. The work that we see Hand D doing in the text is interesting in terms of any attempt to reconstruct what went on in an early modern writing 'workshop'. Hand D is responsible for a specific scene that casts the character of Thomas More in a particular light but it is clear that when it was being written some of the other details of the wider play were not to hand as the writer uses the phrase 'Others' for speech prefixes and individual characters' names are only entered in at a later stage by Hand C. It is a tantalising glimpse of writers, Shakespeare and others, at work, performing their particular professional handicraft, and the result is an improved theatrical product.[9]

Chapter 6

Satire

Biting, aggressive, corrosive, excoriating, scornful, scourging, whipping, drubbing, abrasive: these are all terms that have at some point in time been used to refer to or to conjure up the effects and modes of satire as a literary genre. In the Induction to Jonson's 1599 play *Every Man Out of His Humour*, Asper, a character described in the print edition as 'eager and constant in reproof, without fear controlling the world's abuses' (Characters, 11–12), makes the following assertions:

> Who can behold such prodigies as these
> And have his lips sealed up? Not I. My soul
> Was never ground into such oily colours
> To flatter vice and daub iniquity,
> But with an armed and resolved hand
> I'll strip the ragged follies of the time
> Naked as at their birth . . .
>   and with a whip of steel
> Print wounding lashes in their iron ribs.
>   (Induction, 10–16, 17–18)

This is the self-assigned role of the satirist, then, to right the wrongs of a supposedly wicked age – 'this impious world' as Asper describes it in his opening lines (Induction, 2) – and as a result the medicalised language of purging and curing, as well as the more violent vocabulary of whipping and biting, naturally attaches itself to the satirist's discourse. Asper commits to 'scourge the age' and offer 'physic of the mind' (Induction, 127, 131). The visceral nature of his intentions is both striking and noteworthy in terms of establishing a tone for the genre as it develops on the early modern commercial stage:

>   My strict hand
> Was made to seize on vice, and, with a gripe,
> Crush out the humour of such spongy souls
> As lick up every idle vanity.
>
>   (Induction, 142–5)

Asper's focus on the 'humour' of his targets is itself a medicalised reference and brings into play the particular framework for understanding character that the theory of the four humours provided. The theory was that the body was made up of four chief liquids – choler, melancholy, phlegm and blood – and that the relative balance or imbalance of these in any individual contributed to personality and character. Jonson used this as an inspirational framework for early plays such as *Every Man In His Humour* and *Every Man Out of His Humour* and would return to it later in his career with plays like *The Magnetic Lady* (1632) but it was also visible in Middleton's contributions to the early modern repertoire.

What humours comedy did was to take social types to an extreme on the stage so that individuals and their actions were dominated by their tendency to, for example, the melancholic or the choleric, or indeed, by extension, to other extremes of emotion and position. While exaggeration is part of the overall effect, what was achieved by this kind of stage portraiture was social satire at its most active – the particular obsessions and fads of the age could be picked up and parodied through this kind of overt dramatic characterisation. Greed, for example, became a favoured trope in a number of social satires ranging from the avaricious farmer Sordido in *Every Man Out of His Humour* who hoards his grain specifically in order to make a profit at the expense of the suffering in times of bad harvest and dearth, 'a precious, filthy damnèd rogue, / That fats himself with expectation / Of rotten weather and unseasoned hours' (1.3.23–5), to Volpone the fox coveting his riches at the beginning of Jonson's eponymous 1606 play (see Case study C), and from Shakespeare and Middleton's *Timon of Athens* (*c.* 1605) to Massinger's superbly excessive creation the monopolist and encloser Sir Giles Overreach in *A New Way to Pay Old Debts* (1625).

Classical precedents

Satire as a genre had strong classical provenance and origins; the works of Seneca, Martial, Juvenal all provided textual precedents and models and, as we saw with some of the examples of satirical tragedy that we looked at under the heading of 'revenge drama' in Chapter 2, several key exponents of the form were associated with the malcontent type and with a particular brand of nihilism. Jonson, in particular, was clearly interested in investigating and testing the possibilities of satire on the stage and he was influenced in this action both by a general tendency towards experimentation in his work and by a particular set of social and political circumstances in which he found himself as a writer. His 'comicall satire' formulation – he assigned three of his early plays this label (*Cynthia's Revels, Poetaster* and *Every Man Out of His Humour*) – was a specific theatrical innovation that sought to bring the concerns and approaches of non-dramatic satire into a stage context. There were strong classical precedents for his experimentations with the form, in particular stemming from Horace (65–8 BCE) and Juvenal (late first to second century CE).

Horatian satire is generally regarded as being at the gentler end of the spectrum, indulging in ridicule rather than out-and-out reproof and aimed at reparation, whereas the Juvenalian manifestation is more abrasive and linked to specific position-taking such as misogyny and misanthropy. Though at various stages in his career Jonson would associate himself with Horace as a writer (most notably in his 1601 play *Poetaster*), it is the Juvenalian form that is perhaps most evident in his satiric comedies. *Epicene*, for example, written and staged in 1609 and the first of Jonson's solo plays to make a virtue out of its verisimilar London staging, features a witty but cynical central character called Truewit, who not only embodies a Juvenalian mindset on the stage but in several key moments directly adapts Juvenalian texts in his discourse. At 2.2 he arrives at the household of Morose, who has made known his intention to marry; Truewit is keen to dissuade him from this course of action, not least because he fears that his close friend and associate Dauphine, Morose's nephew, will be disinherited in the process, presumably curtailing some of the economic security enjoyed by Truewit's (homo)social circle. He arrives, therefore, carrying significant hand properties, a noose and a post-horn. Blowing on the horn is simply intended to aggravate the obsessive-compulsive older man who has a deep aversion to noise of any kind, notwithstanding his decision to live in one of the noisiest areas of London, near the Strand; the noose, however, signifies a means to achieve the suicide that Truewit advocates as preferable to the subjected state of marriage or the 'goblin matrimony' (2.2.25) as he terms it. In the process of his verbal fireworks display Truewit directly cites Juvenal's sixth *Satire*, updating its references to match the contemporary London geography in which *Epicene* so self-consciously locates itself:

> Marry, your friends do wonder, sir, the Thames being so near, wherein you may drown yourself so handsomely or London Bridge at a low fall with a fine leap, to hurry you down the stream; or such a delicate steeple i'the town as Bow, to vault from; or a braver height as Paul's; or if you affected to do it nearer to home and a shorter way, an excellent garret window into the street... (2.2.16–20)

Truewit outlines at length how Morose's prospective wife will come to humiliate and overrule him in his own home; as one recent editor, Richard Dutton, has noted: 'The energy of the play is directed not towards sexual union but towards its undoing.'[1] This negative energy (even the play's fifth-act 'reveal' is an undoing in the midst of a divorce scene) could suggest that satire is never constructive in its ends or aims, but there are different impulses at work in the way that early modern playwrights engage with the form at different moments in their writing careers.

Randall Martin has suggested that it was the kind of topical polemics that circulated in the form of religious pamphlets in the 1580s that activated an interest in classical Roman satire.[2] But on 1 June 1599 (the year that Jonson wrote and staged *Every Man Out of His Humour*) a ban on all prose and poetic satires had been ordered by the Bishops of Canterbury and London, who were the chief press censors of the day. As a result of their edict to the Stationers' Company, many works were seized and burned at Stationers' Hall (the Guildhall) in a public statement of intent, including works by names we recognise all too well – Christopher Marlowe, Thomas Middleton and John Marston. Book-burning should always give us pause; so it is important to ask why satire as a genre was perceived as containing such a threat to the authorities and to religious authorities in particular? Martin has questioned whether the entire genre was in fact the focus of the so-called Bishops' Ban, suggesting that it was instead 'new levels of generally sexualised and scatological content' that were causing most concern.[3] Whatever the exact truth of the matter, Jonson clearly seized on a particular opportunity to rethink the satirical form through drama, and his innovative brand of social satirical comedy was to gain considerable credence on the early modern stage in the ensuing decades. While satire certainly found its voice and place in tragedy through the specific figure of the malcontent, it is in alignment to comedy that early modern audiences most readily understood the satiric impulse.

But what happens to the biting, aggressive nature of satire when it is allied to the conventions and forms of dramatic comedy? And what became its specific social satirical targets in the early seventeenth century and why? The rest of this chapter will take as its informing sample a selection of plays by Jonson, Middleton and Massinger, several of which have also been categorised as 'city comedy' (the subgenre looked at in detail in the previous chapter) or, in the specific case of *A New Way to Pay Old Debts*, as a play about what happens to rural communities when they are impacted by urban practices and value systems. These plays sought to satirise the urban experience that, as we saw previously, was proving such a novel, challenging and unsettling phenomenon for early modern England.

Urban(e) satire

The 1590s vogue for verse satire that in part led to the 1599 Bishops' Ban was very much associated with a particular geographical locale, the Inns of Court where future barristers were trained (and previously a subject in the discussion of revenge drama in Chapter 2). Often referred to as the 'third university' (in addition to Oxford and Cambridge, the two formal higher education institutions of the day), it was the breeding ground for several of the playwrights we are thinking about here, not least Marston, Middleton, Webster and Shirley, and many other writers, including Jonson and the poet John Donne, were part of its wider social networks. Inns-men and their associates circulated poetry in manuscript form among select groups of readers and this identifiable clique or network perhaps starts to explain the prevalence of trial scenes and legal humour in a number of the successful commercial dramas of the day: from *Epicene*'s manufactured divorce hearing to the double trial of *Volpone*, the legal hearing at the heart of *The Merchant of Venice* to Middleton's *Michaelmas Term*, whose very title refers to the yearly cycle of four study terms for the students of the Inns which helped increasingly to define the London 'season' when people would be in town to pursue lawsuits or receive legal training and, of course, to attend plays in the meantime.

An Inns training had its own quasi-theatrical elements and content with legal learning effected not only through staged debates and dialogues but through the active use of theatre for personal recreation and public relations purposes, so we can register an Inns of Court influence at the level of both theatrical form and venue.[4] Equally significant though is the influence of Inns discourse at the level of language as it appears in commercial drama, from the fustian Latin of *Epicene* and *The White Devil* to the particularly masculine and biting edge of satirical verse which clearly feeds into the plays we are unpacking in this particular section and into specific character types such as the malcontents we considered earlier in Chapter 2, such as Bosola and Vindice from *The Duchess of Malfi* and *The Revenger's Tragedy* respectively. The ultimate embodiment of this can be seen in Duke Altofront's performance as Malevole, the malcontent of Inns-man and verse satirist Marston's eponymous play, first published in 1604. This was, as we have already seen, a play that was influential in generic fields that might at first seem entirely distinct, shaping revenge tragedies and satirical comedies and even, via an unexpected flirtation with the pastoral tradition, feeding into the emergence of tragicomedy as a genre in its own right in the early seventeenth century.

Wit, irony and sarcasm were, then, the modes of speech and attitudinal stances most frequently associated with the satirist and in *Epicene* they are the qualities most associated with the aforementioned character of Truewit. Sometimes over-simplistically assumed to be Jonson's mouthpiece, Truewit's part is undoubtedly the star actor's turn in the play and this is one of the reasons why critics and editors have speculated that the part may have been taken by Nathan Field, one of the most experienced actors of the Children of the Revels by the time of *Epicene*'s first performance in late 1609 to early 1610. Field was a favourite of Jonson's who would go on to be a playwright in his own right as well as a significant adult performer.[5] If Field was Truewit this would confirm the sense, in reading or seeing this play, that it is he who establishes an all-important relationship with the audience through the mechanism of his knowing discourse. We might read this kind of role across to a figure like Jaques, the black-clad satirist who seems deliberately out of place in Shakespeare's pastoral comedy *As You Like It*. The significance of Jaques's back-story is that he seems to know cities and urban spaces as well as courtly enclaves and speaks in the medicalised phrases of the melancholic satirist as a result:

> Give me leave
> To speak my mind, and I will through and through
> Cleanse the foul body of th'infected world,
> If they will patiently receive my medicine.
>
> (2.7.58–61)

In this respect satire as a genre cuts across all others, sharing its space with poetry and drama, with comedy as well as tragedy.

The edge of the stage

As well as being a deft means of locating Morose's household, the central locale of *Epicene* as a play, its epicentre if you like, in its London surroundings – the proximity of the Thames as well as of significant local churches is economically achieved – 2.2 is a scene of devastating bite and wit that demonstrates early on to the audience Truewit's (seemingly) consummate control of both language and situation. This relationship with the audience is not quite the intimacy that we have witnessed in action with characters in other generic contexts in this study – perhaps satire prohibits true intimacy by its very nature – but it is certainly one that draws the sometimes guilty laughter of spectators; witness Truewit's merciless description of the Morose marriage at 4.1:

> The spitting, the coughing, the laughter, the neezing, the farting, dancing, noise of the music, and her masculine and loud commanding and urging the whole family, makes him [Morose] think he has married a Fury. (4.1.8–11)

The control freakery that Truewit exhibits over the Morose nuptials (initially he wants to prevent them, then when they take place he insists on their raucous celebration) is a stance that we will see him repeat in the carefully stage-managed duel between the two hapless social climbers Sir Jack Daw and Sir Amorous La Foole in 4.5. Here he sets up Clerimont and Dauphine as observers, as 'chorus behind the arras' (32):

> Do you observe this gallery or rather lobby, indeed? Here are a couple of studies, at each end one: here I will act such a tragicomedy between the Guelphs and the Ghibellines, Daw and La Foole. Which of 'em comes out first will I seize on. (4.5.27–31)

Truewit effects something similar in the equally theatrical legal shenanigans of the divorce scene where we witness Cutbeard the barber and drunkard Thomas Otter, disguised as a lawyer and a parson respectively, subjecting Morose to a humiliating hearing in which he is forced to confess impotency in public: 'If you have *manifestam frigiditatem* you are well, sir' (5.3.172–3). The extended mockery in this particular scene of legal Latin is further evidence, were it needed, of Truewit's discursive control. The denouement of the fifth act, however, proves he is not as in control as he likes to think. The big reveal of Epicene's true sex (and his related plotting) by Dauphine – '*He takes off Epicene's peruke*' (5.4.207 s.d.) – is as much a surprise to Truewit as it is to his conspiratorial audiences.

Undeterred, Truewit seizes the last lines of the whole play, inviting the audience to applaud in a final act of confederacy. Banishing Daw and La Foole from the stage and rebuking the Ladies' Collegiate, who have also been taken in by Epicene's disguise to the point of self-disclosure, he then steps forward and invites spectators to continue the taunting of Morose through the making of noise (applause). Jonson, Shakespeare and Middleton were well aware of the politics of according their epilogues; the character to whom they give the last word can often undercut what seem otherwise to be neat moral endings. The Epilogue to *Volpone* is a fine example. Jonson's play is often remarked on for its somewhat brutal, unsentimental resolution of the plot: one that sees Volpone incarcerated, Mosca sent to the galleys and various of the gulls subject to ritualistic public humiliation. But in the closing moments of any performance, Volpone breaks the frame of the play, steps out to the edge of the stage and directly addresses the audience as a court of appeal:

> The seasoning of a play is the applause.
> Now, though the Fox be punished by the laws,
> He yet doth hope there is no suff'ring due
> For any fact [crime] which he hath done 'gainst you . . .
>
> (5.12.152–5)

It is telling that in satirical comedy the undercutting and subversive tendencies persist right to the very edge of the performance and into the space of the epilogue. Just as Truewit, Volpone and other satirical protagonists strive throughout their respective dramas to control the action, so too we might see something here of the playwright-satirist's control of the materials of performance.

Social cartographies and domestic space

Volpone is a play that can be usefully interpreted through the mechanisms of its social and spatial cartographies and the mapping of society that it performs in the course of its satire. Much attention has been paid to Jonson's careful evocation of the Venetian city setting and the resulting exposé of 'La Serenissima', as the great Venetian republic was known in the context of European politics, but equally important to the play is the way in which space operates at the level of individual households and residences: indoor and outdoor space, the significance of doors, windows and thresholds, are all crucial to the plot of Jonson's carefully crafted satire.[6] The impressively pacy plotline of *Volpone* is pushed ever forwards both by Volpone's restless personality – most obviously articulated in an exchange with his servant Mosca in the opening scene:

> Yet I glory
> More in the cunning purchase of my wealth
> Than in the glad possession, since
> I gain no common way . . .   (1.1.30–3)

– and overt plot mechanisms such as knocks at the door of the magnifico's Venetian palazzo. In a manner that harks back to the spatial semantics of the Roman New Comedy that we have already suggested was a shaping influence on early modern comedy, the crossing of any threshold in *Volpone* is continually fraught with meaning and with danger;[7] Volpone exhibits impressive control of the space of his bedroom in the early scenes with the conniving gulls Corvino,

Corbaccio and Voltore who come to prey on his wealth, believing him to be a dying man, but once he steps out into the less amenable space of the city itself his control begins to be wrested from him (not least by his equally aspirational and scheming house-servant Mosca). Other characters in the play seem confined and contained by household space; when Volpone performs his virtuoso show at 2.2 as the mountebank Doctor Scoto of Mantua in the Venetian streets, Celia can only look out from the portal of the residence where her sadistic husband Corvino so clearly dominates.

The handkerchief Celia drops from the window is yet another telling plot mechanism and a poignant intertheatrical moment if audiences read it, as they surely could have, alongside Shakespeare's play of just a few years earlier, *Othello*, a counterpart tragic rendition of an entrapped and endangered wife for whom a dropped handkerchief spells danger and misinterpretation. Corvino's rage is palpable –

> Death of mine honour, with the city's fool?
> A juggling, tooth-drawing, prating mountebank?
> And at a public window?   (2.5.1–3)

– and his punishment swift and spatially prescribed:

> thy restraint before was liberty
> To what I now decree . . .
> First, I will have this bawdy light dammed up,
> And, till't be done, some two or three yards off
> I'll chalk a line; o'er which if thou but (chance
> To) set thy desp'rate foot, more hell, more horror,
> More wild, remorseless rage shall seize on thee
> Than on a conjurer that had heedless left
> His circle's safety ere his devil was laid.
>
> (2.5. 48–56)

He then proceeds to hang a chastity belt on Celia. Clare McManus has rightly understood this scene in terms of wider anxieties about sexual and social mobility in the early modern period, as well as connecting the moment back to the specific signifier of the balcony, which was linked to the stereotype of the Venetian courtesan.[8]

Thomasine, restless wife of the avaricious woollen draper Quomodo in Middleton's *Michaelmas Term*, is another female character associated with the space of the window or balcony lookout. Like Celia, she is largely defined by the overbearing personality of her spouse as well as the demands of his profession – their residence, as the play makes clear, is a typical early modern blended residence in which the shopfront directly abuts the family spaces, and is a space Thomasine is expected to occupy and to 'work' in on his behalf not least by selling their daughter Susan to the highest bidder in the marriage market. Finding his wife and daughter together at 2.3, Quomodo comments:

> How now, what prating have we here? Whispers? Dumb shows? Why, Thomasine, go to; my shop is not altogether so dark as some of my neighbours', where a man may be made cuckold at one end while he's measuring with his yard at t'other. (2.3.35–9)

Ironically, Quomodo renders himself a cuckold later in the play when by counterfeiting his own death he enables the remarriage of Thomasine to Easy. The audience has, tellingly, been won round to a sympathetic reading of Thomasine's actions by the speeches and observations she has shared with us in the form of telling asides from her sighted but restricted space of the stage 'above', the household window or gallery. Interestingly, though, like her counterpart Celia, it is through the liminal or porous space of the balcony that Thomasine gains access to different possibilities and personalities, in particular in the shape of Easy, the Essex countryman whom Quomodo gulls mercilessly out of his lands in the course of the play but whom Thomasine comes to pity and eventually to love in the process:

> [*aside*] Why stand I here (as late our graceless dames
> That found no eyes) to see that gentleman
> Alive, in state and credit executed,
> Help to rip up himself, does all he can?
> Why am I wife to him that is no man?
> I suffer in that gentleman's confusion. (2.3.226–31)

The balcony mutates in this moment to something not purely indicative of sexual mobility but an alternative moral and gendered space, one that allows for the possibility of empathy. The comparison that Thomasine makes with the 'graceless dames / That found no eyes' is a direct reference to spectators for public executions who witnessed horrible cruelties visited upon individual bodies (see Case study K on 1605 and the hanging, drawing and quartering of the Gunpowder Plotters whose executions had taken place in the year of *Michaelmas Term*'s composition and first performances). There is a testing of the theatre audience to also see alternative possibilities for action and ethics in this moment. She returns to her theme at the end of the scene in a further aside, reflecting on how easily Easy has been persuaded to sign away his life and lands in this scene of staged temptation (Quomodo has falsely lured him with the promise of great wealth to be made from a particular cloth trading deal): 'Now he is quart'ring out; the executioner / Strides over him; with his own blood he writes. / I am no dame that can endure such sights' (2.3.378–80). Thomasine's and Celia's responses to public spaces and the behaviours they enable also offers a contrasted version of neighbourhood and civic responsibility to the competitive one-upmanship of overreaching protagonists such as Quomodo or Volpone or, indeed, their later counterpart Overreach in Massinger's *A New Way to Pay Old Debts*, to whom we will return in the final section of this chapter.

Satire is, like its kin-genre city comedy, deeply invested in the meanings and possibilities of households of various kinds; these households extend from family residences and estates to the more public households of inns and alehouses. Each of these spaces has its own hierarchies and the roles of servants provide a particular dynamic for these plays. The significance of Volpone's man-servant Mosca to the dynamic of that play has already been hinted at and is nowhere better encapsulated than by his 3.1 soliloquy where he shares with the audience his determination to trick and in the process to out-master his patron:

> I fear I shall begin to grow in love
> With my dear self and my most prosp'rous parts,
> They do so spring and burgeon . . .
>   I could skip
> Out of my skin now, like a subtle snake,
> I am so limber.   (3.1.1–3, 5–7)

Here we can see in action not only Mosca's linguistic dexterity in the tricksy alliteration and the brilliant use of enjambment and rhythm but also his theatrical lineage in the false but witty servant figure from Roman satire, and in yet another of the generic bleedings that we have seen as typical of early modern drama in this study we can also see that role reconfigured in tragic space in the shape of De Flores in *The Changeling* or Iago in *Othello*.

An interest in master–servant relationships within households also brings to plays of this nature an upstairs–downstairs dynamic as we witness the activities and operations of various parts of the household and the particular servants linked to them; for example, stewards and the resource-heavy site of the buttery surface in plays from *Twelfth Night* to *A New Way to Pay Old Debts*. As we see in the evocation of Lady Alworth's household in the latter play, where the memory of her late husband is a tangible marker of virtue and older forms of hospitality, these cultural geographies are also always sites of memory: they recall or make visible sometimes by their absence the customary practices of an older, more rural community, the very community that by the time of the permanent playhouses was increasingly migrating to the urban centres and adapting to the new market economies of that place and space. The final section turns, then, to the ways in which the country as a concept and a social force is contrasted with urban values in satirical drama in the early seventeenth century and the point of entry that can give us to the ethical and moral dilemmas of the time.

Landscape, metaphor and metonymy

The city is, as we have seen, a space to be confronted and moved through, at the heart of dramatic satire of this period, and in this way dramatic satire meets with city comedy as a form or category and the generic distinctions once again begin to blur in productive and suggestive ways. In *Epicene* the city is used as a veritable weapon with which to beat the obsessional Morose. Truewit hires bearwards (keepers of bears used in the popular entertainment of bear-baiting) to stand under Morose's window with their dogs and make a racket (1.1.171–6); this action gives us access not only to the satirist's perverse enjoyment of Morose's distress but also a vivid sense of the actual noise of the early modern city. Bearwards did indeed parade the streets of London, advertising upcoming shows, but we are also transported by this reference to the bear-baiting sites of the Bankside and in particular Paris Garden, famously a locale shared with the popular commercial theatre of the day. This is the very area of the city that Tom Otter preferred to spend his time in, naming his drinking cups fondly after the bull-baiting and bear-baiting arenas he haunted (2.6.511, and see Case study D). Morose's pathological objection to the daily soundscape of the city paints for us a detailed picture of its quotidian practices, from the Babel of languages to be heard in the law courts of Westminster to the coaches, bells and street criers of the city's narrow thoroughfares to its waterside wharves, its thriving markets and its theatres:

> And that I did supererogatory penance, in a belfry, at Westminster Hall, i'the Cockpit, at the fall of a stag, the Tower Wharf... London Bridge, Paris Garden, Billingsgate, when the noises are at their height and loudest. Nay, I would sit out a play that were nothing but fights at sea, drum, trumpet and target!   (4.4.12–18)[9]

Satire sounds the space, then, of the emergent capital city in very particular and resonant ways but it also engages with the spaces and places of the nation which interact with, contribute to and are in turn shaped by urban culture: the provinces and regions and their very particular landscapes, social and physical. What is particularly interesting here is the way in which land and landscape on the stage – always already inevitably substituted for by language and description on the relatively bare stage of the early modern commercial theatre – also functions as a metaphor or metonymy for various social concerns and social issues.

In *Michaelmas Term* this can most readily be witnessed in operation in Quomodo's yearning for Easy's Essex property and lands, which he quickly imagines converting into new resources of a very particular kind:

> [*aside*] Now I begin to set one foot upon the land. Methinks I am felling of trees already; we shall have some Essex logs yet to keep Christmas with, and that's a comfort.   (2.3.373–7)

Quomodo's particular interest in acquiring and in turn converting Easy's forests performs several functions in the play as performed. These kinds of rural imagining inevitably transport an urban theatre audience to the country and invite spectators to think of the status of these other kinds of space and society in the process. We are invited to think about the country estates of noblemen and the kinds of social performances they engaged in. Quomodo extends this example when he imagines travelling to his new estate in a thinly veiled version of a royal progress (these were occasions when monarchs such as Elizabeth I and James VI and I made lengthy summer journeys to visit their noble subjects and their estates and households, often benefiting from lavish hospitality in the process):[10]

> A fine journey in the Whitsun holidays, i'faith, to ride down with a number of citizens, and their wives, some upon pillions, some upon sidesaddles. I and little Thomasine i'th' middle, our son and heir, Sim Quomodo, in a peach-colour taffeta jacket, some horse-length or a long yard before us. There will be a fine show on's, I can tell you, where we citizens will laugh and lie down, get all our wives with child against a bank, and get up again.   (*Michaelmas Term*, 4.1.77–85)

But what Quomodo's plan to immediately convert 'his' forests into firewood to fuel his hearth at a lavish Christmas gathering indicates is not only his desire to perform this kind of textbook role as a country estate-holder but also the ready conversion of one kind of property into another in the new moral and financial economy of early modern England. Garrett A. Sullivan, Jr has described the way in which land operates as a 'fluid and alchemical' emblem in drama of this kind, with land frequently described as being converted into clothing and other material goods through acts of trade and exchange.[11] Truewit describes this likelihood to Morose in *Epicene*:

[Your would-be wife] must have that rich gown for such a great day; a
new one for the next, a richer for the third; be served in silver . . . while
she feels not how the land drops away, nor the acres melt, nor foresees
the change when the mercer has your woods for her velvets.   (2.2.77–83)

In *Michaelmas Term* Quomodo, a professional draper, tellingly attempts to
acquire his land through a transaction over textiles, just as the mention of the
mercer alludes to in the *Epicene* quotation, so in some ways Easy's stands of
Essex trees are converted twice over – into the bond that secures the country
landholder his share in the (illusory) fabric enterprise and into Quomodo's
dreamed-of household fire, emblem itself of wealth and newly acquired status:
'I'll have 'em lopped immediately; I long / To warm myself by th' wood'
(4.1.75–6).

Households and lands signified strongly on the stages of early modern
drama and in satire in particular became a vehicle through which heightened
anxieties around social and financial mobility could be voiced and explored.
Massinger's Nottinghamshire-based play *A New Way to Pay Old Debts* engages
with this idea through the pointed staging of two counterpoised households
and value systems: the avaricious nouveau riche property of urban incomer Sir
Giles Overreach, who transports with him the questionable economic values
of the city, and that of the long-term member of the local nobility, Lady
Alworth, whose table is always well stocked and welcoming to visitors: 'if this
morning / I am visited by any, entertain 'em' (1.2.60–1). The social satire
extends beyond the contrasted behaviours of these households to a deeper
investigation of rapacious landlords and the complicity of the law in such
activity, as manifested in the aptly named role of Justice Greedy. Overreach is
shameless in his approach to land rights: 'I must have all men sellers, / And I
the only purchaser' (2.1.32–3):

I'll therefore buy some cottage near his manor,
Which done, I'll make my men break ope his fences;
Ride o'er his standing corn, and in the night
Set fire on his barns; or break his cattle's legs.
These trespasses draw on suits, and suits expenses,
Which I can spare, but will soon beggar him.
When I have harried him thus two, or three year,
Though he sue *in forma pauperis*, in spite
Of all his thrift, and care he'll grow behind-hand . . .
Then with the favour of my man of law,
I will pretend some title: want will force him
To put it to arbitrement: then if he sell
For half the value, he shall have ready money,
And I possess his land.   (2.1.34–42, 44–8)

Overreach, as his name suggests, and in a dramaturgic arc that links him directly to the epic rises and falls of tragic protagonists such as Doctor Faustus, grows too gargantuan in his greed and by the fifth act of the play is seen initially in a vain Faustus-like attempt to stave off his fate –

> Why, is not the whole world
> Included in my self? to what use then
> Are friends, and servants? (5.1.355–7)

– and then in a state of complete physical and mental collapse:

> Ha! I am feeble:
> Some undone widow sits upon mine arm,
> And takes away the use of't; and my sword
> Glu'd to my scabbard, with wrong'd orphans' tears,
> Will not be drawn.   (5.1.361–5)

Social satire and tragic and comic imperatives meet here in a single character and a single powerful dramatic moment on the stage. Overreach has in a sense rejected the household and societal spaces that have proved to be the very lifeblood of the stage genre in which he finds himself and as a result he has no option (like Faustus) but to be forced from the stage. Satire bites and it encourages larger than life protagonists but its ultimate impulse is always towards reform.

Topical theatre and 1605–6: 'Remember, remember the fifth of November'

On Tuesday 5 November 1605, Guy (Guido) Fawkes was discovered in a vault beneath Westminster along with sufficient explosive materials to blow up and obliterate not only the Houses of Parliament but also a considerable amount of the surrounding area and its resident population. A narrative was subsequently uncovered of conspiratorial plotting in London inns and of the renting under false identities of rooms and houses in which to store gunpowder and other materials with which to create a terrorist explosion, and from which to dig the underground system through which to reach their target. What had been uncovered was the so-called 'Gunpowder Plot', a supposed conspiracy of fundamentalist Catholics to undermine the heart of government and along with it the security of the reign of the recently new King of England, James I, who had acceded to the throne from his kingdom in Scotland just two years earlier (see Figure 8). The impact of the 'Plot' finds direct modern parallels in an event like the London Tube bombings of 2005 which continues to circulate in both the popular press and public memory many months and even years afterwards.

The stories that unfurled around Guy Fawkes and his fellow conspirators both during their trial and subsequent to their grisly public executions (the men were hanged, drawn and quartered) had an enormous impact on the contemporary cultural imagination and nowhere could this be better registered than on the public theatre stages themselves. We have already begun to think in this study about the value of considering early modern drama in terms of repertoire – in terms of the other plays that plays appeared with and alongside in the programming or offer of particular London theatres. James Shapiro's engaging study *1599* also encourages us to think about a single year as a moment in early modern experience that we might zoom in on and unpack in specific ways.[1] If we apply both these ideas to 1605–6, then, it proves insightful to look at those plays which were being staged at the Globe Theatre on Bankside and which might reasonably be expected to reflect some of the anxieties and ideas whipped up by the contemporary fascination with the Gunpowder Plot and its chief protagonists, Father

8. Conspiracy and the cultural imaginary

Henry Garnet, Robert Catesby, Fawkes and all. Shakespeare's *Macbeth* and Jonson's *Volpone*, one a formal tragedy, one a satirical city comedy, both had their premieres in the weeks and months following the Plot's discovery and both seem in some way to respond to that cultural moment in specific ways, through language, action and effect. Jonson may even have rushed to write his satiric comedy in the relatively short time of five weeks precisely in order to capitalise on the commercial potential of that moment (see *Volpone*, Prologue, 16).[2]

Language is, as ever, instructive in thinking about topical resonance. Keywords that circulated in many of the textual responses to the Plot that were being read and discussed in London and elsewhere in the country sound themselves in significant ways in both plays. 'Grind', 'powder' and 'blow' all find their place in the opening speeches of *Volpone* – '[I] have no mills for iron, / Oil, corn, or men, to *grind* 'em into *powder*; / I *blow* no subtle glass' (1.1.35–7, my italics) – and Richard Dutton has suggested that Lady Politic Would-be's use of 'assassinates' or Sir Pol's 'fantasies about tinder-boxes in the *Arsenale*' later in the play (3.4.112, 4.1.86–91) would certainly have resonated sharply with audiences in 1606 when it was first performed and printed.[3] *Macbeth* speaks in his 'If it were done' soliloquy at 1.7.27, which ruminates on regicide or the killing of a king, specifically of 'vaulting ambition', thereby directly conjuring the underground space in which Guy Fawkes was discovered. Both plays concern themselves at length with plots and counterplots, conspiracy and treason; and *Macbeth*, in particular, abounds with a general air of subterfuge and darkness, popular associations with stereotypes of Jesuit conspirators in the early modern popular press.

The critic Jonathan Gil Harris has gone one stage further and suggested that Globe audiences watching *Macbeth* may have been spurred by more than language to remember recent events. Performing a type of criticism known as 'historical phenomenology', Harris invites us to imagine what a production of *Macbeth* might have smelt like and how that would have stirred the spectators' fervent imaginations.[4] The play's opening stage direction reads '*Thunder and lightning*' and Harris's point is that squibs (small fireworks created by throwing rosin powder at candles) would have been let off in the theatre at this moment, creating a sulphurous smell. That smell, appealing to what Harris refers to as the 'receptive horizons' of the audience, would have brought to mind age-old associations with the devil and, indeed, theatrical modes and methods for creating onstage devils that stretched back to the medieval cycle plays Shakespeare would have known in his own childhood and which would have been repeated to great effect in the special effects of plays like Marlowe's *Doctor Faustus*.[5] But, more specifically, the smell of sulphur could have sparked the recent and raw memory of the narrowly averted Gunpowder Plot, whose participants were themselves regularly branded as satanic and devilish in texts by polemical pamphleteers and in Protestant sermons delivered in London churches: 'Because the sulphurous odor of *Macbeth*'s fireworks was every bit as strong as their bright flash and loud crackle, early modern audiences would have begun the experience of the play with a keen awareness of the smell of gunpowder. This must have been a highly charged encounter in the wake of recent events.'[6] What Harris brilliantly draws our attention to here is the potent role of memory in the production of topical meaning in the theatre and how such memories might combine with the very practical physical and sensory affects induced by theatre special effects.

It is in 2.3 or the so-called 'Porter scene' that this topical undertow to *Macbeth* can perhaps most clearly be traced. Responding to the same knocking heard by Macbeth himself at the end of the preceding scene, the

Porter seems to function on two levels as both the literal porter of this fateful Scottish castle where a king has just been savagely killed offstage and as the archetypal 'porter of Hell gate' (2.3.1–2). His dialogue is shot through with references and allusions to the events of 1605, to which Globe spectators' 'receptive horizons' would have been open. He talks, for example, of seeing an 'equivocator'; Father Henry Garnet justified his use of equivocation at his interrogation and trial for his role in the Plot. That Garnet (who hanged for his crimes) had also deployed the pseudonym of 'Farmer' as part of the Plot may in part explain the Porter's reference a few lines earlier to 'a farmer, that hanged himself on th'expectation of plenty' (2.3.4–5). It is this kind of contemporary relevance that helps us to understand the interpolation of a scene like that involving the Porter which on the surface might seem to have little to do with advancing the plot of the play. He exits exhorting us to 'remember the porter' and in many respects this short scene is a masterclass in the sheer power of memory's operations in a theatrical context.

Macbeth seems to have had an immediate appeal to Globe audiences. It was revived on a regular basis and some critics have gone so far as to suggest that Jonson was in such a rush to write *Volpone* in order to respond to the frisson of that particular play as well as the moment more generally. Whatever the truth of that claim, and it should be remembered that as a practising Catholic at various times in his life, and one who was questioned directly by the authorities about the Gunpowder Plot, Jonson had more reasons than many to want to respond to that event through his writings, it is evident that 1606, and indeed the years subsequent, witnessed many theatrical responses, both direct and embedded, to the events and effects of 5 November 1605.

'Little eyases': the children's companies and repertoire

In the 1623 folio edition of Shakespeare's *Hamlet* an exchange takes place between Hamlet and 'Rosincrance' (*sic*) on traditions of playing, presumably in the Elsinore of the play's setting, though many have identified a direct allusion to playing practices in Shakespeare's contemporary London:

> **ROSINCRANCE** ... there is, sir, an eyrie of children, little eyases that cry out on the top of question and are most tyrannically clapped for't. These are now the fashion and so berattle the common stages... that many wearing rapiers are afraid of goose-quills and dare scarce come thither.
>
> **HAMLET** What, are they children? Who maintains 'em? How are they escotted? Will they pursue the quality no longer than they can sing? Will they not say afterwards if they should grow themselves to common players – as it is most like if their means are no better – their writers do wrong them to make them exclaim against their own succession?
>
> (*Hamlet*, F 2.2.337–49)

This exchange (which does not appear in earlier printed quarto editions of the play) has proved a rich seam of conjecture for theatre scholars. The topical reference (at least in the early years of the play's performances) appears to be to the particular phenomenon of the children-only companies which had their roots in choir schools but which by the time of *Hamlet* were already becoming more professional and commercialised, and which took up residence at St Paul's and at the Blackfriars and the Whitefriars Theatres, most notably in the first decade of the seventeenth century. The Children of Paul's, the Children of the Chapel and, later, the Children of the Queen's Revels became associated with particular kinds of repertory and particular kinds of playing style that bear more detailed attention in understanding how certain early modern plays might have operated on the stage in their initial performances. This case study builds, then, on important recent work in the area of 'repertory studies' which argues for company-based

175

understandings of bodies of plays that were commissioned and authored at this time rather than a single-author focus which tends to extract us from deeper consideration of specific contexts and contingencies that shape the success of certain genres and styles of playing at particular times.[1]

It is an interesting challenge to the modern interpreter of playtexts performed by the children's companies to imagine how the effect of particular plays and indeed generic categories were impacted by the specific convention of having all the parts taken by child actors: age, gender and rank were all being 'performed' in a state of heightened awareness for audiences. As Lucy Munro has evidenced, however, the phrase 'children' may itself be something of a misnomer as the age range of the performers varied between early to late teens, and sometimes even early twenties in some of the later plays, and certainly as the companies aged so did some of their star performers, a number of them – Nathan Field, for example – advancing to become adult company performers in due course.[2] In turn, their ability to perform in more flexible and subtle ways may also have meant that the approach to specific genres or themes may have adapted or altered.[3] What we do know is that this was a very successful form of playing for a brief period in London's commercial theatre history and that the companies drew large audiences to their productions and encouraged several of the key playwrights of the day to write for them. Certainly, the competitive atmosphere of the London commercial theatre scene is evident in Hamlet's pointed references to the rivalry between the adult and the children's companies, with the prince, himself a great exponent of the skills of performing in this play, questioning as he does in the passage quoted above the rationale of the child players putting down the adult actors they are themselves destined to become.

Middleton's *Michaelmas Term*, the collaboratively authored *Eastward Ho!* and Jonson's *Epicene* were all initially designed for performance by the boy performers of the Children of Paul's (*Michaelmas Term*) and the Children of the Queen's Revels (*Eastward Ho!* and *Epicene*) and it is worth thinking about how these initial playing conditions may have impacted the way in which certain scenes, moments or characters would have been understood by spectators. Munro has in her detailed and important study of the repertory of the Revels Company made the case for the 'innovatory' aspect of their programming, with plays in almost every major genre and mode.[4] *Michaelmas Term*, *Eastward Ho!* and *Epicene* are also all, as we have seen, city comedies of sorts and plays that satirise – with different levels of geniality and savagery at different moments – the deep desire in the capital at this time for upward social and economic mobility. Touchstone's daughter Gertrude with her obsessive desire for a coach and a castle is just one of the more obvious embodiments of this in *Eastward Ho!*: 'My coach for the love of heaven, my coach! In good truth, I shall swoon else.... As I am a lady, I think I am with child already, I long for a coach so' (3.2.24–7). Gertrude is, of course – like her counterpart character Quicksilver, the goldsmith's apprentice who feels demeaned by his subservient social role in view of his upbringing and tries with somewhat disastrous consequences to live the life of a city gallant by illegal means (the fifth act of the play, as we have seen, finds him in debtor's prison) – humiliated in the course of the play's plotlines for these aspirations, but it perhaps adds to the slightly brutal comedy of these scenes if we imagine all of these roles taken by younger male actors.

Epicene is a play that is usually mentioned in the same breath as castigating Jonson for overt misogyny. Certainly the female characters in this play do not come off well, but actually, as already noted, in this drama of false appearances and counterfeit performances, absolutely everyone (and indeed everything, including major institutions such as the church and the law) is satirised by the close. As the play's editor Richard Dutton notes, 'the play's most overt misogyny comes, as it were, in inverted commas'.[5] Perhaps, once again, this levelling effect was made all the more achievable when every performance was of necessity multi-layered as in a children's company show: boys cross-dress here not only as the monstrous regiment of the Ladies' Collegiate, or as the ambitious city shopkeeper Mistress Otter (whose very name like so many in this play hints at ambiguity: the otter being an animal that thrives in both wet and dry elements) or indeed as Epicene him/herself, but as older men like the misanthropic Morose, as courtiers and wits such as Dauphine and Truewit, and as hapless social wannabees like Sir Amorous La Foole.

The opening scene of *Epicene* sets up with savage efficiency the realm of layered socio-sexual confusion that will define the play's representations with the exquisite knowingness that seems typical of the children's companies' repertoires – a knowingness we have already encountered in examples like Marston's *The Malcontent* and its archly self-conscious take on revenge drama tradition. Clerimont's boy describes the games of dressing up that society women play with him:

> The gentlewomen play with me and throw me o'the bed, and carry me in to my lady and she kisses me with her oiled face, and puts a peruke o'my head, and asks me an' I will wear her gown, and I say no; and then she hits me a blow o'the ear and calls me innocent and lets me go. (*Epicene*, 1.1.12–17)

The force of this description as a point of entry into understanding the highly performative sexual and social politics of the West End London community represented in the play is augmented by the fact that the first stage direction tells us that Clerimont enters onstage '*making himself ready*' (1.1.0 s.d.), that is, putting on his own cosmetic mask to face the world. The play persistently draws attention to the constructedness of identity, from make-up to wigs to social performance in its broadest sense (note, for example, the 'oiled face', perukes and gowns of the Boy's description here). It is a hyper-real world of artificialities and superficialities in which Jonson's satire seems to light on everyone rather than one specific social grouping. The children's company repertoires, which engaged with every possible genre but in the same knowing way in which satire and city comedy are approached in the examples offered here, were consciously experimental and innovative in the way that they approached dramatic form for the very reason that their performance conventions invited audiences to be self-aware about the stage pictures being put before them.

Chapter 7

Tragicomedy

Tragicomedy has been described as the 'Cinderella' of early modern genres[1] and certainly watching a tragicomic drama unfold can sometimes feel like a highly uncomfortable combination of fantastic events, high melodrama, impossible outcomes and see-sawing emotions. In trying to pin down what exactly the tragicomic aesthetic is in comparison to the other dramatic genres and sub-genres we have discussed so far in this study, perhaps it is this notion of a slightly uncomfortable hybrid of multiple genres that takes us nearest to the essence. Tragicomedy, as its compound title suggests, is full of happenings and events that seem to be steering us on a full-blown course to tragedy and death only to be suddenly and sometimes miraculously subverted or resolved happily at the midnight hour; tragicomedies, while frequently set in the same Italianate courts full of rival monarchs, sycophants, pretenders and favourites, and featuring the same inevitable imperilled lovers as the revenge drama of Webster or Middleton explored in Chapter 2, in contrast to those plays feature multiple 'resurrections' – the case of Hermione's statue in Shakespeare's *The Winter's Tale* is perhaps the best-known example – and pretended or faked deaths as opposed to the stage scattered with corpses more familiar from revenge tragedy. In discussing the emergence of tragicomedy as form in the early seventeenth century, then, we will necessarily have recourse to other texts to which the plays in this mode refer or allude and often, as we shall see, actively rewrite. We begin from the supposition that tragicomedy is a highly intertextual and indeed intertheatrical force and that from this stems much of its performative energy. This demands yet again an attentive spectatorship that can build on and make meaning from these intertextual angles but also one that, as the above descriptive terms indicate, is unsettled and unseated by the often deliberate dissonance or strangeness of what is taking place before their eyes.

Precedent and provenance: *The Malcontent,*
The Faithful Shepherdess and *Il pastor fido*

Having already in part defined tragicomedy as a hybrid genre that self-consciously fashions itself from melding the conventions and motifs of other genres, from tragedy to revenge drama and from romance to comedy, it is also worth identifying its particular origin and precedents on the English stage. The key source text is an Italian one, which may in part explain the penchant for Italianate locales that tragicomic dramatists manifest (in this chapter alone, for example, we will refer to three plays written across three decades at least partially set in Sicily: *Philaster*, *The Winter's Tale* and *The Queen and Concubine*). Giovanni Battista Guarini's *Il pastor fido* (1590), or *The Faithful Shepherd*, first staged in the context of a royal wedding in Ferrara, proved to have considerable influence on early modern drama across Europe and also inspired several musical settings and responses. It was ostensibly a pastoral tragicomedy and it was the absorption of the pastoral conventions that we were exploring in Chapter 4 within the context of broader and darker political settings, more familiar from tragic drama, which proved a key element of the English development of tragicomedy.

There are two seminal playtexts in the story of the evolution of English tragicomedy, though at first glance this pair seem far removed from one another in terms of concerns, style and effect: John Marston's *The Malcontent*, published in 1604, first performed by the Children of the Blackfriars and later adopted and adapted by the King's Men, previously discussed in Chapter 2 as part of the revenge drama stable; and John Fletcher's anglicised take on Guarini's play, *The Faithful Shepherdess*, first staged in 1608, also by the Children of the Blackfriars, though much more successfully revived, as we shall see, in the context of the Caroline penchant for pastoral in the 1630s. As so often, then, the connection between these seemingly generically distinct plays can be found through a careful consideration of repertoire and theatre company context.

The Malcontent is by its own admission a bitter satire; the metatheatrical Induction to the augmented King's Men version, supposed by many to have been authored by John Webster rather than Marston himself, apologises for this fact.[2] The deposed Duke Altofront returns to the court disguised as Malevole and wreaks havoc amidst the corruption and decadence he identifies there. By contrast, Fletcher's play is set in the semi-literary ancient Greek domain of Thessaly and features shepherds and shepherdesses as main characters. Fletcher's play builds on the precedent of Guarini and the Italian tradition while also continuing the development of the Spenserian tradition of pastoral that we touched on in Chapter 4. In his address to the reader which prefaced the print edition of the play, Fletcher sought, however, to define what was meant by 'pastoral tragicomedy' in particular by stressing that this was far from conventional pastoral drama even though it built on some of its settings, characterisations, methods and tropes (finding in the process an excuse for the poor reception the play received in 1608):

> It is a pastorall Tragie-comedie, which the people seeing when it was plaid, having ever had a singuler guift in defining, concluded to be a play of country hired Shepheards, in gray cloakes, with curtaild dogs in strings, sometimes laughing together, and sometimes killing one another: And missing whitsun ales, creame, wassel and morris-dances, began to be angry.[3]

If the connection, then, is the introduction of the political and satirical context and the move away from a purely rural or even idealised locale, there already begins to be a greater kinship between Fletcher's project and Marston's own just a few years earlier. In fact, Marston's play was recorded in the Stationers' Register of 1604 as a 'tragiecomedia'.[4] This understanding of a kinship between Fletcher's and Marston's plays and projects is further reinforced when we recognise *The Malcontent*'s own deep foundations in Guarini's *Il pastor fido*. For, as several critics have demonstrated, Marston's play was strongly influenced by Guarini's drama, containing as it does upwards of twenty direct references and quotations. While some critics dispute whether Marston accessed Guarini's text in the original or at one stage removed through an English translation effected by one of the two Dymock brothers in 1602, the point remains that *The Malcontent* in a sense provides the working template for the combination of pastoral with satiric conventions that we will come to see as a defining feature of English tragicomic drama.[5] It was very successful on its initial performances and the aspiring young playwright John Fletcher must have been aware of this when he attempted his own dramatic intervention in the form.

Generic combinations

Tragicomedy's bringing together of pastoral (and by extension romantic) and satiric conventions (abutting therefore existing work from both the tragic and comic domains) was viewed by earlier twentieth-century critics as simply evidence of a form lacking its own identity. In 1952, Eugene M. Waith claimed that: 'The net effect of the combination of satire and romance upon the pattern of tragicomedy can be described as a major increase in formalisation and a corresponding decrease in meaning.'[6] More recently, however, tragicomedy's combining impulse has been credited with introducing a deeper vein of political thinking into these plays and it can be argued that this is best witnessed at the level of engagement with issues of rank, gender and power. The ways in which individual playwrights or writing teams engage with these issues remain, though, subject to the particular circumstances, cultural and political, of the time in which they were working, and for that reason this chapter seeks to explore and test tragicomedy's innovations and oddities across an extended time period in the commercial theatre.

In the process the influence of these experimentations on Shakespeare's late-career encounters with this more mixed generic mode, in particular in his *The Winter's Tale*, becomes evident. Increasingly it seems likely that Beaumont and Fletcher's *Philaster*, with its cross-dressing themes and its representation of a fractured court family, influenced Shakespeare's 1610–11 tragicomedy, which opens in a winter-bound Sicily. It is perhaps no mere coincidence that Shakespeare was collaborating with the younger John Fletcher at this very point in time (in 1613 on *The Two Noble Kinsmen* and most importantly on *Henry VIII, or All is True* which as connective tissue in this network of influence and response also brings the genre of the history play into the heady mix). *The Winter's Tale* in turn enjoyed its own influence and reworking by other tragicomic playwrights: as we shall see, the jealous King and his placing of his innocent Queen on trial in Brome's Sicilian play *The Queen and Concubine* is deeply aware, in 1635, of its Shakespearean predecessor.

In the process of effecting these intertextual and intertheatrical readings, however, we will see that commercial drama itself was not a hermetically sealed space, influential and influenced only within its own circuit, but drew elements from courtly and regional theatrical productions and from other evolving genres such as the masque. These interactions would themselves have distinguishable impact on the handling of topics such as gender in these plays, from Shakespeare's late romances, not least *The Winter's Tale*, to Brome's and, indeed, Shirley's revisiting of the form in the Caroline era in plays such as *The Bird in a Cage* (1633), performed at the height of Queen Henrietta Maria's own experiments with theatre at the English court.

Rank, gender and power

Perhaps unsurprisingly in light of the accretive nature of tragicomedy that we have heretofore been establishing, plays classified in this mode feature a welter of tropes and devices already familiar from companion genres. From comedy, and not least from pastoral and romance, we have cross-dressing and all of the gender ambiguities and social and sexual uncertainties that inevitably result. The complicated love triangle of Philaster, Arethusa and Bellario/Euphrasia in Beaumont and Fletcher's drama is a reimagining of the triad of Orsino, Olivia and Viola/Cesario in Shakespeare's *Twelfth Night*. Philaster offers Arethusa his page as her companion in his absence when their relationship is thwarted by the political and dynastic ambitions of her father the King. In a manner directly derived from pastoral, Bellario is described as 'Sent by the gods' and linked to a sub-Ovidian landscape:

> I have a boy
> Sent by the gods, I hope, to this intent,
> Not yet seen in the court. Hunting the buck
> I found him sitting by a fountain's side,
> Of which he borrowed some to quench his thirst
> And paid the nymph again as much in tears.
> A garland lay him by, made by himself,
> Of many several flowers bred in the vale . . .
>
> (*Philaster*, 1.2.111–18)

We have the sub-Petrarchan motif of the hunt familiar from romantic comedy signalled here from the beginning. Also linked from the start with a form of pastoral innocence free from court corruption, Bellario is many times described by characters exposed to his charms in the text as 'angel-like' (2.4.18) and his 'pretty' talk (2.3.7) is much remarked on. Unlike the *Twelfth Night* plotline surrounding Viola's protective disguise as Cesario in order to serve as the Duke Orsino's page in his Illyrian court, the audience is never formally let into the secret of Bellario's female identity (s/he is really Euphrasia, lost daughter of courtier Dion).

There are interesting kinships once again with comical satire and specifically with the Whitefriars boys' play authored by Jonson at much the same time as Beaumont and Fletcher were collaborating on *Philaster*. *Epicene*, with its gender-bending social satire and fifth-act reveal of the 'silent woman' of the play's subtitle as a boy (see Chapter 6). There are also links with the ways in which *Twelfth Night*'s Viola and her cross-dressed companions of Shakespearean comedy are described and were presumably performed by boy actors in the roles; this 'sad-talking boy' (2.3.7) has much in common with Viola in his seeming melancholia and vulnerability. As *Philaster*'s modern editor Suzanne Gossett indicates, if the intertextuality which we are arguing is a principal arm of tragicomic effect was brought into active play by spectators, they might well have registered clues throughout the dialogue that hint at Bellario's female side: 'The tears, the garlands, the gentleness, prettiness and tenderness are all clues that the "boy" is female.'[7] For alert audience members Philaster's infuriated line to Bellario at 4.3.27 – 'Go sell these misbeseeming clothes thou wearest' – could also signify cross-dressing at some level. Peter Berek makes the point, however, that although Beaumont and Fletcher seem attracted to cross-dressing as a potentially subversive or transgressive theatrical device and to the issues of gender fluidity that it raises, there are more often than not in their plays, and not least in *Philaster*, substantive moves to recontain any real sense of threat from the female agency and independence that the motif of cross-dressing might release. There is no epilogue for Bellario that can be compared to Rosalind's Epilogue in *As You Like It* or, indeed, the vision of Viola/Cesario still in her boy's attire at the close of *Twelfth Night*. Berek suggests that this attraction to the unstable was part of Beaumont and Fletcher's experimentation with 'the new and puzzling genre' of tragicomedy but that the end results, for all the flirtation with instability and inconsistency, are politically (and sexually) conservative. Berek stresses that unlike satire, which seems directly confrontational in its movements, tragicomedy does not really want the audience to ask deep questions but rather to see the social and cultural anxieties of the day staged and contained, or at least staged without too many follow-on questions being asked: 'Tragicomedic dramaturgy lends itself to the social function of embodying rather than resolving contradictions . . . Absence of meaning, or ambiguity of meaning, pleases audiences by offering them the delights of conflicting ideas without any necessity for a conceptual resolution.'[8] It is perhaps too neat a formula to reduce the work of a single playwriting team to a fixed reading in this way, but what is clear is that tragicomedy is often read in directly opposing ways by critics: Shirley's *The Bird in a Cage*, for example, has been viewed by some critics as an act of recontainment of female power akin to that argued for by Berek as typifying the Beaumount and Fletcher canon, while others have identified in its playacting motifs a potentially empowering approach to female subjectivity, not least when read in its political and cultural context.[9]

Certainly women are persistently placed in danger or under scrutiny in tragicomedy. Philaster's gift of Bellario to Arethusa is sharper-edged than it at first appears; he has set the page to function as a kind of spy in order to test his lover's fidelity and what ensues in terms of plot as malicious court rumours are spread by women jealous of Arethusa's position is a fairly typical tragicomic narrative of jealousy. Philaster believes the worst of his partner and descends into a violent rage. Similarly rapid declines into obsessive jealousy (which in turn recall the behaviours of Othello and Leontes in the Shakespearean canon) occur in Brome's much later and derivative tragicomedy, *The Queen and*

Concubine, and a similar testing of a woman's chastity is conducted in Shirley's *The Bird in a Cage* when Philenzo disguises himself as the court cynic Rolliardo and delivers himself in the titular birdcage to the Princess Eugenia's bedroom. What makes the ramifications of these emotional plotlines so huge is that they are usually conducted by rulers or heirs to various thrones and kingdoms so that the family breakdown has wider political and state implications and consequences.[10]

It is in this deft combining of the romantic plotline with heightened political drama that Gossett and others see the real originality of tragicomedy. This, at least in part, explains why it gained increasing credence and popularity as a form: as Gossett notes, 'Despite the see-sawing emotions, the danger and the rescue, the disguise and the revelation, *Philaster* remains tied to a natural-istic world of political intrigue, citizen "can-carriers" and sexual infidelity.'[11] Tied up with the romantic storylines represented through thwarted relation-ships, refuge taken in disguise and cross-dressing, and pastoral exiles, then, we have concurrently running themes of usurpation and rightful succession more familiar perhaps from tragic and historical drama, and it is through the latter strategies that these plays gesture at least towards a form of contemporary political commentary.

Jacobean and Caroline political and cultural contexts

The plotline of *Philaster* provides us with a weak king who is trying to rule two kingdoms and who is vexed by troubled questions of succession. It is as a result of this that he is attempting to marry his daughter Arethusa off to the philandering Spanish Prince Pharamond (he is memorably described as a 'pernicious petticoat prince', 2.2.145) against her wishes. It is worth pausing to consider the resonances these topics might have found at this particular point (1609–10) in the relatively new Jacobean reign. Scottish King James VI had succeeded to the English throne as James I only in 1603 and not without controversy in view of painful memories of his mother, Mary Queen of Scots, and challenges to the legitimacy of the Elizabethan reign, as well as very current debates about the possible union of England and Scotland in what James himself termed the 'Britannia' project. We can see how all of these topics, from anxiety around female rule and succession to political union, hover around the edges of *Philaster* as a play while never operating as naïve political allegory in any way. Berek and others have also suggested that James's interest in promoting his family as a royal family in stark contrast to the iconography that had surrounded his predecessor the 'Virgin Queen', but also in contradistinction to his own propensity to male favourites and companions at court, rendered tragicomedy's interest in the relationship between family and state and between sexual and high politics intriguing at the very least: 'In the years after 1603, there may have been a special frisson associated with the idea that what we would now call biological maleness was reassuringly linked to bravery and social stability.'[12]

Philaster is clearly the people's choice to rule in Beaumont and Fletcher's play as well as Arethusa's preferred partner in marriage, much to the chagrin of the King her father. The play's opening scene has courtiers discussing this political situation, filling in the audience with the necessary information:

> the King, of late, made a hazard of both the kingdoms – of Sicily and his own – with offering but to imprison Philaster. At which the city was in arms, not to be charmed down by any state order or proclamation till they saw Philaster ride through the streets, pleased and without a guard. At which they threw their hats and their arms from them, some to make bonfires, some to drink, all for his deliverance.   (1.1.34–43)

The role of the citizenry in this play is palpable and this both renders *Philaster* an immediately politicised play, despite the faraway Italianate setting, and connects it with chronicle histories such as the two parts of Heywood's *Edward IV* which, as we saw in Chapter 3, made great play of the connection between the citizens of its historical recollection and those present in the theatre audience. The courtier Dion's declaration of intent towards the braver citizens who rise up against rebels in the play is revealing of this connection, alluding to them as it does explicitly as shopkeepers and water-bearers (parodying their cry 'what-ye-lacks' and referring to them, as already mentioned, as 'can-carriers') which are terms more suggestive of contemporary London than any romance setting. He suggests that he will see them chronicled in popular forms ranging from ballads to sonnets:

> Are your swords sharp? Well, my dear countrymen what-ye-lacks, if you continue and fall not back upon the first broken shin, I'll have ye chronicled and chronicled, and cut and chronicled, and all-to-be priced, and sung in sonnets, and bathed in new brave ballads, that all tongues shall troll you in *saccula saeculorum*, my kind can-carriers...
>
> (5.3.125–32)

Dion also commits henceforth to buy only their products from within the city walls and again this particular geography conjures the mercantile London of the 1610 of the play's early performances rather than any ostensible Sicilian setting:

> Oh, my brave countrymen! As I live, I will not buy a pin out of your
> walls for this; nay, you shall cozen me, and I will thank you and send you
> brawn and bacon and soil you every long vacation a brace of foremen
> that at Michaelmas shall come up fat and kicking.   (5.3.161–7)

In these textual and performative gestures we can then recognise at least a
willingness for the events of tragicomedy to be connected to the contemporary
political and cultural scene.

The section of the play that sees the captured Pharamond threatened with
extreme violence and indeed execution by his citizen captors also has a strain of
vocabulary worth unpacking in this regard. The elderly Captain who seems to
govern the citizen uprisers refers to his men as 'what-do-you-lack' shopkeepers
as well (5.4.3) and his discourse is governed by a series of metaphors and images
derived from London's thriving textile trade (he refers to their 'chamlets', silks,
copper thread and so on); but it is in his description of the violent intent towards
the captured Pharamond that the city's customary geographies are most vividly
drawn. The intention is to render the Spanish prince quite literally into city
goods through the act of hanging, drawing and quartering, a form of public
evisceration that early modern theatre spectators would have connected with
readily through active recollection of the public executions they would likely
have witnessed in their own streets (see Case study D). As well as hanging
Pharamond 'cross legged / Like a hare at a poulters' (5.4.36–7), they will
render his intestines into gut for stringing and fashion whips and laces from
his entrails. A petrified Pharamond rails against the 'Uncivil trades' (5.4.91)
these artisanal hands now intend to practise. Shades of chronicle history and
city comedy hedge round these scenes and add to the complexity of tone that
characterises tragicomedy as a form.[13]

There was, as already noted, an immediate appeal in this kind of material for
members of the audience to whom these quotidian details were all too recognisable, a moment of frame-breaking familiarity that spurs a different kind of
encounter with the vaguely fantastical storyline of the play. Bradbrook's inspirational idea as to how commercial theatre audiences were trained over time
helps us to see the kinds of dramatic economy and shorthand that tragicomedy
in its most appropriative and acquisitional mode could rely on – audiences were
by the early part of the seventeenth century trained to read across repertoires
and indeed across genres.

Philaster does open with familiar themes and topics from tragedy and
revenge drama. This seems almost knowingly to be signalled by the embedded
allusions to *Hamlet* that occur in the characterisation of Philaster himself.
In mourning for his late father ('oh I had a father / Whose memory I bow

to', 1.1.187–8), whom he considers to have been the rightful claimant to the Sicilian throne, and whose presence he describes as 'A dangerous spirit in the room' (282) – a line that surely reminds regular theatregoers of Old Hamlet's ghost – Philaster unsettles the court in ways which directly recall the actions of the grieving Danish prince in Shakespeare's tragedy: his rival Pharamond labels him 'mad' (202) and later he will exhibit the same tendency to misogyny as his Shakespearean heroic counterpart (he instructs Arethusa to 'dig a cave, and preach to birds and beasts / What woman is, and help to save them from you', 3.2.111–12). It might seem a rather extravagant claim to make that a play staged earlier in the same decade could already have such currency in theatrical memory that shorthand allusions of this kind could function successfully in an experimental tragicomedy but we know that *Hamlet* was being referred to and parodied almost as soon as it hit the boards (the collaborative *Eastward Ho!* features a charmingly distracted footman called Hamlet, in 1605).[14] I would argue that Beaumont and Fletcher also expect their audiences to make the connections with revenge drama (and not least the tragicomic precedent of *The Malcontent*) and with pastoral romance that their play mobilises in such creative and challenging ways. Tragicomedy from this angle becomes a mode that encourages a lively and alert rather than a desensitised audience.

A brief example of this kind of knowing invocation of other plays and generic practices can be found in the fourth-act hunting scene of this play, which as we might expect makes immediate recourse to pastoral drama. We encounter a new character at this stage, one who does not appear at any other point in the play. A 'Country Fellow' is wandering in the woods at the same time as the hunt is taking place. He has heard that the King's party is present and has come along out of curiosity to see his monarch in the flesh and with a genuine sense of celebrity spotting (a different kind of hunt as he himself observes):

> I'll see the King if he be in the forest. I have hunted him these two hours.
> If I should come home and not see him, my sisters would laugh at me. I
> can see nothing but people better horsed than myself that outride me. I
> can hear nothing but shouting.   (4.5.75–9)

Instead, what the Fellow encounters, in a grim inversion of the pastoral idyll we might have expected, is the sight of Philaster stabbing Arethusa in the woods after a fraught encounter in which he has yet again misinterpreted the relationship between her and Bellario, and, as a result, as witness to this affray, the Fellow gets to meet the King under very different circumstances. It is a striking if brief moment when 'real-life' and everyday attitudes to monarchy are allowed a voice on the stage in ways that positively invite the early modern audiences to make connections with their own present space, place and time. As the discussion elsewhere in this study of the title page that accompanied the 1620 printing of this play indicates (see Case study G), the fact that this 'moment' was chosen by the printing-house for depiction and therefore remembrance in the woodcut suggests that contemporary audiences did register this as a pivotal section of the play.

Violence is common on the tragicomic stage, as the multiple stabbings of *Philaster* alone suggest, though its full impact and consequence are often diverted or repulsed in ways that swerve away from the fully tragic at the last moment. While there are many wounds in this play, none of them prove fatal. In *The Bird in a Cage* Philenzo is not really dead but has merely taken a sleeping draught that makes him appear so; in *The Queen and Concubine* no actual deaths occur – Sforza's execution is averted and Prince Gonzago finds refuge in the Palerman countryside along with his exiled mother, the Queen. Even when the kangaroo court assembled by the jester Andrea and others looks likely to execute the villain Flavello with much blood and torment, Queen Eulalia arrives to halt proceedings. This might be seen as the default mode of tragicomedy: the halted violent act, the swerve from the darkest action into reconciliation. If we were to take all our readings from the final act of a play we might infer a depoliticised approach to plotlines and a movement away from deep social questions to easy resolution and recontainment. But that would be to ignore the force of what precedes. In tragicomedy, as in the form of the court masque and courtly pastoral theatre from which it took considerable energy and ideas, it is not entirely possible to banish what has gone before in the wrapping up of complex plotlines.

Restaging the pastoral

If, as we saw in Chapter 4, pastoral space is frequently a space of sanctuary or retreat in conventional versions of the genre, it remains true that in tragicomedy it is into pastoral space that the bruised and damaged still seem to retreat: the nation of Bohemia with its sheep-shearing festival in the fourth act of *The Winter's Tale* is just an extreme version of that dramatic and spatial arc. In Beaumont and Fletcher's *Philaster* the pastoral opportunity is represented by the woodlands through which Arethusa, Bellario, Philaster and others stumble as a hunt takes place. The hunt motif alone connects the staging back to the Petrarchan metaphors made tangible that we identified in the earlier discussion of pastoral and romantic comedies in Chapter 4. We might also recognise in this a slightly more twisted and threatening version of the labyrinthine Athenian woods through which the confused lovers of Shakespeare's *A Midsummer Night's Dream* wander and trip.

If pastoral space is sometimes designated by characters as innocent space, the plays which mobilise the possibilities of the genre are, as we have seen, deeply bound up with issues of rank as well as gender, and in *Philaster's* particular remaking of the dramatic trope of the hunt, questions of rank and of ethical behaviour come very forcefully into play, not only in how the hunt is staged but also in the ways in which different individuals choose to perform within the context of this ritual. We encounter two woodsmen whose job it has been prior to their physical entrance onto the stage to 'lodge' the deer so that it can be easily shot by the aristocrats 'playing' at the formerly life-and-death activity of hunting for food. This easy routeway is, notably, Pharamond's preferred course of action, whereas Arethusa proves of bolder spirit and personal agency and chooses to 'hunt fully'.

As with Shakespeare's forest of Arden, the woodlands of this Beaumont and Fletcher play prove to be a highly mixed economy of pastoral cliché, working farmland, elite hunting ground and, as a result, of real-life contradictions. Philaster may yearn for this to be a stereotypical pastoral space of unconfused innocence and 'a life / Free from vexation' (4.3.12–13) where he could have loved a chaste 'mountain girl' (4.3.7), but it is in reality anything but this kind of place; the rank-inscribed customs of the hunt prove this from the start of this sequence, and Philaster's cynical, misogynistic vocabulary merely confirms this as an already fallen world:

> Oh, that I had been nourished in these woods
> With milk of goats and acorns, and not known
> The right of crowns nor the dissembling trains
> Of women's locks, but digged myself a cave
> Where I, my fire, my cattle and my bed
> Might have been shut together in one shed.
>
> (4.3.1–6)

A further interesting point to register in looking at this particular speech is that it is adapted from a satirical rather than obviously pastoral source: Juvenal's Sixth Satire, which we have elsewhere heard reworked on the early modern stage in the cynical mouth of Truewit in Jonson's *Epicene* in the scene where he railed on the subject of the 'goblin matrimony' (2.2.25; see the more detailed analysis in Chapter 6). *Philaster* and *Epicene* were performed in reasonably quick succession in the 1609–10 seasons at the Globe and the Blackfriars and at the Whitefriars Theatres respectively and both bear in addition legible intertextual and staging influences from Jonson's earlier wedding masque for the female courtier Lady Frances Howard at the time of her ill-fated first marriage to the Earl of Essex, the 1606 *Hymenaei*. In *Philaster* 5.3, the love triangle of Philaster, Arethusa and Bellario appears in bridal guise with Bellario him/herself deliberately dressed with robe and garland as an attendant of Hymen, such as appeared in Jonson's masque;[15] and the King responds by calling this a 'masque' at this point as if to stimulate the association for the watching theatre audience. Through this kind of connectivity we can again witness tragicomedy as a dramatic mode being informed as much by satire as by the courtly theatrical tastes associated with pastoral and romance. Once again the significance of the network of plays, masques and entertainments provided by both commercial and courtly repertoires at particular moments in time allows us to gain sight of the ways in which different playwrights responded to and were influenced by each other, but also the ways in which different venues and acting companies responded to and remade those repertoires, riffing off each other's work in highly creative fashion.

Lucy Munro has written astutely of the 'actively recycling theatrical culture in the 1630s', revealing in the process 'a theatre industry in which the plays of a dramatist's predecessors retained a living, breathing presence'.[16] An important key to understanding that 'recycling culture', as she notes, is the impact of theatre revivals and 'repeats' of new plays. Brome's pastoral tragicomedy *The Queen and Concubine* was written and performed *c.* 1635. It clearly responds to the contemporary vogue for tragicomedy and especially for pastoral tragi-comedy informed by the particular tastes and predilections of the French Queen Consort Henrietta Maria, who was by this date not only commission-ing but performing in her own court drama, including Sir Walter Montagu's eight-hour-long pastoral experiment *The Shepherd's Paradise* in 1633. Court masques reflected these interests as well; Jonson's *Chloridia* (1631) and Aurelian Townshend's *Tempe Restored* (1632) are both much cited examples. On the commercial stage, Shirley had recently adapted Sir Philip Sidney's prose pas-toral *The Arcadia*. As previously observed, Fletcher's first pioneering pas-toral experimentation in English, *The Faithful Shepherdess*, which had been a resounding failure when it was first written, found newly receptive audiences both at court and in the public theatres at this time and it is as part of this wider 'network' that Brome's play, which might otherwise seem somewhat against the grain of his grittier Jonson-influenced city comedies, is best understood and interpreted. *The Queen and Concubine*, which subjects its protagonist Queen, Eulalia, to false accusation and trial and the supposed death of her loved ones, has immediate kinships with Shakespeare's *The Winter's Tale*; indeed, Matthew Steggle has called Brome's play 'an open and creative misappropriation of Shakespeare's'.[17] But there are additional links to other plays that test pastoral conventions almost to breaking point, not least *As You Like It* and *King Lear* and some of the forest community plays discussed in Chapter 4, including Massinger's *The Guardian* performed just a couple of years earlier.

The opening moments of *The Queen and Concubine* establish a certain expectation of engagement with the pastoral genre, if only as a motif, through the language of the courtier Lodovico in the first scene when he describes the newly arrived time of peace in the Sicilian court following a period of warfare from which the King is just about to return:

> Now the court
> Puts on her rich attire, and, like fresh flora
> After the blasts of winter, spreads her mantle
> Decked with delightful colours to receive
> The jocund spring that brings her this new life.
>   (1.1, speech 2)

But after events have taken an immediate turn for the worse – when the returning monarch is drawn sexually to his wife's childhood companion Alinda and in the process seems to find reason for his infidelity in an unfounded suspicion of Eulalia's adultery with Alinda's father Duke Sforza – the pastoral becomes a very real scenario in the play. Eulalia, following a public trial in which corrupt servants of the court slander her name (and which of course mirrors the treatment of her counterpart character Hermione in *The Winter's Tale*), is banished to the rural region of Palermo (of course now Sicily's chief urban centre). Her first speech in her soon-to-be-adopted homeland occurs at the beginning of Act 3, tellingly at the heart of the action, which again trains the audience to understand much by this significant structural location of the pastoral encounter. In her own words, 'Turned out of all and cast into the world' (3.1, speech 437), she hears birds chirping:

> Birds chirp.
> What music had the court compared to this;
> Or what comparison can all their sports
> And revels hold with those of kids and fawns,
> And frisking lambs upon the country lawns,
> Which are my hourly pleasant entertainments
> In all my wanderings.   (3.1. speech 437)

We can hear in these lines the age-old opposition of court and country values that drove the majority of pastoral poetics in the Elizabethan and Jacobean periods and which clearly persisted into the Caroline theatrical era, albeit increasingly hedged round with the realism and pragmatism that we saw in play in the Corin–Touchstone dialogue of *As You Like It* (3.2; discussed in detail in Chapter 4). Certainly, Eulalia finds a welcome here that stands in stark contrast to the suspicions and betrayals of the court, and she praises the 'plainness' of this place (4.1, speech 759) in contrast to the 'bells and bonfires, tilts and tournaments... feats and banquets, music and costly shows' (759) of the court. As we will explore further in Case study M, the use of dumb show and what the play's editor Lucy Munro calls 'visual rhetoric' is directly informed by the traditions and techniques of court masquing and it would be a naïve reading of any play at this time that assumed an outright condemnation of court practices and culture. Nevertheless there is a determined presentation of 'simpler' pastoral practices in the show that Eulalia stages to welcome her former husband's progress to the region. The King is accompanied by his troubled and murderous new wife Alinda, who by this stage is overcome with paranoia and on the verge of mental collapse – 'I fear she has a moonflaw in her brains' is how one character terms it (4.3, speech 958) – adding to the dissonance of courtly values in this scene. The handiwork and musical skill of the village women as well as Eulalia's own are presented before the King as an impressive statement of female independence and competency. An odd stage direction, which some critics have taken as an indication that Brome intended additional dialogue for Eulalia at this stage in the action, particularly if the play was staged in a venue where it would be hard for the audience to see the detail of the material properties being deployed, tells us that she:

> *Shows her works, and makes a brave description of pieces: as sale-work, day-work, night-work, wrought night-caps, coifs, stomachers.*
>
> (5.3, s.d. 1131)[18]

This is a striking moment that effects its own connection to yet another genre for which Brome was perhaps better known at this time: city comedy with its trade products as props and its entrepreneurial working-women characters like Rebecca Brittleware and Alice Saleware of *The Sparagus Garden* and *A Mad Couple Well Matched* (*c.* 1637–9) respectively (see fuller discussion in Chapter 5 of this phenomenon, though it is worth noting that Brome was clearly working on *The Sparagus Garden* at much the same time as *The Queen and Concubine*, which allows for a certain degree of crossover and cross-fertilisation). Tragicomedy is magpie-like in its attraction to other genres and subgenres, and the further allusions to both court masque and rural festivity in this moment merely underscore this perception. Eulalia's own son the Prince Gonzago leads (veiled and cross-dressed) a country dance of the local women as a kind of May Queen in a gender-bending performance that deliberately echoes and draws attention to his own mother's quasi-monarchical role in the rural community. It should perhaps also be noted that Gonzago was earlier feared dead and therefore serves as a further example of tragicomedy's generic tendency to acts of resurrection, of which Hermione's statue come to life in *The Winter's Tale* is just the best known.

Tragicomedy's absorption of both pastoral and satiric tendencies can perhaps then be best understood as part of a broader appropriative tendency in the genre as a whole but also as an indication of the specifically accumulative approach of individual plays and playwrights to drama in the repertoire at the time of composition, new work and revivals alike. The way in which this complex matrix of influences plays a shaping role in the plots and outcomes of these plays can usefully be explored through the particular theme of female agency and representation in Caroline 1630s forays into the tragicomic mode.

Female competencies

In *The Queen and Concubine*, in what reads to me like a direct nod to *As You Like It*, Eulalia is accompanied into rural exile by her devoted fool Andrea, and this enables some later scenes of mock-justice in the play which themselves echo the work of another fool in exile with his maltreated monarch, Lear's Fool. Perhaps even more significant, though, is the healing and educative effect Eulalia appears to have on the Palerman community which takes her to its heart, even when they know what they risk by sheltering the outcast Queen. In a remarkable sequence of scenes in which Eulalia seems to be almost sanctified by that local community for having a curing touch, she also learns through supernatural intervention – a Genius of the Place gives her hands these powers as she takes some much needed rest – how to earn her living through manual labour (most notably the needlework that we have already seen her present in the fifth-act entertainment for the visiting King). Furthermore, she deploys her own elite education to the advantage of the village daughters who acquire literacies and competencies of various kinds in her classroom. It is this learning and these moral and educational gains that the girls effectively present back to the King in 5.3 in the form of textile and musical skill, but this stand-out moment in the play shares real kinships with a much earlier masque-like entertainment that was staged for the benefit of King James VI and I's wife, Queen Anna of Denmark, in 1610 at Greenwich by members of one of the prime academies for female education at that time, Deptford Ladies Hall: Robert White's *Cupid's Banishment*.[19] Brome seems to have wanted to place a very particular emphasis on female education in this play; Lucy Munro notes his deliberate expansion of his source text (Robert Greene's *Penelope's Web*) in this respect, so we should perhaps not be surprised to see a legacy of female masquing and agency in performance (Anna was directly credited by Jonson as a co-creator of the first full Jacobean masque, *The Masque of Blackness*, in 1605)[20] being actively remade alongside pastoral convention in this play.

We might want to trace a direct line in female representation from Rosalind's assertive and stage-claiming Epilogue in *As You Like It* (discussed in Case study H) to the extensive parts written for both Eulalia and Alinda in Brome's play, mediated as they are in turn through direct intertextual referents, in Eulalia's case to other persecuted and prosecuted queens on the stage, from Hermione in *The Winter's Tale* to Katherine of Aragon in Shakespeare and Fletcher's *Henry VIII*, and in Alinda's to other female characters who go insane onstage from Ophelia to Brome's own delightful creation Constance in *The Northern Lass* (1629). Munro suggests that the roles of both Queen and concubine in Brome's 1635 play indicate the presence of highly competent boy actors in the Salisbury Court company at the time.[21] What is also clear, however, is that these roles need to be understood within the wider context of Caroline theatre where both on the commercial stage and at court women were increasingly active in the commissioning and performance and sometimes even the writing of theatre, which seems to have been reflected in the expansion of female opportunities on the public stages, albeit in roles still ventriloquised by boy actors. Not everyone was content with this state of affairs of course and the same kinds of anti-theatricalist who had railed in published pamphlets against the public theatre when it first opened in England in the 1590s resurfaced in the 1630s. The most notorious of these was William Prynne, the fundamentalist Protestant, who in 1633 published the thousand-page diatribe *Histriomastix* in which female actors were castigated and indeed indexed as 'notorious whores'.[22] Prynne was punished severely, not least for his implicit criticism of the Queen, and his books were burned, but it was in this febrile atmosphere that James Shirley composed his play all about female performance, *The Bird in a Cage*, which he sarcastically dedicated to Prynne who was languishing in his own prison cage at the time. At the heart of this play we have yet another incarcerated and tested princess, Eugenia, who along with her ladies-in-waiting decides to stage a play to pass the time. Much discussion of acting competencies and no small amount of sexual bawdy ensue as the women play out a version of the Jupiter–Danae myth that clearly parallels Eugenia's own situation:

> **DONELLA** You like this story best then?
> **EUGENIA** That of Jupiter and Danae comes near our own.   (4.2.1–2)

In a way that confirms earlier assertions of tragicomedy's knowing mixing of romance and myth with realpolitik readings, the Danae myth – which tells of a princess imprisoned to protect her from the perceived threat of being made pregnant by a god, only for the brazen tower in which she is locked to be penetrated by Jupiter in the guise of a shower of gold – is made material as a storyline in this play through the attempts by Morello and other courtiers to bribe the female guards of Eugenia's tower in order to gain access to the imprisoned women. Pharamond voices a similarly down-to-earth version of the myth in *Philaster*:

> [*aside*] This is a crafty wench. I like her wit well . . . She's a Danae must be courted in a shower of gold . . .
>
> (2.2.43–5)

As the double-edged handling of the Danae myth and the theme of female sexuality in these two plays suggests, it would be wrong to suppose that the treatment or representation of women is either wholly empowering or wholly restrictive in tragicomedy. As with this acquisitive and referential genre's approach to all other themes and topics, female agency is handled in multiple, multi-levelled and sometimes conflicting ways. Nevertheless the female voice is heard strongly on the stage of tragicomedies, most strikingly so as the decades progress and in particular in the Caroline 1630s. Again, it would be too simplistic to suggest that the theatre-fond and theatre-active Caroline Queen alone drove these shifts in practice, in terms either of generic adaptation or of female representation, but as we are beginning to see, it is all part of a complex matrix of influences that we need to bring to bear in understanding early modern drama and the magpie mode of tragicomedy in particular.[23] The 'Cinderella' of genres may yet be invited to the ball after all.

Case study M

The visual rhetoric of dumb show

When Hamlet elects to stage 'The Murder of Gonzago' before King Claudius and the Danish court in Act 3 of Shakespeare's tragedy, the spoken version of the play is preceded by a dumb show enactment of the main action: a king and queen embrace, the sleeping king is then poisoned in the ear by another man who in the process steals his crown, and the poisoner is then witnessed in a passionate embrace with that same queen. Ophelia, one of the court spectators to this production, turns to Hamlet and asks 'What means this, my lord?' (*Hamlet*, 3.2.130) and the real theatre audience is at that moment presumably several steps ahead of her in construing that Hamlet is staging before his uncle Claudius and his new wife, Hamlet's mother Gertrude, exactly what he believes happened to his own father.[1] The dumb show is a 'speaking picture', a picture without words that condenses and as a result renders even more shocking the story that needs to be told.

Jacobean tragedy had a particular taste for using dumb show to present some of its most shocking actions and events. In John Webster's *The White Devil* (c. 1612), the device is used to depict some of the most extravagantly engineered deaths of the play (shown to the Duke Brachiano, and thereby to the audience, in the form of a dumb show by a conjurer), including the poisoning of the Duke's wife Isabella by means of a poisoned painting and the grotesque murder of his mistress's husband Camillo in a gymnasium: '*as Camillo is about to vault, Flamineo pitcheth upon his neck, and with the help of the rest, writhes his neck about, seems to see if it be broke, makes shows to call for help*' (2.2.37 s.d.). What might have stretched the imagination if staged for real is both denaturalised and heightened in its horror by its rendition in this form. Death made pictorial and spectacular was clearly an effect that Webster appreciated, since he redeployed dumb show to great effect in *The Duchess of Malfi*. This is, then, the stage tradition which Caroline dramatist Richard Brome was able to build on and to benefit from in assuming a skilful 'interpreting' audience when he deployed dumb show in his experimental tragicomedy *The Queen and Concubine* in 1635.

Act 2, scene 1 of that play opens with a version of dumb show that is best understood as melodrama in the true sense. Loud music plays throughout a lengthy period of stylised action:

> *Loud Music.*
>
> *Enter four* LORDS [*including* LODOVICO, HORATIO, *and* FLAVELLO,] *two* BISHOPS, KING [*and*] PRINCE [GONZAGO], *they sit;* EULALIA *in black, crowned, a golden wand in her hand, led between two* FRIARS. *She kneels* [*to*] *the* KING; *he rejects her with his hand. Enter at the other door, a* DOCTOR *of physic, a* MIDWIFE [FABIO *and* STROZZO]. *The* KING *points them to the* BISHOPS; *they each deliver papers, kiss the* BISHOPS' *books, and are dismissed. The papers are given to the* KING. *He with his finger menaces* EULALIA *and sends her the papers; she looks meekly. The* BISHOPS *take her crown and wand,* [*and*] *give her a wreath of cypress, and a white wand. All the* LORDS *peruse the papers. They show her various countenances, some seem to applaud the* KING, *some pity* EULALIA.
>
> *Music ceases.* KING *speaks.*

(2.1.0 s.d.)

This dumb show does much of its work through the by now familiar the-atrical devices of spoken early modern theatre – costume, properties and gesture – but something about the silent (and, as we shall see, silencing) nature of the scene heightens the attention which we pay these devices and therefore the meanings they make onstage.

This is, in terms of the play, the moment when the King publicly and formally rejects his wife the Queen Eulalia in favour of a new mistress (she, Alinda, will, with shocking haste, enter as a bride within moments of this action unfolding before spectators' eyes). Eulalia's humiliation and rejection delivered in the form of dumb show, however, asks us to pay particular attention to the visual rhetoric of the scene. Her costuming in black, crowned and holding a golden wand in her hands, is an immediate signifier of her rank and would presumably add to the shock of her public deposition in this scene. This is reinforced by surrounding her with figures of institutional religion, the bishops and friars who should presumably protect her interests as the ruling monarch. The play's most recent editor, Lucy Munro, has also suggested a multi-layered aspect to this particular costume decision in that the significant prop of the '*golden wand*' might not only suggest a queen's sceptre but more specifically invoke mythical associations with the sorceress Circe whose wand had the power to transform humanity and whose image we know was being actively deployed in court masques at this time, not least in Aurelian Townshend's *Tempe Restored* in 1632. We may as a result, she suggests, be being asked through this association to appreciate

9. An ensemble of actors workshopping dumb show movements in a Caroline play.

the ways in which the King consistently constructs Eulalia in negative terms from this point in the play onwards. Certainly these trappings of Eulalia's power, positive or negative in force, are seized from her grasp and she is presented instead with '*a wreath of cypress, and a white wand*'. These are, by contrast, the handheld properties that a penitent female sinner would be made to carry in public rituals.

In particular, though, I want to explore the role of hands in this dumb show. We are informed that the King gives many of his instructions manually, pointing to individuals like the bishops and with his finger 'menacing' or making a threatening gesture at Eulalia herself. Her response to this is typical of the passive and essentially obedient if not necessarily submissive stance she adopts throughout the play; we are told that she '*looks meekly*'. We know from printed manuals of hand gestures that particular positionings of hands were understood to represent specific emotions or emotional responses on the stage,[2] and from contemporary workshopping of the scene we can also see how actors might put this kind of gesturing into practice (see Figures 9 and 10).[3] John Bulwer published *Chirologia, or The Natural Language of the Hand* and a second part *Chironomia, or The Art of Manual*

10. Legible hand gestures in dumb show.

Rhetoric in 1644.[4] Though published later than the date of performance, these manuals are a compendium of earlier practices, and both contain images of hand positions that seem to correlate with this moment in the action of Brome's play; Eulalia's '*meekly*' may have been conveyed through the position of *supplico*, which involved stretching out both hands or holding both hands together in front of the body. It is intriguing that later in the scene when the King speaks he draws attention back to Eulalia's hands in a statement about depriving her of voice and agency. It is striking that dumb show has been deployed by Brome to enact the fiercest kind of silencing of this innocent Queen. Dumb show is a device to which he returns on several occasions in *The Queen and Concubine* and this suggests that a cue is established early on in this play for audiences of this tragicomedy to be alert at all times to the complex speaking pictures being placed before them and, like the courtiers of '*various countenances*' in this example, to come to their own conclusions.

Conclusion: The wind and the rain: the wider landscape of early modern performance

In thinking about the visual culture of the early modern period, we have grown accustomed to reproducing the panoramas of London created in the seventeenth century by the likes of Wenceslaus Hollar or the anonymous examples produced by Dutch publisher Claes Jansz Visscher and the impressive sense they give of an emergent capital city, with all its complications, juxtapositions and possibilities.[1] It is worth, however, looking at such vistas with fresh eyes in the light of the discussions that have gone before in this volume and noting again the significant presence of the purpose-built theatres of the Bankside. We have already seen how their neighbourhood and waterside geography was crucial to the development of early modern commercial theatre: the status of the Clink prison precinct and Paris Garden as liberties, the neighbourhood of Southwark itself with its tanners and weavers, the proximity of the river and access to the City proper just across the water and the necessary audiences that helped to provide. We have also turned at regular intervals to the increasing importance of the indoor playhouses to the story of that development, and the panoramas also help us to register the shift of emphasis towards their locations on the north side of the Thames as the children's companies' success blossomed and almost as quickly yielded their power and their venues to the dominant adult companies such as the King's Men.

While there is considerable mileage in thinking about how plays were written with some of these theatres – and the particular possibilities and restrictions of their design as well as the companies that worked in them – in mind, plays were not site-restricted, so any understanding of site-specific writing at this time needs to be tempered by a recognition of the need for adaptability, flexibility, portability and movement.[2] Not only did some plays and companies shuttle between the Bankside and the Blackfriars, and from outdoor arena to indoor venue in the process, as in the case of the King's Men, plays were more often than not brought to the court's residences at Whitehall, Greenwich and Richmond for performance or taken on tour to the provinces and regions, visiting in the process the houses of nobles and significant courtiers but also playing in humbler venues such as town guildhalls and inn courtyards. This much more nuanced and complex view of early modern playing, one which brings into its embrace everything from street jugglers and puppet masters to waxwork shows, has been enhanced beyond recognition by the scholarship enshrined in the *REED* project: *Records of Early English Drama* (and now in Welsh and Scottish drama also).[3] Even within London, there are additional sites of performance to consider such as the Inns of Court and the city streets and thoroughfares, including the great Thames itself on the days of civic and royal ceremonial.[4] To conclude, then, I would like us to expand our own horizons and consider the wider panorama of performance in the period in question and the influence it undoubtedly had on the commercial theatre plays we have thus far been considering.

Court theatre and the masque

Court theatre, broadly conceived, is also a crucial part of that panorama. If at times court theatre operated in opposition to commercial outlets and manifested seemingly oppositional values in many other respects, it had a strong influence on them. John Astington has written a highly evocative essay in which he imagines the movements of performers in a *c.* 1598 production of *Love's Labour's Lost* in a single day, stretching from an afternoon performance at the Curtain in Shoreditch to an evening production at Whitehall Palace: 'Once the play was over [at the Curtain], the actors might have packed their costumes and properties in bags and baskets, and made their way the 2 miles or so from their theatre to Whitehall.'[5] Implicit in this reconstructive history is a sense of properties and costumes on the move which conjures a very dynamic picture of London with players traversing its streets between venues and transporting the tools of their trade. Of course, court theatre also enabled access to a very different kind of wealth and therefore to costumes, props and theatre machinery of a potentially higher order and there has been some suggestion that the commercial companies could have taken advantage of this by being loaned items for a court performance. Similar cases have been made for the borrowing of locally appropriate items when companies were performing in provincial households, and one play, Middleton's *A Mad World, My Masters* (1604–7), makes comic capital of this in a plotline in which Sir Bounteous Progress receives travelling players at his household, only to find that they purloin these borrowed items from him: 'I lent the rascals properties to furnish out their play, a chain, a jewel, and a watch, and they watched out their time, and rid quite away with them' (5.2.246–9).

We do know for certain that there was an intriguing traffic in dramatic materials at the level of costumes. In Jonson's 1629 Blackfriars play *The New Inn*, one aristocratic character, Lady Frances Frampul, is envisaging a 'day's sports' (1.6.44) in which she will dress up her own chambermaid Prudence as a queen for twenty-four hours. For this purpose she lends Prudence items from her own wardrobe, though it is clear she cannot envisage then being seen in public wearing dresses that have been worn by a commoner. Her solution is clear: 'Twill fit the players yet / When thou hast done with it, and yield thee somewhat' (2.1.35–6).

This moment in the play is enhanced by its delivery during a scene of dressing-up in which Lady Frances is attempting to lace the presumably larger or curvier Prudence into her dress and connects to real-life practice. Contemporary commentator Thomas Platter observed in his diary: 'The actors are most expensively and elaborately costumed; for it is the English usage for eminent lords or knights at their decease to bequeath and leave almost the best of their clothes to their serving men, which it is unseemly for the latter to wear, so that they offer them for sale for a small sum to the actors.'[6] Remembering the entrepreneurial basis of early modern theatre that we sketched in the Introduction to this volume and Henslowe's second career as a pawnbroker and dyer, we can see how theatre costumes can tell a very real story of social circulation and interaction – between places and people – in this period.[7] A further illuminating example of this kind of practical theatrical exchange can be traced in the performance at the Caroline court in 1633 of Sir Walter Montagu's specially commissioned play (it ran for more than eight hours) *The Shepherd's Paradise* by Queen Henrietta Maria and her court women.[8] The particular theatrical frisson and innovation of a queen in a speaking role is something we will return to in a moment but what is also known is that the costumes made for this lavish production were recycled for a successful revival of John Fletcher's experimental pastoral tragicomedy *The Faithful Shepherdess*, staged at court at the Queen's behest.[9]

Ideas were also part of this active knowledge exchange process between city, provinces and court and it is perhaps no coincidence that Beaumont and Fletcher's canon evidences very strong marks of influence from courtly theatre practices, since we know Beaumont was actively involved in masque-making for the nobility. There is not space enough in a conclusion to adequately account for the complex history of the court masque as a form but it is one strongly associated with Ben Jonson, who elsewhere in this volume has been seen as deeply embedded in the practices and customs of the public theatres. Jonson collaborated, albeit in a tense and highly competitive relationship, with the architect and theatre designer Inigo Jones to produce these lavish multimedia spectacles for King James and Queen Anna, as well as for their sons Prince Henry and Prince Charles, and subsequently for Charles when he became King in 1625 and for his French Queen Henrietta Maria, who brought with her from the Paris court a strong interest in and commitment to live performance.[10]

The Jones–Jonson masques were inextricably tied up with the site of the Banqueting House (decorated by Jones) where the majority of them were performed. That this was also the venue in which court-commissioned performances of public theatre plays took place meant there was yet further opportunity for crossover of practical experience and thinking. Even though Shakespeare never formally wrote a royal masque or entertainment, he was influenced by their theatrical idiom in this way. Arthur Kinney makes the lucid point that 'Fashioning plays after 1603, Shakespeare probably kept [the Banqueting House] in mind in scripting and blocking his works.'[11] This kind of potent cross-fertilisation can also still be seen in the architecture of the city of London itself: Jones allowed his theatrical experiences to bleed into the way he thought about designing public space, and this can best be witnessed in the Italianate piazza of Covent Garden with its consciously theatrical sightlines.[12] That this 1630s location itself became the raw material for public theatre drama by Brome and Nabbes – *The Weeding of Covent Garden* (1632) and *Covent Garden* (1633) respectively[13] – is yet further evidence of the rich cultural dialogue that was taking place between different performativities, forms, genres and contexts throughout the period in focus. The lavish masquing costumes, also designed for court masques and entertainments by Jones, as well as other items from the Royal Wardrobe, were stored in buildings located at Blackfriars, just across a bridge from the playhouse precinct itself, and this was therefore a very possible site of cross-directional traffic. Actors and company workers would very likely have been seen on the days of performance and of royal pageants transporting materials across the water (the site was bordered by the Fleet Ditch). In this respect, with its concern with clothing, with who might wear what and to what end, and the ways in which people might counterfeit identities through the work of a tailor (in this play a dubious character named Nick Stuff), Jonson's *The New Inn* seems hypersensitive to the cultural and physical contexts of its own performance.[14]

Masques were, as already noted, multimedia productions and while the visuals of stage machinery and costume were clearly deeply impressive and memorable (contemporary ambassadorial accounts often dwell on such details and Jonson was careful to provide intricate descriptions of the same in printed versions of the masque texts), dance and music were also crucial components in the overall effect. The intrinsic and extensive role of instrumental music and song in masques formed an obvious connection to the enhanced presence of music in the indoor playhouse venues such as the Blackfriars and helps to explain why plays for these particular theatres showed a special predilection for restaging masques in the course of their plotlines and action. Shakespeare's *The Tempest* (1610–11), with its wedding masque of Iris and Ceres staged for Miranda and Ferdinand by the magus Prospero (the mythical content of which was a direct allusion to the kinds of narrative staged by Jonson and Jones for the Jacobean and later the Caroline court), is often singled out in these discussions but many more such examples can be furnished, including Shakespeare's *Cymbeline* (*c.* 1611), Shakespeare and Fletcher's collaborative *The Two Noble Kinsmen* (1613), which directly reworked passages and ideas from Beaumont's *Masque of the Inner Temple and Grays Inn*, a masque staged as part of royal wedding celebrations for Princess Elizabeth in 1613, Beaumont and Fletcher's *The Maid's Tragedy* (*c.* 1619), Ford's *The Broken Heart* (1632) and Massinger's *The City Madam* (1632). The scene of Hermione's statue come to life in Act 5 of *The Winter's Tale* can also be read as part of this wider allusive tradition, reworking as it does the 'animated statues' that were a favoured form of masque storytelling.[15] This particular version of metatheatricality was of course a natural extension of early uses of inset drama and plays within plays, a veritable explosion of which we saw in the revenge drama tradition (see Chapter 2) but it was also answering to a particular clamour from public theatre audiences to see at least a version of the court drama they heard so much about but could never see for themselves at firsthand.[16] Reworkings and remakings need not be deferential of course and Jonson himself proved more apt to parody than to praise the masque form in his public theatre drama: the puppet play of *Bartholomew Fair*, staged both at the newly opened Hope Theatre and at the court in 1614, albeit with altered, presumably venue- and audience-specific prologues, stages a Bankside version of the court masque. Hero and Leander are based now on the Thames rather than the Hellespont and converse in local idiom to boot. The puppet play sequence was also a wonderful opportunity for Jonson to take a swipe at his great rival Jones in the figure of puppet master and showmaker, Lantern Leatherhead:

> **LANTERN** *It is Hero.*
> *Of the Bankside, he saith – to tell you without erring –*
> *Is come over into Fish Street to eat some fresh herring.*
>
> (5.4.123–5)

One of the other arenas in which the development of the masque as a prime mode of performance at the court played a major part was the introduction of women actors into the English tradition. Though women were prohibited from performing on the public stage by law, thereby creating the particular inventiveness of the boy actor tradition (which we explored in Case study H), there were no such restrictions at court. The move to female theatrical agency was incremental; when Queen Anna of Denmark performed in Jonson and Jones's pioneering *The Masque of Blackness* in 1605 she was a silent woman (another feature potentially parodied by Jonson in the boys' company play *Epicene* with its supposedly silent 'female' protagonist who is persistently compared to the kinds of classical and mythical character performed by women in the masque tradition). It was not until Henrietta Maria's importation of French theatrical practice, where professional women actors were the norm, that speech entered the skill-set of courtly women performers, but nevertheless we can register the reasonably rapid influence of this development in practice in the enhanced female roles of 1630s Caroline drama on the public stages.[17]

Civic drama and pageantry

While the cross-fertilisation between masque and public drama was a particularly rich one, there was not a simple binary of court versus commercial theatre in the London context. If we have already begun to map the ways in which playwrights like Jonson and indeed Beaumont and Fletcher occupied these spaces and forms, writing masques as well as plays, and also how companies like the King's Men enjoyed a shared repertoire, the built environment of the city provided a site of performance beyond the purpose-built playhouses per se. Bear-baitings, public punishments and executions, sermons and preaching, marketsellers' cries can and have all been read as modes of performance that impact upon and are impacted by early modern theatre. But we might also note the existence of the very specific civic dramatic form of the pageant, a 'participatory ritual of civic affirmation' to use Anne Lancashire's suggestive phrase.[18] Chief among this category were the annual Lord Mayor's Pageants, amphibious performances which traversed both the waterways and major streets and thoroughfares of London and provided multiple sites for theatrical display and entertainments which themselves adapted and provided conscious counterpoints to the conventions of court masques. Heywood, Munday, Dekker and Middleton can all be found producing work in this arena at the same time as they were working as professional playwrights so a degree of crossover seems inevitable.[19]

The Lord Mayor's Pageants with their processional quality made the most of key locales in the city including the Thames, Cheapside and increasingly in the seventeenth century the West End thoroughfare of the Strand with its multiple signifying sites such as the Royal Exchange, a space of consumption and exchange in its broadest sense, and the noble houses that enjoyed both streetside and waterside facades. We have already seen through engagement with the specific mode of city comedy how early modern drama made the most of the possibilities of place in its representational modes. If Middleton's plays are fascinated by the artisanal workshops of Cheapside and the Thames, so too are Jonson's and Brome's plays which, full as they are of court aspirants and the socially mobile, locate themselves in and around the Strand.[20] We might also register the influence on their work and that of others of both these playwrights' contributions to another form of processional city pageant, the royal entry; both Jonson and Middleton, along with Dekker, were prominent in producing work for the formal entry of James VI and I to London in 1603.[21]

Commercial playhouses and the story of their development in the Introduction to this volume were necessarily London focused, and as the diverse account provided here of sites of performance in the capital proves, it would be naïve, foolhardy even, to pretend that the city of London is not central to this story – as venue and often as subject matter for early modern commercial theatre. A chapter exploring the genre of city comedy but also discussions of chronicle history (and indeed comedy in the case of *The Shoemaker's Holiday*) have already served to evidence this fact. But London was not an island. Its hybrid community was a product of many incomers, some from the European mainland (the Huguenot refugee textile works we saw figuring in plays like Dekker's *The Shoemaker's Holiday*) but many from the regions and provinces of the nation itself. Oddly enough it is one particular London location and community, the Inns of Court (whose influence on theatregoing in general and on the satirical form in particular was explored in Chapters 2 and 6), which provides a wonderful point of entry to this fact. The Inns served as a virtual microcosm of the nation's regional relationships and associations. Particular regions were represented in particular Inns and so future movers and shakers in the world of politics and literature came to identify themselves not only as Inns-men but through their own provincial provenance or connections – connections formed through patronage and through the practical experiences of touring theatre, as we shall see. In the heavily nostalgic exchanges between

Shallow and Silence in Shakespeare's *Henry IV, Part 2*, we see this version of cultural geography brought vividly to life:

> **SHALLOW** I was one of Clement's Inn, where I think they will talk of mad Shallow yet... There was I, and little John Doit of Staffordshire and black George Barnes, and Francis Pickbone and Will Squeal, a Cotswold man...
>
> (3.1.12–14, 18–20)

Inns of Court drama also found kinship with other theatre that took place in and was formed out of educational and pedagogic contexts, from the university drama of Oxford and Cambridge, to the schools drama tradition from which both metropolitan and regional examples are extant.[22]

Household drama in London and the provinces

If court masques had a tangible influence on early modern drama, so too did the longstanding traditions of household theatre.[23] Middleton's *A Mad World, My Masters* and the arrival of touring players at Sir Bounteous Progress's estate (albeit that in practice they prove to be the conspiratorial cohorts of Progress's morally bankrupt nephew Follywit) has already been mentioned as one example of a direct reference to provincial touring in commercial London theatre. Several other plays evidence an awareness and an interest in household performance as yet another theatrical mode: in Marston's *Histriomastix* (1610) Sir Oliver Owlet's players memorably complain that they 'travel, with pumps full of gravel' (2.1, sig. C3^v);[24] elsewhere, the metatheatrical framing to Shakespeare's *The Taming of the Shrew* depicts a company of travelling players arriving at an unnamed lord's household, and Brome's *The Antipodes* (1636–8) and *A Jovial Crew* (1642) both feature specifically commissioned household performances. This is all far less surprising or unusual as an occurrence if we recognise the regular exposure to actors returning from provincial tours that those working in the public theatres would necessarily have had. As Peter Greenfield has noted, thanks to the scholarship of the *REED* project and individuals such as Sally Beth McLean and Scott McMillin: 'Research on performing outside London has... found much new evidence to show that touring was a regular, expected practice of even the most successful companies.'[25] It is, of course, entirely possible that Jonson, Brome, Shirley and others had hands-on experience as touring players or, at the very least, visited particular provincial households engaged in theatre as part of the patronage groupings and literary circles in which they were involved, and may even in the process have been exposed to regional entertainment networks that in turn influenced their work and dramatic composition.[26]

Regional playing is not simply a story of London 'hit' plays being taken out to the regions, in possibly pared down or stripped back versions, though this is undoubtedly one important part of the jigsaw. Regional families and households were active in reading and staging drama – key individuals like Sir Edward Dering in Kent and John Newdigate III in Nottinghamshire purchased a large number of play and masque texts during working trips to London. In Dering's case we know he also reworked these for staging in his household, including Shakespeare's two parts of *Henry IV* which he appears to have conflated into a single play performance in 1623, and Newdigate may even have authored some significant drama as well as poetry during his lifetime.[27] We know that at Skipton Castle in 1636 localised revivals of Beaumont's *The Knight of the Burning Pestle* (1613), with its Waltham Forest scenes presumably retold for a Yorkshire audience, and Massinger's Nottinghamshire-based *A New Way to Pay Old Debts*, took place. What did audiences make of these plays? How many spectators had a previous theatrical memory of these plays in particular or others like them to bring to bear? How much were they simply remade in the moment of the particular performance event? In telling the story of professional theatre, then, we need to keep in our sights the crossover with amateur and non-professional sites and playing contexts at all times if we want to gain the fullest possible understanding of lines of circulation, communication and influence.

No performance artist, style or convention exists in splendid isolation: in the early modern period, the commercial and the courtly, the civic and the artisanal, the metropolitan and the provincial, all overlap and feed into each other in significant ways. The genre of masques and entertainments also had its own regional variations which in turn fed back and influenced the metropolitan and courtly traditions. For all of the specific arguments made about the commercial context for theatre in the early modern period and the significance of the purpose-built playhouses to the story of its development, this conclusion is a plea to avoid reading early modern commercial theatre as hermetically sealed. The tendrils of theatre and the influence of performance culture were extremely wide-reaching in the early modern period. They did not suddenly bloom overnight. Strongly influenced by traditions and practices inherited from earlier medieval and Tudor traditions of playing, as well as by European courtly experiments and advances, the changes that were undoubtedly wrought by the professionalisation and commercialisation of the form, and the establishment of the purpose-built playing houses, are significant but must be read in the context of these other simultaneous stories of theatrical experimentation.

Endings and epilogues

At this point it also seems apposite to make a point about endings. As the witty epilogues of plays like *Volpone* and *The Tempest* acknowledge, a fifth act is only an ending if we allow it to be so; life carries on beyond that artificial stop, other choices can be made, actors can be resurrected to perform the same ending, perhaps inflected slightly differently, the next day, even the same evening. This book had in its own way to set certain date parameters. We end our study in 1642, when as theatre history tells us, due to the advancing tensions in London that would eventually break out in full-blown civil war that would run for seven years, the commercial playhouses were closed down and public playing prohibited. The wars themselves would end with a dramatic scene of their own, the carefully staged execution of King Charles I in front of the very Inigo Jones designed Banqueting House in which his extravagant court theatricals and masques had been staged just a few years earlier. Politics and theatre are hard to distinguish at this point. In different places and spaces however, and in different formats, performance and indeed theatre survived on into the 1640s and 1650s, stretching across the period of the English republic and feeding into what is often referred to as the 'restored' theatre of 1660, when other changes in practice would also arrive on the commercial stage, including professional women actors and indeed playwrights.

There are, then, different ways of ending a story and, as was made clear at the start of this study, different ways of navigating through the work presented here. It is to be hoped that readers and users of this material will produce their own versions and accounts both of the period in question and of the material presented here. What I hope to have furnished you with are different, perhaps even sometimes contradictory, ways to work, multiple angles from which to approach an event or a text or a moment, multiple ways in which to apply the case study models provided here. There is no one, nor indeed right, way of thinking about early modern theatre; that is perhaps why we are constantly drawn back to it as a subject of study. And yet there is, perhaps, another reason why we are drawn back again and again to this particular moment in English theatre that needs to be sounded here: this is a really special, incredibly exciting moment in the history of the English theatre; it is almost as if, as we start to reconstruct the performances of plays from this time, they start to crackle with life and we begin to register the mind-expanding, heart-expanding experience that they were for contemporary spectators, who themselves came back again and again to the theatre to watch plays and to be inspired by them. It is worth thinking about why there was the kind of explosion of dramatic energy and linguistic and intellectual and indeed acting talent that was seen on the stages of the Globe and the Blackfriars, that led people to push wagons along rutted, muddy country roads to perform plays in great halls in regions as far afield as Nottinghamshire and Lancashire, that caused other people, and sometimes the same ones, to carry clothing and props across the bridge from the Royal Wardrobe to prepare for a performance in the Blackfriars, that rendered citizens willing to wait for hours on bridges to catch brief glimpses of a royal or a civic procession, that inspired queens to act, and bricklayers to write.

Early modern theatre enjoyed, positively revelled in, moments of frame-breaking and self-awareness about the conditions of performance, moments when as a form it could call attention to its power to *transform*, to conjure and to affect. A statue comes to life, a man is taken down to hell by devils, having sold his soul, a girl turns out to have been a boy all along, lives are lost, loves are found, all in a space of 'two hours' traffic of our stage' (*Romeo and Juliet*, Prologue, 12). No wonder spectators came back again and again to sit or stand, in sun, in rain or by candlelight; to laugh, to cry, to be petrified, to be appalled, to be confused, to be challenged and, hopefully, eventually to applaud. Because even the best shows have to end …

> The seasoning of a play is the applause.
> Now, though the Fox be punished by the laws,
> He yet, doth hope there is no suffering due
> For any fact, which he hath done 'gainst you.
> If there be, censure him: here he doubtful stands.
> If not, fare jovially, and clap your hands.
> 　　　　　　　　　　(*Volpone*, Epilogue, 152–7)

> Now my charms are all o'erthrown
> And what strength I have's mine own,
> Which is most faint …
> As you from crimes would pardoned be,
> Let your indulgence set me free.
> 　　　　(*The Tempest*, Epilogue, 1–3, 19–20)

> Though we are now no beggars of the crew
> We count it not a shame to beg of you.
> The justice here has given his pass free
> To all the rest unpunished; only we
> Are under censure, till we do obtain
> Your suffrages that we may beg again
> And often in the course we took today

Which was intended for your mirth; a play
Not without action and a little wit,
Therefore we beg your pass for us and it.
    (*A Jovial Crew*, Epilogue, speech 1078)

A great while ago the world begun
With hey, ho, the wind and the rain.
But that's all one, our play is done,
And we'll strive to please you every day.
            (*Twelfth Night*, 5.1.401–4)

Chronology

Year	Plays	Events and other publications
1558		Death of Mary I; accession of Elizabeth I
1561–2	Sackville and Norton, *Gorboduc*	
1572		Last recorded production of religious drama in York
1574		Blundeville, *The True Order and Methode of Wryting and Reading Histories*
1576		The Theatre built; Children of Chapel Royal begin performing at first Blackfriars Theatre
1577		The Curtain opens; Holinshed, *Chronicles of England, Scotland and Ireland*; Drake sails around the world
1579		Gosson, *School of Abuse* published; Spenser, *The Shepheardes Calender*
1580		Last performance of Coventry Corpus Christi plays
1582		Gosson, *Plays Confuted in Five Actions* published
1583		Queen's Men founded; Stubbes, *Anatomy of Abuses* published
1583–4	Lyly, *Campaspe, Sappho and Phao*	
1585	Lyly, *Galatea*	First English colony in Virginia
1585–6	Marlowe and Nashe, *Dido, Queen of Carthage*; Kyd, *The Spanish Tragedy*	

(*continued*)

Year	Plays	Events and other publications
1587		Rose Theatre built; execution of Mary Queen of Scots; Greene, *Penelope's Web*
1587–8	Marlowe, *1* and *2 Tamburlaine*	
1588	Lyly, *Endymion*	Spanish Armada defeated
c. 1588	*Sir John Oldcastle*	
1588?	Marlowe, *Doctor Faustus*	
1589	Lyly, *Midas*	Puttenham, *The Arte of English Poesie*
1589–90	Greene, *Friar Bacon and Friar Bungay*	
c. 1589–90	Marlowe, *The Jew of Malta*	
1590	Guarini, *Il pastor fido*; Greene, *The Scottish History of James IV*	Paul's Boys stop playing; Lodge, *Rosalynde*
1590–1	Shakespeare, *The Two Gentlemen of Verona*	
1590–2	Shakespeare, *The Taming of the Shrew*	
1591	Shakespeare, *2* and *3 Henry VI, Richard III*	
c. 1591	Peele, *The Battle of Alcazar*	
1591–3	Marlowe, *Edward II*	
1592	*Arden of Faversham*; Nashe, *Pierce Pennilesse*; Shakespeare (and Nashe?), *1 Henry VI*	
1592–3	Munday *et al.*, *Sir Thomas More*	
1593	Marlowe, *The Massacre at Paris*; Shakespeare and Peele, *Titus Andronicus*	Death of Marlowe
1594	Shakespeare, *The Comedy of Errors*	Admiral's Men and Chamberlain's Men given Privy Council licence
c. 1594?	Heywood, *The Four Prentices of London*	
1594–5	Shakespeare, *Love's Labour's Lost*	
1595	Shakespeare, *Richard II, Romeo and Juliet, A Midsummer Night's Dream*	The Swan built; Sidney, *Apology for Poetry* published

Year	Plays	Events and other publications
1596	Shakespeare, *King John*	De Witt's sketch of the Swan; second Blackfriars built (not used until 1600)
1596–7	Shakespeare, *1 Henry IV*, *The Merchant of Venice*	
1597	Chapman, *An Humorous Day's Mirth*; Jonson, *The Case is Altered*; Jonson and Nashe, *The Isle of Dogs*	*The Isle of Dogs* controversy; lease on the Theatre lapses; playhouse due for demolition
1597–8	Shakespeare, *The Merry Wives of Windsor*	Boar's Head converted into theatre
1597–9	Shakespeare, *2 Henry IV*	
1598	Haughton, *Englishmen for My Money*; Jonson, *Every Man In His Humour*	Materials from the Theatre moved for new Globe Theatre
1598–9	Shakespeare, *Henry V*, *Much Ado About Nothing*	
1599	Dekker, *The Shoemaker's Holiday*; Heywood, *1* and *2 Edward IV*; Jonson, *Every Man Out of His Humour*; Shakespeare, *Julius Caesar*	Opening of Globe Theatre; Paul's Boys resume playing
1599–1600	Marston, *Antonio and Mellida*	
1600	Marston, *Antonio's Revenge*; Shakespeare, *As You Like It*; *A Yorkshire Tragedy*	The Fortune built; innyard performance prohibited; Chapel Children begin performing at Blackfriars
1600–1	Jonson, *Cynthia's Revels*; Shakespeare, *Hamlet*	
1601	Dekker, *Satiromastix*; Jonson, *Poetaster*; Marston, *What You Will*	
c. 1601	Shakespeare, *Twelfth Night*	
1602	Shakespeare, *Troilus and Cressida*	
c. 1602–3	Chapman, *The Gentleman Usher*	

(*continued*)

Year	Plays	Events and other publications
1603	Chapman, *The Old Joiner of Aldgate*; Jonson, *Sejanus*; Heywood, *A Woman Killed with Kindness*	Death of Elizabeth; accession of James I; patent for King's Men; Admiral's Men become Prince Henry's Men
1603–4	Shakespeare, *Measure for Measure*, *Othello*	
1603–5	Marston, *The Dutch Courtesan*	
1604	Dekker and Middleton, *1 The Honest Whore*; Dekker and Webster, *Westward Ho*; Marston, *The Malcontent*; Middleton, *Michaelmas Term*	Children of Chapel Royal become Children of the Queen's Revels
1604–5	Chapman, *Bussy D'Ambois*, *The Widow's Tears*; Dekker and Middleton, *2 The Honest Whore*	
1604–7	Middleton, *A Mad World, My Masters*	
1605	Chapman, Jonson and Marston, *Eastward Ho!*; Dekker and Webster, *Northward Ho!*; Middleton, *A Trick to Catch the Old One*	The Gunpowder Plot; Red Bull built; Anna of Denmark involved in commissioning of *The Masque of Blackness* from Ben Jonson and Inigo Jones for performance at court
c. 1605	Shakespeare and Middleton, *Timon of Athens*; Shakespeare, *King Lear*	
1605–6	Middleton, *The Revenger's Tragedy*; Shakespeare, *Macbeth*; Ben Jonson, *Volpone*	
1606		Whitefriars Theatre built (not used until 1609)?
1607	Middleton, *Your Five Gallants*	Paul's Boys stop playing

Year	Plays	Events and other publications
1608	Fletcher, *The Faithful Shepherdess*; Shakespeare, *Coriolanus*	Blackfriars children move to Whitefriars; King's Men in Blackfriars
1609	Jonson, *Epicene*	Cockpit (or Phoenix) built (not used as theatre until 1616)
1610	Beaumont and Fletcher, *Philaster*; Jonson, *The Alchemist*; Marston, *Histriomastix*	Foundation of Jamestown, Virginia; White, *Cupid's Banishment* performed at court
1610–11	Shakespeare, *The Tempest*, *The Winter's Tale*	
1611	Dekker and Middleton, *The Roaring Girl*; Jonson, *Catiline*	
c. 1611	Shakespeare, *Cymbeline*	
1612		Death of Prince Henry; execution of the Lancashire Witches; Heywood, *Apology for Actors* published
c. 1612	Webster, *The White Devil*	
1612–13	Webster, *The Duchess of Malfi*	
1613	Beaumont, *The Knight of the Burning Pestle*; Middleton, *A Chaste Maid in Cheapside*; Shakespeare and Fletcher, *Henry VIII, or All is True*, *The Two Noble Kinsmen*	Globe Theatre burns down; Marriage of Princess Elizabeth to Frederick, Elector Palatine; Children of the Revels and Lady Elizabeth's Men join
c. 1613–16	Middleton, *The Witch*	
1614	Jonson, *Bartholomew Fair*	The Hope built; second Globe built
c. 1616		The Phoenix used as a theatre
1616	Jonson, *The Devil Is an Ass*	Jonson's *Works* published in folio
1617		Fynes Morison, *Travels in Britain and Europe*
1617–21	Webster, *The Devil's Law-Case*	
1619		Banqueting House burns down; Inigo Jones begins work on new one
c. 1619	Beaumont and Fletcher, *The Maid's Tragedy*	

(*continued*)

Year	Plays	Events and other publications
1619–21	Fletcher, *The Island Princess*	
1621	Dekker, Ford and Rowley, *The Witch of Edmonton*	Fortune Theatre burns down
1622	Middleton and Rowley, *The Changeling*	
1622–3		Fortune Theatre rebuilt
1623		Shakespeare's plays published in folio
1623–4	Middleton, *Women Beware Women*	
1624	Middleton, *A Game at Chess*; Webster and Ford, *Keep the Widow Waking or The Late Murder of the Sone upon the Mother*	So-called 'Spanish Match' when Prince Charles's attempts at a marriage into the Spanish royal family founder
1625	Massinger, *A New Way to Pay Old Debts*	Death of James I; accession of Charles I and marriage by proxy to Princess Henrietta Maria of France
1626	Jonson, *The Staple of News*; Massinger, *The Roman Actor*	
1629	Brome, *The Northern Lass*; Jonson, *The New Inn*	Salisbury Court Theatre built; Charles I begins 11-year rule without calling Parliament (so-called 'Personal Rule')
1629–32	Brome, *The City Wit*	
1630?	Ford, *'Tis Pity She's a Whore*	
c. 1630–1	Heywood, *The Fair Maid of the West*	
1632	Ford, *The Broken Heart*; Jonson, *The Magnetic Lady*; Massinger, *The City Madam*; Shirley, *Hyde Park*; Brome, *The Weeding of Covent Garden*	
1632–3	Ford, *Love's Sacrifice*	
1632–4	Ford, *Perkin Warbeck*	

Year	Plays	Events and other publications
1633	Ford, *The Lover's Melancholy*; Jonson, *A Tale of a Tub*; Massinger, *The Guardian*; Montagu, *The Shepherd's Paradise*; Nabbes, *Tottenham Court, Covent Garden*; Shirley, *The Bird in a Cage*	Prynne's *Histriomastix* published
1634	Brome and Heywood, *The Late Lancashire Witches*; Shirley, *The Arcadia*	
1635	Brome, *The Queen and Concubine, The Sparagus Garden, A Mad Couple Well Matched*; Shirley, *The Lady of Pleasure*	
1636–8	Brome, *The Antipodes*	
1637	Jonson, *The Sad Shepherd*	Ship Money tax introduced
c. 1637–9	Brome, *A Mad Couple Well Matched*	
1639–40	Brome, *The Court Beggar*	
1641	Shirley, *The Cardinal*	
1641–2	Brome, *A Jovial Crew*	
1642	Shirley, *The Sisters*	King leaves London; hostilities begin between parliamentary opposition supporters and supporters of the crown; theatres closed by parliamentary ordinance
1644		Bulwer, *Chirologia, or The Natural Language of the Hand*; *Chironomia, or The Art of Manual Rhetoric*
1649		Execution of King Charles I in front of the Banqueting House, Whitehall

Notes

Preface

1 See my Introduction to the edition of the play in *CWBJ*, vol. VI, pp. 167–76.
2 Rosalyn L. Knutson, *Playing Companies and Commerce in Shakespeare's Time* (Cambridge University Press, 2001), p. 15.
3 Jean E. Howard, *Theater of a City: The Places of London Comedy, 1598–1642* (Philadelphia: University of Pennsylvania Press, 2007), pp. 19–20.
4 Janette Dillon, *The Cambridge Introduction to Early English Theatre* (Cambridge University Press, 2006), pp. 141, 161.
5 Howard, *Theater of a City*, p. 20.

Introduction

1 Fynes Morison, *An Itinerary . . . containing his ten yeeres travel through the twelve dominions*, 3 vols. (London, 1617); cited in Andrew Gurr, *The Shakespearean Stage, 1574–1642*, 3rd edn (Cambridge University Press, 1992), p. 10.
2 Dillon, *Cambridge Introduction to Early English Theatre*, pp. 161–2.
3 Andrew Gurr, *The Shakespeare Company, 1594–1642* (Cambridge University Press, 2004), p. 1.
4 Scott McMillin and Sally-Beth McLean, *The Queen's Men and Their Plays* (Cambridge University Press, 1998); and also Helen Ostovich, Holger Schott Syme and Andrew Griffin (eds.), *Locating the Queen's Men, 1583–1603: Material Practices and Conditions of Playing* (Aldershot: Ashgate, 2009). On Lyly, see Mike Pincombe, *The Plays of John Lyly: Eros and Eliza* (Manchester University Press, 1996).
5 Cf. Arthur Kinney, *Shakespeare By Stages: An Historical Introduction* (Oxford: Blackwell, 2003), p. 2.
6 See Nigel Smith, *Literature and Revolution in England, 1640–1660* (New Haven, CT: Yale University Press, 1994); and Susan Wiseman, *Drama and Politics in the English Civil War* (Cambridge University Press, 1998).
7 In taking this approach to my material I have my own strong sense of a critical legacy to acknowledge. The work of Muriel Bradbrook in the twentieth century was, to my mind, pioneering in the developmental case it made for the rise of formal playing traditions during this period and the kind of hands-on, experiential training that members of the

220

audience got in watching plays of all genres, often in close proximity, and performed by an increasingly well-known and recognised body of actors on the purpose-built stages. She argues in effect for an emergent set of theatrical competencies on the part of both practitioners and audiences, which is both persuasive and significant in identifying why theatre was the focus of such creative energy at this time. It has been fascinating and insightful to return to that work in the course of writing this book. See, in particular, M. C. Bradbrook, *The Rise of the Common Player: A Study of Actor and Society in Shakespeare's England* (London: Chatto & Windus, 1962), but also *Elizabethan Stage Conditions: A Study of Their Place in the Interpretation of Shakespeare's Plays* (Cambridge University Press, 1968). Her *John Webster, Citizen and Dramatist* (London: Weidenfeld & Nicolson, 1980) is to my mind a pioneering example of cultural geography in the attention it pays to the agency of the place, space and environment in which a playwright operates.

8 Cited in Glynne Wickham, Herbert Berry and William Ingram (eds.), *English Professional Theatre, 1530–1660* (Cambridge University Press, 2000), p. 535.

9 Dillon, *Cambridge Introduction to Early English Theatre*, p. 46.

10 For a more extensive discussion of the soundscapes of early modern theatre, see Bruce R. Smith, *The Acoustic World of Early Modern England: Attending to the 'O' Factor* (University of Chicago Press, 1999).

11 William Ingram, *The Business of Playing: The Beginnings of the Adult Professional Theatre in Elizabethan London* (Ithaca, NY: Cornell University Press, 1992).

12 The full title was in fact 'Master of the Royal Game of Bears, Bulls, and Mastiff Dogs'; see S. P. Cerasano, 'Henslowe, Philip (c. 1555–1616)', *Oxford Dictionary of National Biography* (Oxford University Press, 2004), online edn, www.oxforddnb.com/view/article/12991 (accessed 27 January 2013).

13 Cerasano, *ibid.*, notes the complex history of these papers, housed in the Wodehouse Library at Dulwich College, and what has gone missing over time as well as issues of forgeries. See also the online *Henslowe-Alleyn Digitisation Project*, www.henslowe-alleyn.org.uk/index.html (accessed 27 January 2013).

14 On the significance of Jonson's bricklaying background to his canon of work, see Laurie Ellinghausen, *Labor and Writing in Early Modern England, 1567–1667* (Aldershot: Ashgate, 2008), esp. pp. 63–92.

15 For a more extensive list and analysis, see Knutson, *Playing Companies*, p. 22; see also Kinney, *Shakespeare By Stages*, p. 34.

16 Carol Chillington Rutter (ed.), *Documents of the Rose Playhouse* (Manchester University Press, 1984), p. 136.

17 See Thomas Platter, *Travels in England, 1599*, trans. Clare Williams (London: Jonathan Cape, 1937), pp. 166–7. Platter is also a source for evidence on the different ticket entry prices at the outdoor theatres.

18 Stephen Greenblatt, *Renaissance Self-Fashioning: From More to Shakespeare* (University of Chicago Press, 1980), p. 195.

19 Susan Bennett, *Theatre Audiences: A Theory of Production and Reception*, 2nd edn (London: Routledge, 1987).

20 Dillon, *Cambridge Introduction to Early English Theatre*, p. 76.

21 Kinney, *Shakespeare By Stages*, p. vii.

22 Dillon, *Cambridge Introduction to Early English Theatre*, p. 49.

23 For a fuller account, see Gurr, *Shakespeare Company*, p. 6.

24 Lucy Munro, 'Music and Sound', in Richard Dutton (ed.), *The Oxford Handbook of Early Modern Theatre* (Oxford University Press, 2009), pp. 543–59 (549).

25 Martin White's work is especially helpful in this respect; see *Renaissance Drama in Action: An Introduction to Aspects of Theatre Practice and Performance* (London: Routledge, 1998), esp. pp. 147–50.

26 Rosalyn L. Knutson, *The Repertory of Shakespeare's Company, 1594–1613* (Fayetteville: University of Arkansas Press, 1991), and her *Playing Companies*. See also Lucy Munro, *Children of the Queen's Revels: A Jacobean Theatre Repertory* (Cambridge University Press, 2005).

27 Rutter (ed.), *Documents of the Rose Playhouse*, p. 94.

28 *Ibid.*, p. 94: 'Henslowe's schedule suggests that the schedule was not known in advance, for he entered his receipts day by day or he listed a column of dates, which he sometimes changed, and filled in the titles later.'

29 Simon Palfrey and Tiffany Stern, *Shakespeare in Parts* (Oxford University Press, 2007), discusses the ways in which actors received scripts of 'parts' with cue lines.

30 Gurr, *Shakespeare Company*, p. 15.

31 See Roy Strong, *The Cult of Elizabeth: Elizabethan Portraits and Pageantry*, 2nd edn (London: Pimlico, 1999); Philippa Berry, *Of Chastity and Power: Elizabethan Literature and the Unmarried Queen* (London: Routledge, 1994); and Helen Hackett, *Virgin Mother, Maiden Queen: Elizabeth I and the Cult of the Virgin Mary* (Basingstoke: Macmillan, 1996).

32 See, for example, Andrew Hadfield, *Literature, Travel and Colonial Writing in the English Renaissance, 1545–1625* (Oxford University Press, 2007).

33 See, for example, Janette Dillon, *Shakespeare and the Staging of English History* (Oxford University Press, 2012); and Warren Chernaik, *The Cambridge Introduction to Shakespeare's History Plays* (Cambridge University Press, 2007).

34 See, for example, Clare McManus's work on Anna's involvement in the Ben Jonson–Inigo Jones court masques that came to typify Jacobean court theatre, in *Women on the Renaissance Stage: Anna of Denmark and Female Masquing in the Stuart Court (1590–1619)* (Manchester University Press, 2002).

35 Plays of 1613 that deal with unexpected deaths of young heroes would include, for example, the Shakespeare and Fletcher collaboration, *The Two Noble Kinsmen*. See also Roy Strong, *Henry, Prince of Wales and England's Lost Renaissance* (London: Pimlico, 2000).

36 See Linda Levy Peck (ed.), *The Mental World of the Jacobean Court* (Cambridge University Press, 2005); and Curtis Perry, *The Making of Jacobean Culture: James I and the Renegotiation of Elizabethan Literary Practice* (Cambridge University Press, 1997).

37 Gurr, *Shakespeare Company*, pp. 42–5 (44).

38 See, for example, Martin Butler, *Theatre and Crisis, 1632–1642* (Cambridge University Press, 1984); and Julie Sanders, *Caroline Drama* (Plymouth: Northcote House, 1999).

39 Darryll Grantley, 'Middleton's Comedy and the Geography of London', in Suzanne Gossett (ed.), *Thomas Middleton in Context* (Cambridge University Press, 2011), pp. 28–36 (28).

40 Matthew Steggle, *Wars of the Theatres: The Poetics of Personation in the Age of Jonson* (Victoria, BC: English Literary Studies, 1998).

41 Tiffany Stern, '"On each Wall / And Corner Post": Playbills, Title-pages, and Advertising in Early Modern London', *English Literary Renaissance*, 36 (2006), 57–85.

42 Stubbes's *The Anatomy of Abuses* went through five editions between 1583 and 1595; see E. K. Chambers, *The Elizabethan Stage*, 4 vols. (Oxford: Clarendon Press, 1965), vol. IV, pp. 223–4; cited in Kinney, *Shakespeare By Stages*, p. 130.

43 Alfred Harbage, *As They Liked It* (London and New York: Macmillan, 1947), p. 3.

44 Brian Walsh, 'Performing Histories in Dekker's *Shoemaker's Holiday*', *Studies in English Literature*, 46 (2006), 323–46 (341).

Case study B An outdoor theatre repertoire: the Rose on Bankside

1 R. A. Foakes (ed.), *Henslowe's Diary*, 2nd edn (Cambridge University Press, 2002). See also Rutter (ed.), *Documents of the Rose Playhouse*.

2 S. P. Cerasano, 'Tamburlaine and Edward Alleyn's Ring', *Shakespeare Survey*, 47 (1994), 171–9. Alleyn is also discussed in detail in Chapter 1.

3 Andrew Gurr, *Shakespeare's Opposites: The Admiral's Company, 1594–1625* (Cambridge University Press, 2009), p. 31; James Knowles, Introduction to his edition with Eugene Giddens of *The Roaring Girl and Other City Comedies* (Oxford University Press, 2001), p. xi.

4 This estimate is Gurr's, *Shakespeare's Opposites*, p. 2.

5 S. P. Cerasano, 'The Geography of Henslowe's Diary', *Shakespeare Quarterly*, 56 (2005), 328–53; and Julian Bowsher and Patricia Miller, *The Rose and the Globe: Playhouses of Tudor Bankside, Southwark: Excavations 1988–91* (Museum of London, 2009).

6 Gurr, *Shakespeare's Opposites*, p. 157.

7 James Shapiro, '"Tragedies naturally performed": Kyd's Representation of Violence', in David Scott Kastan and Peter Stallybrass (eds.), *Staging the Renaissance: Reinterpretations of Elizabethan and Jacobean Drama* (London: Routledge, 1991), pp. 99–113. Peele's play is probably that referred to in Henslowe's *Diary* as 'Muly Molucco'.

8 See Gurr, *Shakespeare's Opposites*, pp. 132–3.

1   Tragedy

1 Cf. Farah Karim Cooper and Tiffany Stern (eds.), *Shakespeare's Theatres and the Effects of Performance* (London: Arden Shakespeare, 2013).

2 See Catherine Belsey, *The Subject of Tragedy: Identity and Experience in Renaissance Drama* (London: Routledge, 1991).

3 A. C. Bradley, *Shakespearean Tragedy: Lectures on 'Hamlet', 'Othello', 'King Lear', 'Macbeth'* (London: Penguin, 1991; 1st edn 1904), p. 25.

4 L. C. Knights, 'How Many Children had Lady Macbeth? An Essay in the Theory and Practice of Shakespeare Criticism', in *Explorations* (London: Chatto & Windus, 1945), pp. 1–39.

5 Carol Chillington Rutter, 'Remind Me: How Many Children Had Lady Macbeth?', *Shakespeare Survey 57* (2004), 38–53 (38).

6 Mario Di Gangi, *Sexual Types: Embodiment, Agency and Dramatic Character from Shakespeare to Shirley* (Philadelphia: University of Pennsylvania Press, 2011); and the Continuum series on *Character Studies*, especially the volume on *Twelfth Night* by Graham Atkin (London and New York: Continuum, 2008), and Michael Davies, *Hamlet: Character Studies* (London and New York: Continuum, 2008).

7 Greenblatt, *Renaissance Self-Fashioning*, p. 212; and on 'cultural poetics', see his 'Towards a Poetics of Culture', *Southern Review*, 20 (1987), 3–15. For an overview of the influence and range of Greenblatt's criticism, see Mark Robson, *Stephen Greenblatt* (London: Routledge, 2007).

8 See S. P. Cerasano, 'Alleyn, Edward (1566–1626)', *Oxford Dictionary of National Biography* (Oxford University Press, 2004), online edn, www.oxforddnb.com/view/article/398 (accessed 28 January 2013), and her 'Tamburlaine and Edward Alleyn's Ring'. My thanks also to Tiffany Stern for discussions of this topic.

9 For a related argument, see Gurr, *Shakespeare's Opposites*, esp. pp. 1–2.

10 The oft-made claim that a real devil had appeared onstage at the Bel Savage Inn during a performance of *Doctor Faustus* was repeated in print by William Prynne in his 1633 antitheatricalist tract, *Histriomastix*. See Genevieve Guenther, 'Why Devils Came When Faustus Called Them', *Modern Philology*, 109 (2011), 46–70 (46).

11 Cited in Bradbrook, *Rise of the Common Player*, p. 200. On Donne and theatregoing, see also Anthony B. Dawson and Paul Yachnin, *The Culture of Playgoing in Shakespeare's England: A Collaborative Debate* (Cambridge University Press, 2001), p. 39. 'The Calm' was a poem much valued by Jonson who mentions it in the *Informations to William Drummond of Hawthornden* (*CWBJ*, vol. V, p. 365.7) and quotes it in a metatheatrical context in the fourth act of *The New Inn* in 1629 (4.4.246).

12 A Hamlet competition that Bradbrook mentions in *Rise of the Common Player*, p. 207, may have involved Burbage himself. In 1605 provincial players were invited to compete with a London player in the role.

13 The phrase 'mighty line' was coined by Jonson in his 1623 folio elegy on Shakespeare.

14 See Harry Levin, *The Overreacher: A Study of Christopher Marlowe* (Cambridge, MA: Harvard University Press, 1952).

15 On the gradual training and professionalising of English audiences as well as players between the late sixteenth and early seventeenth centuries, see Bradbrook, *Rise of the Common Player*.

16 Emma Smith, 'Shakespeare and Early Modern Tragedy', in Garrett A. Sullivan, Jr and Emma Smith (eds.), *The Cambridge Companion to English Renaissance Tragedy* (Cambridge University Press, 2010), pp. 132–49 (esp. 138–42).

17 Cf. Adrian Streete, *Protestantism and Drama in Early Modern England* (Cambridge University Press, 2011).

18 Thomas Healy, '*Doctor Faustus*', in Patrick Cheney (ed.), *The Cambridge Companion to Christopher Marlowe* (Cambridge University Press, 2004), pp. 174–92 (174).

19 *Ibid.*, pp. 180–5; Tom Rutter, *The Cambridge Introduction to Christopher Marlowe* (Cambridge University Press, 2012), pp. 174–92; and Mark Thornton Burnett, '*Doctor Faustus*: Dramaturgy and Disturbance', in Sullivan, Jr and Smith (eds.), *Cambridge Companion to English Renaissance Tragedy*, pp. 163–73.

20 Healy, '*Doctor Faustus*', p. 177.

21 Aristotle, *Poetics*, trans. Malcolm Heath (London: Penguin, 1996).

22 Greenblatt, *Renaissance Self-Fashioning*, p. 216.

23 Bradbrook, *John Webster*, p. 11.

24 See, for example, Robert Ornstein, 'Marlowe and God: The Tragic Theology of *Doctor Faustus*', *PMLA*, 83:5 (1968), 1378–85.

25 On exits and entrances, see Andrew Gurr and Mariko Ichikawa, *Staging in Shakespeare's Theatres* (Oxford University Press, 2000), pp. 72–95.

26 The Royal Shakespeare Company production directed by Barry Kyle in the Swan Theatre in 1987 did exactly this; see J. R. Mulryne and Margaret Shewring, 'The Repertoire of the Swan', in Mulryne and Shewring (eds.), *This Golden Round: The Royal Shakespeare Company at the Swan* (Stratford-upon-Avon: Mulryne and Shewring Ltd, 1989), pp. 23–36.

27 Andrew Power, 'What the Hell is Under the Stage? Trapdoor Use in the English Senecan Tradition', *English*, 60 (2011), 276–96.

28 This section draws directly on Power's analysis of this scene, *ibid.*, pp. 291–2.

29 The edition of *Gorboduc* referred to is in T. W. Craik (ed.), *Minor Elizabethan Tragedies* (London: J. M. Dent & Sons, 1974).

30 Tiffany Stern, *Making Shakespeare: From Stage or Page* (London: Routledge, 2004), p. 25. Cf. Power, 'What the Hell', p. 277.

31 Cf. Power, 'What the Hell', p. 295.

32 White, *Renaissance Drama in Action*, pp. 148–51. My thanks to Martin for numerous subsequent discussions on this topic.

33 Kim Solga, 'Playing *The Changeling* Architecturally', in Susan Bennett and Mary Polito (eds.), *Performing Environments: Site Specificity in Medieval and Early Modern Drama* (Basingstoke: Palgrave Macmillan, forthcoming).

34 Bradbrook, *John Webster*, p. 97.

35 Heather Hirschfeld, 'Collaborating Across Generations: Thomas Heywood, Richard Brome, and the Production of *The Late Lancashire Witches*', *Journal of Medieval and Early Modern Studies*, 30:2 (2000), 339–74.

Case study C Opening scenes

1 John Donne, *Selected Poetry*, ed. John Carey (Oxford University Press, 1996).

2 See, for example, Margaret Fetzer, *John Donne's Performances: Sermons, Poems, Letters, and Devotions* (Manchester University Press, 2010); and Hugh Adlington, Peter McCullough and Emma Rhatigan (eds.), *The Oxford Handbook of the Early Modern Sermon* (Oxford University Press, 2011).

3 For a recent exploration of beginnings, see 'Section 1: Close Reading Beginnings', in Russ McDonald, Nicholas D. Nace and Travis D. Williams (eds.), *Shakespeare Up Close: Reading Early Modern Texts* (London: Arden Shakespeare, 2012), pp. 1–24.

4 The Royal Shakespeare Company took exactly this decision in the staging of the play in the Swan Theatre, Stratford-upon-Avon, in 1987. See Mulryne and Shewring, 'The Repertoire of the Swan', pp. 32–3.

Case study D Staging violence and the space of the stage

1 Andreas Höfele, *Stage, Stake and Scaffold: Humans and Animals in Shakespeare's Theatre* (Oxford University Press, 2011), p. 208.

2 On the different textual versions and variants of *King Lear*, see Gary Taylor and Michael Warren (eds.), *The Division of the Kingdoms: Shakespeare's Two Versions of 'King Lear'* (Oxford University Press, 1983).

3 Höfele, *Stage, Stake and Scaffold*, p. 13.

4 *Ibid.*, p. 3.

5 S. P. Cerasano, 'The Master of the Bears in Art and Enterprise', *Medieval and Renaissance Drama in England*, 5 (1991), 195–209.

6 Höfele, *Stage, Stake and Scaffold*, p. 7.

7 See Christine Eccles, *The Rose Theatre* (London: Routledge, 1990), p. 230; cited in Höfele, *Stage, Stake and Scaffold*, p. 1, note 1.

8 Höfele, *Stage, Stake and Scaffold*, pp. 45–6.

9 Julie Sanders, *The Cultural Geography of Early Modern Drama, 1620–1650* (Cambridge University Press, 2011), p. 5; and Mark Brayshay, 'Waits, Musicians, Bearwards, and Players: The Inter-Urban Road, Travel and Performances of Itinerant Entertainers in Sixteenth and Seventeenth Century England', *Journal of Historical Geography*, 31:3 (2005), 430–58.

10 Quoted by Höfele, *Stage, Stake and Scaffold*, p. 11; cited from *Paul Hentzner's Travels in England, during the Reign of Queen Elizabeth*, trans. Horace Walpole (London: Edward Jeffery, 1797), p. 30.

11 Thomas Dekker, *Worke for Armourers, or The peace is broken* (London, 1609), sig. B1^{v}–B2^{r}.

12 *Ibid.*, sig. B1^{v}.

13 *Ibid.*, sig. B2^{r}; cf. Höfele, *Stage, Stake and Scaffold*, pp. 59–60.

2 Revenge drama

1 John Frow, *Genre* (London: Routledge, 2006), p. 10; and Tzvetan Todorov, *Genres in Discourse*, trans. Catherine Porter (Cambridge University Press, 1990), p. 18.

2 Jacques Derrida, 'The Law of Genre', trans. Avital Ronell, *Glyph*, 7 (1980), 202–32 (230).

3 See Steven Mullaney, *The Place of the Stage: Licence, Play and Power in Renaissance England* (Ann Arbor: University of Michigan Press, 1995), on the London liberties and the link between the playhouses on Bankside and the liberty of Southwark, as well as the Blackfriars liberty in the city, where the private theatre of the same name was established. On the broader culture of spaces and communities such as the Inns of Court, see Theodore Leinwand's Introduction to his edition of *Michaelmas Term* in *Oxford Middleton*, p. 334.

4 For details of this close connection to performance, see the *REED* volumes on the Inns of Court: Alan H. Nelson and John R. Elliott, Jr (eds.), *Records of Early English Drama: Inns of Court*, 3 vols. (Cambridge: D. S. Brewer, 2010).

5 Lorna Hutson, *The Invention of Suspicion: Law and Mimesis in Shakespeare and Renaissance Drama* (Oxford University Press, 2011).

6 Marston's play was one of a cluster using this dramatic device of the disguised duke come back to test the community over which he previously ruled; several commentators have observed that these plays occur around the time of the new Jacobean regime and can therefore be seen as a mechanism for exploring notions of good government on the commercial stage. For other examples, see Shakespeare's *Measure for Measure* (1603–4) and Jonson's comic inversion of the idea with his disguised Justice of the Peace, Overdo, who seeks to expose the 'enormities in the fair' (2.1.31–2) in *Bartholomew Fair* (1614). Since a number of these plays enjoyed court as well as commercial performances, this would suggest that James VI and I tolerated debate of this kind, at least to a certain degree within a theatrical context. For a history and exposition of the genre, see Kevin Quarmby, *The Disguised Ruler in Shakespeare and His Contemporaries* (Aldershot: Ashgate, 2012).

7 Tanya Pollard observes that poison as a substance was especially associated with the revenge drama genre; see her 'Drugs, Remedies, Poison and the Theatre', in Gossett (ed.), *Thomas Middleton in Context*, pp. 287–394 (287), and also her *Drugs and Theatre in Early Modern England* (Oxford University Press, 2005).

8 Sir Francis Bacon, *Essayes and counsels, civil and moral whereunto is newly added a table of the colours of good and evil* (London, 1664), p. 19.

9 Q2 in *Hamlet* references indicates additional material found in the second quarto printing of the play.

10 Compare the scene in Middleton's 1623–4 *Women Beware Women* where Bianca's mother-in-law participates in a grim chess game at the court onstage with Livia while she allows her son's wife to be seduced by the all-powerful, all-wealthy Florentine Duke in the above stage space.

11 See Gossett, Introduction to *Philaster*, p. 3.

12 *The Malcontent* exists in two distinct forms as a result of adaptations and additions commissioned when the play passed from the children's company context into the hands of the King's Men. See discussion in Case Study E.

13 Sophie Tomlinson, *Women on Stage in Stuart Drama* (Cambridge University Press, 2005), p. 120.

14 Yearling, Introduction to *The Cardinal*, p. 36.

15 Tomlinson, *Women on Stage in Stuart Drama*, p. 14.

16 *Ibid.*, p. 136, on the Ford text in particular in relation to *The Cardinal.* There is a side comment to make here about the intertheatricality implicit in staging a character suffering from melancholy; this would invoke a whole series of plays from the period, and not least female roles. Many were inspired by the publication of Robert Burton's *The Anatomy of Melancholy* in 1628: for example, Ford's *The Lover's Melancholy* performed that same year, Jonson's *The New Inn* (1629) and Brome's *The Northern Lass* (1629).

17 Tomlinson, *Women on Stage in Stuart Drama*, p. 141.

18 Yearling, Introduction to *The Cardinal*, p. 8.

19 Tomlinson describes the 'courtly regime of observation and performance' witnessed in *The Cardinal* (*Women on Stage in Stuart Drama*, p. 140).

Case study E 'Here, in the Friars': the second Blackfriars indoor playhouse

1 The quotation 'Here, in the Friars' is from *The Alchemist*, 1.1.17. On the locatedness of this play in the Blackfriars parish, see Chapter 5, and also R. L. Smallwood, '"Here in the Friars": Immediacy and Theatricality in *The Alchemist*', *Review of English Studies*, 32:126 (1981), 142–60.

2 QC in references to *The Malcontent* indicates the third quarto print edition of the play which incorporated the additional materials commissioned by the King's Men.

3 For an excellent discussion of this phenomenon of entr'acte action, see Mark Hutchings, 'De Flores Between the Acts', *Studies in Theatre and Performance*, 31:1 (2011), 95–112.

4 Martin White makes the point that indoor theatres probably increased lighting with candles just prior to a scene that required 'darkness' so that a reduction in illumination would create the necessary effect (*Renaissance Drama in Action*, p. 150).

5 David Lindley, 'Blackfriars, Music and Masque: Theatrical Contexts of the Last Plays', in Catherine M. S. Alexander (ed.), *The Cambridge Companion to Shakespeare's Last Plays* (Cambridge University Press, 2009), pp. 29–46.

6 Michelle O'Callaghan, 'Thomas Middleton and the Early Modern Theatre', in Ton Hoenselaars (ed.), *The Cambridge Companion to Shakespeare and Contemporary Dramatists* (Cambridge University Press, 2012), pp. 165–80 (175); and see White, *Renaissance Drama in Action*, and his Arts and Humanities Research Council funded DVD project *The Chamber of Demonstrations*. I am indebted also to the work of Sarah Dustagheer and her 'Repertory and the Production of Theatre Space at the Globe and the Blackfriars, 1599–1613', PhD thesis, King's College, University of London (2012), and to discussions with Sarah on this topic.

7 Jean E. Howard, 'Bettrice's Monkey: Staging Exotica in Early Modern London Comedy', in Jyotsna G. Singh (ed.), *A Companion to the Global Renaissance* (Oxford: Wiley-Blackwell, 2009), pp. 325–39.

8 See my own '"The day's sports devised in the Inn": Jonson's *The New Inn* and Theatrical Politics', *Modern Language Review*, 91:3 (1996), 545–60.

9 The first play was, in 1634, Philip Massinger's *Cleander*; in 1636 she saw, among other productions, Lodowick Carlell's *Arvirargus and Philicia* and in 1638 William Davenant's

The Unfortunate Lovers. Carlell was part of a new breed of courtier dramatists who were seeing their work staged in the public theatres. See Karen Britland, 'Queen Henrietta Maria's Theatrical Patronage', in Erin Griffey (ed.), *Henrietta Maria: Piety, Politics and Patronage* (Aldershot: Ashgate, 2008), pp. 57–72 (58, note 7).

Case study F The social life of things: skulls on the stage

1 Lina Perkins Wilder, *Shakespeare's Memory Theatre: Recollection, Properties, and Character* (Cambridge University Press, 2010), p. 2.
2 Dillon, *Cambridge Introduction to Early English Theatre*, p. 101.
3 Michael Neill, *Issues of Death: Mortality and Identity in English Renaissance Tragedy* (Oxford: Clarendon Press, 1997).
4 Arjun Appadurai (ed.), *The Social Life of Things: Commodities in Cultural Perspective* (Cambridge University Press, 1986), pp. 3–63; see also Jonathan Gil Harris and Natasha Korda (eds.), *Staged Properties in Early Modern English Drama* (Cambridge University Press, 2002); and Catherine Richardson, *Shakespeare and Material Culture* (Oxford University Press, 2011).
5 Steven Mullaney, 'Affective Technologies: Toward an Emotional Logic of the Elizabethan Stage', in Mary Floyd Wilson and Garrett A. Sullivan, Jr (eds.), *Environment and Embodiment in Early Modern England* (Basingstoke: Palgrave Macmillan, 2007), pp. 71–89 (76).
6 Philip Henslowe's inventories for the properties held and used by the Rose Theatre provide another tantalising glimpse into the practical operations of stage props at this time; see Rutter (ed.), *Documents of the Rose Playhouse*, pp. 136–7.
7 Peter Womack, *English Renaissance Drama* (Oxford: Blackwell, 2006), p. 179.

3   Histories

1 See various entries for the 1590s in Foakes (ed.), *Henslowe's Diary*, pp. 16–20; cited in Janette Dillon, *Shakespeare and the Staging of English History*, p. 2.
2 Sidney regarded *Gorboduc* as a much more satisfactory rendering of tragedy than most, since it was 'full of stately speeches and well sounding phrases'; cited in Lawrence Danson, *Shakespeare's Dramatic Genres* (Oxford University Press, 2000), p. 35.
3 Many actors in the part of Buckingham bring this point home by including the real-life audience in the pleas to Richard in the gallery space to accept the crown; the Shakespeare's Globe performance in 2012 was a perfect case in point.
4 Cf. Peter Stallybrass and Ann Jones, *Renaissance Clothing and the Materials of Memory* (Cambridge University Press, 2000).
5 John Jowett, Introduction to William Shakespeare, *Richard III*, ed. Jowett (Oxford University Press, 2000), p. 27.
6 *Ibid.*, p. 27.
7 *Ibid.*, pp. 27–8.

8 See Robert Weimann, 'Performance-Game and Representation in *Richard III*', in Edward Pechter (ed.), *Textual and Theatrical Shakespeare: Questions of Evidence* (University of Iowa Press, 1996), pp. 66–85.

9 Danson, *Shakespeare's Dramatic Genres*, p. 98.

10 Lomax, Introduction to *Ford*, p. xxii.

11 Meg F. Pearson writes of Richard II's 'improvised self-deposition' as the key theatrical moment of Shakespeare's play in her 'Audience as Witness in *Edward II*', in Jennifer Low and Nova Myhill (eds.), *Imagining the Audience in Early Modern Drama, 1558–1642* (Basingstoke: Palgrave Macmillan, 2011), pp. 93–111 (93).

12 *Ibid.*, pp. 103, 93.

13 For a more detailed exposition of this topic in Shakespeare's histories, see Phyllis Rackin and Jean E. Howard, *Engendering a Nation: A Feminist Account of Shakespeare's English Histories* (London: Routledge, 1997).

14 Lomax, Introduction to *Ford*, p. xxiii; see also Lisa Hopkins, *John Ford's Political Theatre* (Manchester University Press, 1994). On Caroline drama and women's roles more generally, see my own *Caroline Drama*.

15 Rackin and Howard, *Engendering a Nation*, pp. 111–12.

16 *Ibid.*, p. 164.

17 Revels editor Richard Rowland notes in his edition of the play that this mention of Nell's Lichfield schooling was a 1590s reference rather than one apposite to the fifteenth-century setting of the play, noting John Brinsley's account of his 1590s experience as a schoolmaster in the Midlands when most villages and market towns began to make schooling available to both boys and girls (*A Consolation for our Grammar Schools*, London, 1622). This marks Hobs out as a very enlightened Staffordshire tanner. See *Edward IV*, p. 147.

18 Dillon, *Shakespeare and the Staging of English History*, p. 5.

19 See Rowland, Introduction to *Edward IV*, *passim*.

20 As well as being a lovingly detailed introduction to the tanning trade that in fact existed in close proximity in the 1590s to the Boar's Head where the play was first performed (residue from bark is essential to the tanning process; and for more on the tanning trade, see Rowland, Introduction to *Edward IV*, esp. pp. 29, 36–8), this exchange parallels Hobs with Jane Shore herself, who later in the play will reject Rufford's demand for a trade monopoly, an action for which he will take bitter revenge in the second part.

21 Cf. Annabel Patterson, *Shakespeare and the Popular Voice* (Oxford: Blackwell, 1989).

22 Danson, *Shakespeare's Dramatic Genres*, p. 90.

23 On chorography, albeit from a rather doggedly nationalist perspective, see Richard Helgerson, *Forms of Nationhood: Elizabethan Writing of England* (University of Chicago Press, 1994); and for a more recent account of the ways in which authors sought to 'write' the English countryside and its road and river networks into being, see Andrew McRae, *Literature and Domestic Travel in Early Modern England* (Cambridge University Press, 2010).

24 Rackin and Howard, *Engendering a Nation*, p. 161.

25 Dillon, *Shakespeare and the Staging of English History*, p. 5.

26 Sonnets were also in vogue in the 1590s and Shakespeare in particular appears to have experimented with them in dramatic settings (see Chapter 4 on comedy).

27 Dillon offers a strong reading of this moment and the 'function' of the Scrivener, in *Shakespeare and the Staging of English History*, p. 18.

28 *Ibid.*, pp. 61, 63.

Case study G Title pages and plays in print

1 Alan Farmer, 'The Playhouse in the Printing House', *Shakespeare and the Book*, www.ccnmtl.columbia.edu/projects/shakespeareandthebook (last accessed 11 January 2013).

2 Stern connects playbills and title pages in this regard in terms of their physical and visible 'intrusion' into city space ('On Each Wall / And Corner Post', esp. pp. 84–5). See also her recent book-length study, *Documents of Performance in Early Modern England* (Cambridge University Press, 2009). See in addition Eleanor F. Shevlin, '"To Reconcile Book and Title and Make 'em Kin to One Another": The Evolution of the Title's Contractual Function', *Book History*, 2 (1999), 42–77 (48).

3 Thomas Postlewait, 'Eyewitnesses to History: Visual Evidence for Theatre in Early Modern England', in Dutton (ed.), *Oxford Handbook of Early Modern Theatre*, pp. 575–606. This article is both wonderfully suggestive and admirably cautious about the use of visual artefacts as evidence.

4 *Ibid.*, p. 602; and see Dillon, *Shakespeare and the Staging of English History*, p. 8, on 'speaking pictures'.

4   Comedy, pastoral and romantic

1 Howard, *Theater of a City*, p. 20.

2 *Ibid.*, p. 19.

3 Mary Thomas Crane, *Shakespeare's Brain: Reading with Cognitive Theory* (Princeton University Press, 2000), esp. pp. 42–50.

4 Of course there is a grim extension of this tendency to realise Petrarchan love metaphors physically onstage: Giovanni carrying the heart of Annabella, the sister he has incestuously desired with such tragic consequences, on a dagger at the close of Ford's *'Tis Pity She's a Whore*.

5 On Ovidian influences on early modern drama, see Jonathan Bate, *Shakespeare and Ovid* (Oxford: Clarendon Press, 1994); and Liz Oakley-Brown, *Ovid and the Cultural Politics of Translation in Early Modern England* (Aldershot: Ashgate, 2006).

6 Jane Kingsley-Smith, *Shakespeare's Drama of Exile* (Basingstoke: Palgrave Macmillan, 2003), p. 100.

7 *Ibid.*

8 See *ibid.*, Chapter 1, for a fuller discussion of these points.

9 My subtitle is a knowing allusion to William Empson's seminal work on pastoral which discussed Shakespeare's engagement with the mode at length, *Some Versions of Pastoral: A Study of Pastoral Form in Literature* (London: Chatto & Windus, 1966).

10 Kingsley-Smith, *Shakespeare's Drama of Exile*, pp. 166–7.

11 Arthur Kinney, 'John Lyly and the University Wits', in Hoenselaars (ed.), *Cambridge Companion to Shakespeare and Contemporary Dramatists*, pp. 1–18 (2).

12 Phyllis Rackin, 'Androgyny, Mimesis, and the Marriage of the Boy Heroine', *PMLA*, 102 (1989), 29–41.

13 Kinney, 'John Lyly', p. 2.

14 On the 'original practices' approach at the reconstructed Globe theatre on London's Bankside, see Christie Carson and Farah Karim Cooper (eds.), *Shakespeare's Globe: A Theatrical Experiment* (Cambridge University Press, 2008).

15 Laura Levine, *Men in Women's Clothing: Anti-Theatricality and Effeminization, 1579– 1642* (Cambridge University Press, 1994).

16 Peter Berek suggests in his article 'Cross-Dressing, Gender, and Absolutism in the Beaumont and Fletcher Plays', *Studies in English Literature*, 44 (2004), 359–77, that Shakespeare's cross-dressing was 'often a strategy for enhancing a woman's ability to discover her own mind' (p. 360), though he goes on to contrast this with what he views as a rather more contained version of the agency of cross-dressing in Beaumont and Fletcher's work.

17 Hunter and Bevington, Introduction to *Galatea*, p. 16.

18 Philip Massinger, *The Guardian* (London, 1633).

19 See, for example, Richard Wilson, 'Like the Old Robin Hood: *As You Like It* and the Enclosure Riots', in his *Will Power: Essays on Shakespearean Authority* (Detroit, MI: Wayne State University Press, 1992), pp. 66–87.

20 For more detailed discussion of this topic, see Rosemary Gaby, 'Of Vagabonds and Commonwealths: *Beggars' Bush, A Jovial Crew*, and *The Sisters*', *Studies in English Literature 1500–1900*, 34 (1994), 401–24; and Julie Sanders, 'Beggars' Commonwealths on the Pre-Civil War stage', *Modern Language Review*, 97 (2002), 1–14. See also related discussion in Butler, *Theatre and Crisis*, pp. 254–64.

21 On early modern theories of hospitality, see Felicity Heal, *Hospitality in Early Modern England* (Oxford: Clarendon Press, 1990); and see also the Introduction to the edition of *A Jovial Crew* by Richard Cave et al. in *Brome Online*.

22 Patricia Fumerton, *Unsettled: The Culture of Mobility and the Working Poor* (University of Chicago Press, 2006); and also the thought-provoking conclusion to Kingsley-Smith, *Shakespeare's Drama of Exile*, p. 175, where she argues that motifs of displacement and exile take on new resonances in the post-Reformation context.

23 Sanders, *Cultural Geography*, pp. 48–52, 84–99; and see Lucy Munro, *Archaic Style in English Literature, 1590–1674* (Cambridge University Press, forthcoming) for discussion of this play in the context of pastoral, linguistic and geographical traditions.

Case study H The boy actor: body, costume and disguise

1 Rutter (ed.), *Documents of the Rose Playhouse*, pp. 135–6.

2 Gurr and Ichikawa, *Staging in Shakespeare's Theatres*, pp. 53–4. On costume, see also Stallybrass and Jones, *Renaissance Clothing*; and Eleanor Lowe, 'Clothing and Fashion in Jonson's Plays', in Julie Sanders (ed.), *Ben Jonson in Context* (Cambridge University Press, 2010), pp. 330–7.

3 Farah Karim Cooper, 'Disguise and Identity in the Plays of Middleton', in Gossett (ed.), *Thomas Middleton in Context*, pp. 279–86 (280).

4 On the counterpart threshold of the prologue in early modern theatre, see Douglas Bruster and Robert Weimann, *Prologues to Shakespeare's Theatre: Performance and Liminality in Early Modern Drama* (Cambridge University Press, 2008).

5 Peter Erickson's 'Sexual Politics and the Social Structure in *As You Like It*', *Massachusetts Review*, 23:1 (1982), 65–83, is a useful working example of this strand of contained readings.

5   City comedies

1 Walsh, 'Performing Histories', p. 323.

2 On Jonson's names and comic nomenclature more generally, see Anne Barton, *The Names of Comedy* (Oxford: Clarendon Press, 1990).

3 Thomas Nashe, *Pierce Pennilesse, His Supplication to the Devil*, ed. G. B. Harrison (Edinburgh University Press, 1966), pp. 325–6; cited in Walsh, 'Performing Histories', p. 326.

4 Christopher Burlinson, 'Money and Consumerism', in Sanders (ed.), *Ben Jonson in Context*, pp. 281–8 (281).

5 *Ibid.*, p. 285.

6 Howard, *Theater of a City*, pp. 138–9.

7 Rebecca Ann Bach, *Colonial Transformations: The Cultural Production of the New Atlantic World, 1580–1640* (Basingstoke: Palgrave, 2000).

8 Donald Lupton, *London and the country carbonadoed and quartered into seuerall characters* (London, 1632), sig. C2ᵛ (p. 20).

9 *Ibid.*, sig. B1ʳ (p. 7).

10 On the cultural geography of this scene, see my edition of the play in *Brome Online* and discussion of it in my *Cultural Geography*, pp. 33–5.

11 Natasha Korda, *Labor's Lost: Women's Work and the Early Modern English Stage* (Philadelphia: University of Pennsylvania Press, 2011), p. 14.

12 Lacy tells Firk to bring Eyre to 'den signe van swannekin', the sign of the Swan' (7.10). John Taylor's *Carriers Cosmography* (London, 1636) listed this inn as one 'inhabited only by Dutchmen' (sig. D7); this point derives from Smallwood and Wells's edition of *The Shoemaker's Holiday* (p. 117).

13 Korda, *Labor's Lost*, p. 2.

14 There is a fascinating kinship between this scene and that in which the disguised King enters the shop of goldsmith Matthew Shore with the intention of wooing his wife, Jane, in Heywood's *Edward IV, Part 1* (scene 17); parallel exchanges on what is for sale and

what can be purchased at a price take place here and connect forward with other city comedy workshop scenes analysed in this chapter, such as those in Middleton's *A Chaste Maid in Cheapside*.

15 Janette Dillon, *Theatre, Court, and City, 1595–1610: Drama and Social Space in London* (Cambridge University Press, 2000); Darryll Grantley, *London in Early Modern English Drama: Representing the Built Environment* (Basingstoke: Palgrave Macmillan, 2008); Howard, *Theater of a City*; and Adam Zucker, *The Places of Wit in Early Modern English Comedy* (Cambridge University Press, 2011).

16 Cf. Howard, *Theater of a City*, p. 21.

17 For a more detailed discussion of this phenomenon, see Sanders, *Cultural Geography*, pp. 226–33.

18 Smallwood and Wells, Introduction to *The Shoemaker's Holiday*, p. 14. See also Smallwood's seminal place-specific reading of Jonson's *The Alchemist*, 'Here in the Friars', *passim*.

19 Walsh, 'Performing Histories', counts thirty-five real locales and place names in this playtext (p. 339).

20 Richard Sennett, *The Craftsman* (London: Allen Lane, 2008); David Scott Kastan, 'Workshop and/as Playhouse: Comedy and Commerce in *The Shoemaker's Holiday*', *Studies in Philology*, 84:3 (1987), 324–37; and Paul S. Seaver, 'Thomas Dekker's *The Shoemaker's Holiday*: The Artisanal World', in David L. Smith, Richard Strier and David Bevington (eds.), *The Theatrical City: Culture, Theatre and Politics in London, 1576–1649* (Cambridge University Press, 1995), pp. 87–100.

21 For a parallel account of the life of temporary lodgers in London at this time, see Charles Nicholl's suggestive biography of Shakespeare's sojourn in Silver Street, lodging with the Mountjoy family: *The Lodger: Shakespeare on Silver Street* (London: Penguin, 2008). This property was itself a workshop where this French Huguenot family of tire-workers plied their trade.

22 Kathleen McLuskie explores the practical and philosophical premises of staging shopping in her essay 'The Shopping Complex: Materiality and the Renaissance Theatre', in Pechter (ed.), *Textual and Theatrical Shakespeare*, pp. 86–101.

23 Cited in Walsh, 'Performing Histories', p. 324.

Case study I The dramaturgy of scenes

1 The edition of this play used is that edited by Simon Trussler for the Royal Shakespeare Company production of the play (London: Methuen, 1987).

2 On exits and entrances, and flow, see Gurr and Ichikawa, *Staging in Shakespeare's Theatres*, pp. 72–95; and on the use of methods of 'defining by analogy' and juxtaposition, see Kinney, *Shakespeare By Stages*, p. 20.

3 Peter Holland, *English Shakespeares: Shakespeare on the English Stage in the 1990s* (Cambridge University Press, 1997), p. 4. He describes early modern drama in terms of a 'single arch' and the 'central plateau' as 'a long sequence of unbreakable action across the centre

of the play'. See also Emrys Jones, *Scenic Form in Shakespeare* (Oxford University Press, 1971).

Case study J Collaborative writing or the literary workshop

1 Sennett, *The Craftsman*, pp. 51, 64.
2 There is a wonderful, exuberant list of many of these professions in Natasha Korda's 'Trade, Work and Workers', in Gossett (ed.), *Thomas Middleton in Context*, pp. 75–82 (79–80).
3 Ton Hoenselaars, 'Shakespeare: Colleagues, Collaborators, Co-authors', in Hoenselaars (ed.), *Cambridge Companion to Shakespeare and Contemporary Dramatists*, pp. 97–119 (99).
4 James P. Bednarz, 'Between Collaboration and Rivalry: Dekker and Marston's Coactive Drama', *Ben Jonson Journal*, 10 (2003), 209–34. See also Heather Hirschfield, '"For the Author's Credit": Issues of Authorship in English Renaissance Drama', in Dutton (ed.), *Oxford Handbook of Early Modern Theatre*, pp. 441–55.
5 Hoenselaars, 'Shakespeare', p. 99.
6 On Jonson and *The Spanish Tragedy*, see Clara Calvo, 'Thomas Kyd and the Elizabethan Blockbuster', in Hoenselaars (ed.), *Cambridge Companion to Shakespeare and Contemporary Dramatists*, pp. 19–33 (27). The specific references in Henslowe's diary appear in September 1601 and June 1602 and refer to payments to Jonson for 'writting of his adicians in geronymo' and for 'new adicyons for Jeronymo' (the play was often referred to by the name of its protagonist, which suggests in itself what worked best on the stage and in audience memories); Foakes (ed.), *Henslowe's Diary*, pp. 182, 203.
7 See, for example, the discussion in Healy, '*Doctor Faustus*'; and Rutter, *Cambridge Introduction to Christopher Marlowe*, pp. 57–60.
8 On Anthony Munday's writing career, see Tracey Hill, *Anthony Munday and Civic Culture* (Manchester University Press, 2004).
9 The play's Revels editors observe: 'The result was a play vastly improved from a theatrical point of view, well constructed, running smoothly and dramatically effective'; Anthony Munday and others, *The Book of Sir Thomas More*, ed. Vittorio Gabrieli and Giorgio Melchiori (Manchester University Press, 1990), Introduction, p. 28.

6   Satire

1 Richard Dutton, Introduction to Ben Jonson, *Epicene, or The Silent Woman*, ed. Dutton (Manchester University Press, 2003), p. 65.
2 Randall Martin, Introduction to his edition of *Epicene*, *CWBJ*, vol. I, p. 236.
3 *Ibid.*, p. 237.
4 Cf. Philip Finkelpearl, *John Marston of the Middle Temple: An Elizabethan Dramatist in His Social Setting* (Cambridge, MA: Harvard University Press, 1969).

5 Dutton, Introduction to *Epicene*, p. 8.

6 See my *Ben Jonson's Theatrical Republics* (Basingstoke: Macmillan, 1998), p. 40.

7 See N. E. Andrews, 'Tragic Re-Presentation and the Semantics of Space in Plautus', *Mnemosyne*, 57:4 (2004), 445–64.

8 Clare McManus, 'Rank', in Sanders (ed.), *Ben Jonson in Context*, pp. 245–53 (248). On later use of the balcony space as social and sexual signifier, see Matthew Steggle, *Richard Brome: Place and Politics on the Caroline Stage* (Manchester University Press, 2004), pp. 49–50.

9 For more on London's theatrical and acoustic soundscape, see Smith, *Acoustic World*, *passim*.

10 Mary Hill Cole, *The Portable Queen: Elizabeth I and the Politics of Ceremony* (Amherst: University of Massachusetts Press, 1999).

11 Garrett A. Sullivan, Jr, 'Land', in Sanders (ed.), *Ben Jonson in Context*, pp. 289–95 (293).

Case study K Topical theatre and 1605–6: 'Remember, remember the fifth of November'

1 James Shapiro, *1599: A Year in the Life of William Shakespeare* (London: Faber and Faber, 2005). See also the special *Shakespeare Quarterly* edition on 1594: 61:4 (2010).

2 Ian Donaldson has also recently explored in detail Jonson's own troubled relationship to the conspiracy; see *Ben Jonson: A Life* (Oxford University Press, 2011), pp. 213–23.

3 Richard Dutton, Introduction to his edition of *Volpone*, *CWBJ*, vol. III, p. 8.

4 For a broader analysis of historical phenomenology as a method, see Bruce R. Smith, *Phenomenal Shakespeare* (Oxford: Wiley-Blackwell, 2010).

5 Jonathan Gil Harris, 'The Smell of *Macbeth*', *Shakespeare Quarterly*, 58:4 (2007), 465–76 (473).

6 *Ibid.*, p. 473. My thanks also to Victoria Buckley's 'The Impact of the Gunpowder Plot on the Jacobean Stage, 1605–16', D.Phil. thesis, University of Sussex (2012) for related ideas.

Case study L 'Little eyases': the children's companies and repertoire

1 See, for example, Rosalyn L. Knutson on 'repertorial strategies' in her essay on 'Adult Playing Companies, 1593–1603', in Dutton (ed.), *Oxford Handbook of Early Modern Theatre*, pp. 66–70.

2 Munro, *Children of the Queen's Revels*, p. 39.

3 *Ibid.*, p. 3.

4 *Ibid.*, p. 3.

5 Dutton, Introduction to his edition of the play in *CWBJ*, vol. III, p. 90.

7 Tragicomedy

1 I owe the phrase to Lucy Munro; see the concluding paragraph to her stimulating Introduction to her edition of Brome's *The Queen and Concubine* in *Brome Online.*

2 For a very thorough account of the three variant versions of the play extant and the generic as well as performative differences between them, see Quarmby, *Disguised Ruler*, Chapter 2, pp. 61–102.

3 John Fletcher, 'To the Reader', 3–8, *The Faithful Shepherdess: A Critical Edition*, ed. Florence Ada Kirk (New York: Garland, 1980).

4 Gossett, Introduction to *Philaster*, p. 3. As Gossett points out, this was not, though, the first use of that term for an English play – that had been in 1598 for an obscurer text by Samuel Brandon called *The Virtuous Octavia*; see Gordon McMullan and Jonathan Hope (eds.), *The Politics of Tragicomedy: Shakespeare and After* (London: Routledge, 1992), p. 19, note 18. On Marston's play as tragicomedy, see Munro, *Children of the Queen's Revels*, p. 106.

5 On the influence of *Il pastor fido* on Marston's work, see Quarmby, *Disguised Ruler*, pp. 66–7, 85; and also Nathaniel C. Leonard, 'Embracing the "Mongrel": John Marston's *The Malcontent*, *Antonio and Mellida* and the Development of English Early Modern Tragicomedy', *Journal for Early Modern Cultural Studies*, 12:3 (2012), 60–87; and Michele Marrapodi (ed.), *Italian Culture in the Drama of Shakespeare and His Contemporaries: Rewriting, Remaking, Refashioning* (Aldershot: Ashgate, 2007). Gossett credits the Dymock translation as Marston's source (Introduction to *Philaster*, p. 3).

6 Eugene M. Waith, *The Pattern of Tragicomedy in Beaumont and Fletcher* (Newhaven, CT: Yale University Press, 1952), p. 85. For a persuasive counterbalance to this argument, see Berek, 'Cross-Dressing', *passim.*

7 Gossett, Introduction to *Philaster*, p. 48.

8 Berek, 'Cross-Dressing', p. 371.

9 For a summary of these critical positions, see Introduction to my edition of the play in Hero Chalmers, Julie Sanders and Sophie Tomlinson (eds.), *Three Seventeenth-Century Plays on Women and Performance* (Manchester University Press, 2006), pp. 21–32.

10 Walter Cohen, 'Prerevolutionary Drama', in McMullan and Hope (eds.), *Politics of Tragicomedy*, pp. 122–50.

11 Gossett, Introduction to *Philaster*, pp. 57–8.

12 Berek, 'Cross-Dressing', pp. 365–6; see also Cohen, 'Prerevolutionary Drama', for a more extended discussion of this topic.

13 Quarmby has made a persuasive argument that the move towards city comedy in tragicomedy begins as early as the King's Men adaptation of the former boys' company play *The Malcontent*, a work he largely attributes to John Webster rather than the putative author Marston; see *Disguised Ruler*, esp. pp. 93–4, 99.

14 Davies, *Hamlet*, pp. 1–2.

15 See Gossett's note, *Philaster*, 5.3.19.

16 Munro, Critical Introduction, *Brome Online.*

17 Steggle, *Richard Brome*, p. 87.

18 Munro suggests the 'brave description' would not necessarily have been needed in the intimate venue of Salisbury Court where the play was first performed; see her Introduction to her edition in *Brome Online*.

19 See edition of the masque contained in Marion Wynne Davies and Susan P. Cerasano (eds.), *Renaissance Drama by Women: Texts and Documents* (London: Routledge, 1996), pp. 83–9; and see discussion in Clare McManus, *Women on the Renaissance Stage*, pp. 179–88, and specifically on embroidery in the performance, pp. 188–201.

20 McManus, *Women on the Renaissance Stage*, pp. 1–17.

21 See Munro's Introduction to her edition of the play in *Brome Online*.

22 See a fuller account of this in Chalmers, Sanders and Tomlinson (eds.), *Three Seventeenth-Century Plays*, pp. 23–4.

23 For a fuller account of Henrietta Maria's engagement with theatre throughout her reign, see Karen Britland, *Drama at the Courts of Queen Henrietta Maria* (Cambridge University Press, 2006).

Case study M The visual rhetoric of dumb show

1 See a close textual reading of the dumb show in *Hamlet* in Tiffany Stern, 'The Dumb Show in *Hamlet*', in McDonald, Nace and Williams (eds.), *Shakespeare Up Close*, pp. 273–81.

2 Andrew Gurr makes this connection between manuals of hand gestures and early modern acting style in *Shakespearean Stage*, pp. 98–101.

3 My reflections here and the supporting images are indebted to collaborative workshopping of this scene by the *Brome Online* project team at Royal Holloway University and in particular to the actors involved in these workshops, the director and photographer Brian Woolland, and the individual editor of this play, Lucy Munro.

4 Bulwer was an early advocate of teaching for the deaf. See Kinney, *Shakespeare By Stages*, pp. 58–62; and also Kristiaan Dekesel, 'John Bulwer: The founding father of BSL', *Signpost*, 5:4 (1992), 11–12.

Conclusion

1 The Guildhall in London has a copy of Visscher's print dated 1616 and the Folger Shakespeare Library in Washington, DC has a 1625 variant. Hollar's long view seen from the tower of what is now Southwark Cathedral dates from 1647 so is retrospective but includes significant details of London Bridge, the bear-baiting arenas of Paris Garden and the adjacent theatres. Visscher's panorama has long been used as a means of reconstructing the early modern geography of the Bankside playhouses but there are now assumed to be some inaccuracies in both the shape and positioning. Nevertheless, as an indicator of the visual significance of the purpose-built theatres in the early modern London landscape these documentary traces still have an important part to

play in reconstructive histories. See also I. A. Shapiro, 'The Bankside Theatres: Early Engravings', *Shakespeare Survey 1* (1947), 25–37. Extensive documentation and resources are available at the Early Modern London Theatres site, www.emlot.kcl.ac.uk. This is a collaboration with the *Records of Early English Drama* project at the University of Toronto, whose own website with supporting materials, including maps, can be found at www.reed.utoronto.ca.

2 See Anna Birch and Joanne Tompkins (eds.), *Performing Site-Specific Theatre: Politics, Place, Practice* (Basingstoke: Palgrave Macmillan, 2012), for reflections on historical understandings of site specificity. Cf. Andrew Sofer, 'Properties', in Dutton (ed.), *Oxford Handbook of Early Modern Theatre*, pp. 560–74, where he argues that if not site-specific exactly, these plays were heavily 'informed by space' (564).

3 Volumes are being added to the extensive *REED* collection all the time.

4 See Anne Lancashire, 'London Street Theatre', in Dutton (ed.), *Oxford Handbook of Early Modern Theatre*, pp. 323–9 (323).

5 John Astington, 'Court Theatre', in Dutton (ed.), *Oxford Handbook of Early Modern Theatre*, pp. 307–22 (308).

6 Platter, *Travels in England*, pp. 166–7; Cited in Kinney, *Shakespeare By Stages*, p. 6.

7 Cf. Stallybrass and Jones, *Renaissance Clothing*. On theories of social circulation, see Stephen Greenblatt, *Shakespearean Negotiations: The Circulation of Social Energy in Renaissance England* (Oxford: Clarendon Press, 1988).

8 Sarah Poynting, '"In the Name of all the Sisters": Henrietta Maria's Notorious Whores', in Clare McManus (ed.), *Women and Culture at the Courts of the Stuart Queens* (Basingstoke: Palgrave Macmillan, 2003), pp. 163–85.

9 Chalmers, Sanders and Tomlinson (eds.), *Three Seventeenth-Century Plays on Women and Performance*, Introduction, p. 5.

10 Britland, *Drama at the Courts of Queen Henrietta Maria*.

11 Kinney, *Shakespeare By Stages*, pp. 11–12.

12 D. J. Hopkins, *City/Stage/Globe: Performance and Space in Shakespeare's London* (London: Routledge, 2007), pp. 184–5.

13 For an extended reading of these plays, see my *Cultural Geography*, pp. 226–33.

14 Lowe, 'Clothing and Fashion', pp. 330–7.

15 In his poem 'An Epistle Answering to One that Asked to be Sealed of the Tribe of Ben', Jonson refers explicitly to the 'animated porcelain of the court' in a masque-soaked allusion (*Underwood*, 47, line 53, *CWBJ*, vol. VII, pp. 188–91); and cf. Sara van den Berg, 'True Relation: The Life and Career of Ben Jonson', in Richard Harp and Stanley Stewart (eds.), *The Cambridge Companion to Ben Jonson* (Cambridge University Press, 2000), pp. 1–14.

16 Gossett, Introduction to *Philaster*, pp. 55–7.

17 Tomlinson, *Women on Stage in Stuart Drama, passim*.

18 Lancashire, 'London Street Theatre', p. 323.

19 Tracey Hill, *Pageantry and Power: A Cultural History of the Early Modern Lord Mayor's Show 1585–1639* (Manchester University Press, 2011), and her *Anthony Munday and Civic Culture*.

20 See, for example, Grantley, 'Middleton's Comedy'; and Steggle, *Richard Brome*.

21 Perry, *Making of Jacobean Culture*, p. 263.

22 See Jonathan Walker, *Early Modern Academic Drama* (Aldershot: Ashgate, 2008); and Alan H. Nelson (ed.), *Records of Early English Drama: Cambridge*, 2 vols. (University of Toronto Press, 1989).

23 Suzanne Westfall, *Patrons and Performance: Early Tudor Household Revels* (Oxford: Clarendon Press, 1990).

24 John Marston, *Histriomastix* (London, 1610), spelling modernised.

25 Peter Greenfield, 'Touring', in Dutton (ed.), *Oxford Handbook of Early Modern Theatre*, pp. 292–306 (292).

26 See Sanders, *Cultural Geography*, pp. 107–19, and my 'Geographies of Performance: An Early Modern Midlands Case Study', in Bennett and Polito (eds.), *Performing Environments* (forthcoming).

27 On Dering, see Michael Dobson, *Shakespeare and Amateur Performance* (Cambridge University Press, 2011), pp. 22–3, 26–30.

Bibliography

Adlington, Hugh, Peter McCullough and Emma Rhatigan (eds.), *The Oxford Handbook of the Early Modern Sermon* (Oxford University Press, 2011)

Andrews, N. E., 'Tragic Re-Presentation and the Semantics of Space in Plautus', *Mnemosyne*, 57:4 (2004), 445–64

Appadurai, Arjun (ed.), *The Social Life of Things: Commodities in Cultural Perspective* (Cambridge University Press, 1986)

Aristotle, *Poetics*, trans. Malcolm Heath (London: Penguin, 1996)

Astington, John, 'Court Theatre', in Dutton (ed.), *Oxford Handbook of Early Modern Theatre*, pp. 307–22

Atkin, Graham, *Twelfth Night: Character Studies* (London and New York: Continuum, 2008)

Bach, Rebecca Ann, *Colonial Transformations: The Cultural Production of the New Atlantic World, 1580–1640* (Basingstoke: Palgrave, 2000)

Bacon, Sir Francis, *Essayes and counsels, civil and moral whereunto is newly added a table of the colours of good and evil* (London, 1664)

Barton, Anne, *The Names of Comedy* (Oxford: Clarendon Press, 1990)

Bate, Jonathan, *Shakespeare and Ovid* (Oxford: Clarendon Press, 1994)

Beaumont, Francis and John Fletcher, *Philaster*, ed. Suzanne Gossett (London: Arden Shakespeare, 2009)

Bednarz, James P., 'Between Collaboration and Rivalry: Dekker and Marston's Coactive Drama', *Ben Jonson Journal*, 10 (2003), 209–34

Belsey, Catherine, *The Subject of Tragedy: Identity and Experience in Renaissance Drama* (London: Routledge, 1991)

Bennett, Susan, *Theatre Audiences: A Theory of Production and Reception*, 2nd edn (London: Routledge, 1987)

Berek, Peter, 'Cross-Dressing, Gender, and Absolutism in the Beaumont and Fletcher Plays', *Studies in English Literature*, 44 (2004), 359–77

Berg, Sara van den, 'True Relation: The Life and Career of Ben Jonson', in Richard Harp and Stanley Stewart (eds.), *The Cambridge Companion to Ben Jonson* (Cambridge University Press, 2000), pp. 1–14

Berry, Philippa, *Of Chastity and Power: Elizabeth Literature and the Unmarried Queen* (London: Routledge, 1994)

Birch, Anna and Joanne Tompkins (eds.), *Performing Site-Specific Theatre: Politics, Place, Practice* (Basingstoke: Palgrave Macmillan, 2012)

Bowsher, Julian and Patricia Miller, *The Rose and the Globe: Playhouses of Tudor Bankside, Southwark: Excavations 1988–91* (Museum of London, 2009)

Bradbrook, M. C., *Elizabethan Stage Conditions: A Study of their Place in the Interpretation of Shakespeare's Plays* (Cambridge University Press, 1968)
   John Webster, Citizen and Dramatist (London: Weidenfeld & Nicolson, 1980)
   The Rise of the Common Player: A Study of Actor and Society in Shakespeare's England (London: Chatto & Windus, 1962)

Bradley, A. C., *Shakespearean Tragedy: Lectures on 'Hamlet', 'Othello', 'King Lear', 'Macbeth'* (London: Penguin, 1991; 1st edn 1904)

Brayshay, Mark, 'Waits, Musicians, Bearwards, and Players: The Inter-Urban Road, Travel and Performances of Itinerant Entertainers in Sixteenth and Seventeenth Century England', *Journal of Historical Geography*, 31:3 (2005), 430–58

Britland, Karen, *Drama at the Courts of Queen Henrietta Maria* (Cambridge University Press, 2006)
   'Queen Henrietta Maria's Theatrical Patronage', in Erin Griffey (ed.), *Henrietta Maria: Piety, Politics and Patronage* (Aldershot: Ashgate, 2008), pp. 57–72

Brome, Richard, *The Complete Works of Richard Brome Online*, gen. ed. Richard Cave, www.hrionline.ac.uk/brome

Bruster, Douglas and Robert Weimann, *Prologues to Shakespeare's Theatre: Performance and Liminality in Early Modern Drama* (Cambridge University Press, 2008)

Buckley, Victoria, 'The Impact of the Gunpowder Plot on the Jacobean Stage, 1605–16', D.Phil. thesis, University of Sussex (2012)

Burlinson, Christopher, 'Money and Consumerism', in Sanders (ed.), *Ben Jonson in Context*, pp. 281–8

Burnett, Mark Thornton, '*Doctor Faustus*: Dramaturgy and Disturbance', in Garrett A. Sullivan, Jr and Emma Smith (eds.), *The Cambridge Companion to English Renaissance Tragedy* (Cambridge University Press, 2010), pp. 163–73

Butler, Martin, *Theatre and Crisis, 1632–42* (Cambridge University Press, 1984)

Calvo, Clara, 'Thomas Kyd and the Elizabethan Blockbuster', in Hoenselaars (ed.), *Cambridge Companion to Shakespeare and Contemporary Dramatists*, pp. 19–33

Carson, Christie and Farah Karim Cooper (eds.), *Shakespeare's Globe: A Theatrical Experiment* (Cambridge University Press, 2008)

Cerasano, S. P., 'Alleyn, Edward (1566–1626)', *Oxford Dictionary of National Biography* (Oxford University Press, 2004), online edn, www.oxforddnb.com/view/article/398
   'The Geography of Henslowe's Diary', *Shakespeare Quarterly*, 56 (2005), 328–53
   'Henslowe, Philip (c. 1555–1616)', *Oxford Dictionary of National Biography* (Oxford University Press, 2004), online edn, www.oxforddnb.com/view/article/12991

'The Master of the Bears in Art and Enterprise', *Medieval and Renaissance Drama in England*, 5 (1991), 195–209

'Tamburlaine and Edward Alleyn's Ring', *Shakespeare Survey 47* (1994), 171–9

Chalmers, Hero, Julie Sanders and Sophie Tomlinson (eds.), *Three Seventeenth-Century Plays on Women and Performance* (Manchester University Press, 2006)

Chambers, E. K., *The Elizabethan Stage*, 4 vols. (Oxford: Clarendon Press, 1965)

Chernaik, Warren, *The Cambridge Introduction to Shakespeare's History Plays* (Cambridge University Press, 2007)

Cohen, Walter, 'Prerevolutionary Drama', in McMullan and Hope (eds.), *Politics of Tragicomedy*, pp. 122–50

Cole, Mary Hill, *The Portable Queen: Elizabeth I and the Politics of Ceremony* (Amherst: University of Massachusetts Press, 1999)

Cooper, Farah Karim, 'Disguise and Identity in the Plays of Middleton', in Gossett (ed.), *Thomas Middleton in Context*, pp. 279–86

Cooper, Farah Karim and Tiffany Stern (eds.), *Shakespeare's Theatres and the Effects of Performance* (London: Arden Shakespeare, 2013)

Craik, T. W. (ed.), *Minor Elizabethan Tragedies* (London: J. M. Dent & Sons, 1974)

Crane, Mary Thomas, *Shakespeare's Brain: Reading with Cognitive Theory* (Princeton University Press, 2000)

Danson, Lawrence, *Shakespeare's Dramatic Genres* (Oxford University Press, 2000)

Davies, Marion Wynne and Susan P. Cerasano (eds.), *Renaissance Drama by Women: Texts and Documents* (London: Routledge, 1996)

Davies, Michael, *Hamlet: Character Studies* (London and New York: Continuum, 2008)

Dawson, Anthony B. and Paul Yachnin, *The Culture of Playgoing in Shakespeare's England: A Collaborative Debate* (Cambridge University Press, 2001)

Dekesel, Kristiaan, 'John Bulwer: The Founding Father of BSL', *Signpost*, 5:4 (1992), 11–12

Dekker, Thomas, *The Shoemaker's Holiday*, ed. R. L. Smallwood and Stanley Wells (Manchester University Press, 1979)

Worke for Armourers, or The peace is broken (London, 1609)

Derrida, Jacques, 'The Law of Genre', trans. Avital Ronell, *Glyph*, 7 (1980), 202–32

Di Gangi, Mario, *Sexual Types: Embodiment, Agency and Dramatic Character from Shakespeare to Shirley* (Philadelphia: University of Pennsylvania Press, 2011)

Dillon, Janette, *The Cambridge Introduction to Early English Theatre* (Cambridge University Press, 2006)

Shakespeare and the Staging of English History (Oxford University Press, 2012)

Theatre, Court, and City, 1595–1610: Drama and Social Space in London (Cambridge University Press, 2000)

Dobson, Michael, *Shakespeare and Amateur Performance* (Cambridge University Press, 2011)

Donaldson, Ian, *Ben Jonson: A Life* (Oxford University Press, 2011)

Donne, John, *Selected Poetry*, ed. John Carey (Oxford University Press, 1996)

Dustagheer, Sarah, 'Repertory and the Production of Theatre Space at the Globe and the Blackfriars, 1599–1613', PhD thesis, King's College, University of London (2012)

Dutton, Richard (ed.), *The Oxford Handbook of Early Modern Theatre* (Oxford University Press, 2009)

Eccles, Christine, *The Rose Theatre* (London: Routledge, 1990)

Ellinghausen, Laurie, *Labor and Writing in Early Modern England, 1567–1667* (Aldershot: Ashgate, 2008)

Empson, William, *Some Versions of Pastoral: A Study of Pastoral Form in Literature* (London: Chatto & Windus, 1966)

Erickson, Peter, 'Sexual Politics and the Social Structure in *As You Like It*', *Massachusetts Review*, 23:1 (1982), 65–83

Farmer, Alan 'The Playhouse in the Printing House', *Shakespeare and the Book*, www.ccnmtl.columbia.edu/projects/shakespeareandthebook

Fetzer, Margaret, *John Donne's Performances: Sermons, Poems, Letters, and Devotions* (Manchester University Press, 2010)

Finkelpearl, Philip, *John Marston of the Middle Temple: An Elizabethan Dramatist in His Social Setting* (Cambridge, MA: Harvard University Press, 1969)

Fletcher, John, *The Faithful Shepherdess*, ed. Florence Ada Kirk (New York: Garland, 1980)

Foakes, R. A. (ed.), *Henslowe's Diary*, 2nd edn (Cambridge University Press, 2002)

Ford, John, *'Tis Pity She's a Whore and Other Plays*, ed. Marion Lomax (Oxford University Press, 1995)

Frow, John, *Genre* (London: Routledge, 2006)

Fumerton, Patricia, *Unsettled: The Culture of Mobility and the Working Poor* (University of Chicago Press, 2006)

Gaby, Rosemary, 'Of Vagabonds and Commonwealths: *Beggars' Bush, A Jovial Crew*, and *The Sisters*', *Studies in English Literature 1500–1900*, 34 (1994), 401–24

Gossett, Suzanne (ed.), *Thomas Middleton in Context* (Cambridge University Press, 2011)

Grantley, Darryll, *London in Early Modern English Drama: Representing the Built Environment* (Basingstoke: Palgrave Macmillan, 2008)

'Middleton's Comedy and the Geography of London', in Gossett (ed.), *Thomas Middleton in Context*, pp. 28–36

Greenblatt, Stephen, *Renaissance Self-Fashioning: From More to Shakespeare* (University of Chicago Press, 1980)

Shakespearean Negotiations: The Circulation of Social Energy in Renaissance England (Oxford: Clarendon Press, 1988)

'Towards a Poetics of Culture', *Southern Review*, 20 (1987), 3–15

Greenfield, Peter, 'Touring', in Dutton (ed.), *Oxford Handbook of Early Modern Theatre*, pp. 292–306

Guenther, Genevieve, 'Why Devils Came When Faustus Called Them', *Modern Philology*, 109 (2011), 46–70

Gurr, Andrew, *The Shakespeare Company, 1594–1642* (Cambridge University Press, 2004)

   The Shakespearean Stage, 1574–1642, 3rd edn (Cambridge University Press, 1992)

   Shakespeare's Opposites: The Admiral's Company, 1594–1625 (Cambridge University Press, 2009)

Gurr, Andrew and Mariko Ichikawa, *Staging in Shakespeare's Theatres* (Oxford University Press, 2000)

Hackett, Helen, *Virgin Mother, Maiden Queen: Elizabeth I and the Cult of the Virgin Mary* (Basingstoke: Macmillan, 1996)

Hadfield, Andrew, *Literature, Travel and Colonial Writing in the English Renaissance, 1545–1625* (Oxford University Press, 2007)

Harbage, Alfred, *As They Liked It* (London and New York: Macmillan, 1947)

Harris, Jonathan Gil, 'The Smell of *Macbeth*', *Shakespeare Quarterly*, 58:4 (2007), 465–76

Harris, Jonathan Gil and Natasha Korda (eds.), *Staged Properties in Early Modern English Drama* (Cambridge University Press, 2002)

Heal, Felicity, *Hospitality in Early Modern England* (Oxford: Clarendon Press, 1990)

Healy, Thomas, 'Doctor Faustus', in Patrick Cheney (ed.), *The Cambridge Companion to Christopher Marlowe* (Cambridge University Press, 2004), pp. 174–92

Helgerson, Richard, *Forms of Nationhood: Elizabethan Writing of England* (University of Chicago Press, 1994)

Heywood, Thomas, *The First and Second Parts of King Edward IV*, ed. Richard Rowland (Manchester University Press, 2005)

Hill, Tracey, *Anthony Munday and Civic Culture* (Manchester University Press, 2004)

   Pageantry and Power: A Cultural History of the Early Modern Lord Mayor's Show 1585–1639 (Manchester University Press, 2011)

Hirschfield, Heather, 'Collaborating Across Generations: Thomas Heywood, Richard Brome, and the Production of *The Late Lancashire Witches*', *Journal of Medieval and Early Modern Studies*, 30:2 (2000), 339–74

   '"For the Author's Credit": Issues of Authorship in English Renaissance Drama', in Dutton (ed.), *Oxford Handbook of Early Modern Theatre*, pp. 441–55

Hoenselaars, Ton, 'Shakespeare: Colleagues, Collaborators, Co-authors', in Hoenselaars (ed.), *Cambridge Companion to Shakespeare and Contemporary Dramatists*, pp. 97–119

   (ed.), *The Cambridge Companion to Shakespeare and Contemporary Dramatists* (Cambridge University Press, 2012)

Höfele, Andreas, *Stage, Stake and Scaffold: Humans and Animals in Shakespeare's Theatre* (Oxford University Press, 2011)

Holland, Peter, *English Shakespeares: Shakespeare on the English Stage in the 1990s* (Cambridge University Press, 1997)

Hopkins, D. J., *City/Stage/Globe: Performance and Space in Shakespeare's London* (London: Routledge, 2007)

Hopkins, Lisa, *John Ford's Political Theatre* (Manchester University Press, 1994)

Howard, Jean E., 'Bettrice's Monkey: Staging Exotica in Early Modern London Comedy', in Jyotsna G. Singh (ed.), *A Companion to the Global Renaissance* (Oxford: Wiley-Blackwell, 2009), pp. 325–39

   Theater of a City: The Places of London Comedy, 1598–1642 (Philadelphia: University of Pennsylvania Press, 2007)

Hutchings, Mark, 'De Flores Between the Acts', *Studies in Theatre and Performance*, 31:1 (2011), 95–112

Hutson, Lorna, *The Invention of Suspicion: Law and Mimesis in Shakespeare and Renaissance Drama* (Oxford University Press, 2011)

Ingram, William, *The Business of Playing: The Beginnings of the Adult Professional Theatre in Elizabethan London* (Ithaca, NY: Cornell University Press, 1992)

Jones, Emrys, *Scenic Form in Shakespeare* (Oxford University Press, 1971)

Jonson, Ben, *The Cambridge Works of Ben Jonson*, gen.eds. David Bevington, Martin Butler and Ian Donaldson, 7 vols. (Cambridge University Press, 2012)

   Epicene, or The Silent Woman, ed. Richard Dutton (Manchester University Press, 2003)

Kastan, David Scott, 'Workshop and/as Playhouse: Comedy and Commerce in *The Shoemaker's Holiday*', *Studies in Philology*, 84:3 (1987), 324–37

Kerrigan, John, *Revenge Tragedy: Aeschylus to Armageddon* (Oxford: Clarendon Press, 1996)

Kingsley-Smith, Jane, *Shakespeare's Drama of Exile* (Basingstoke: Palgrave Macmillan, 2003)

Kinney, Arthur, 'John Lyly and the University Wits', in Hoenselaars (ed.), *Cambridge Companion to Shakespeare and Contemporary Dramatists*, pp. 1–18

   Shakespeare By Stages: An Historical Introduction (Oxford: Blackwell, 2003)

Knights, L. C., 'How Many Children had Lady Macbeth? An Essay in the Theory and Practice of Shakespeare Criticism', in *Explorations* (London: Chatto & Windus, 1945), pp. 1–39

Knowles, James with Eugene Giddens (ed.), *The Roaring Girl and Other City Comedies* (Oxford University Press, 2001)

Knutson, Rosalyn L., 'Adult Playing Companies, 1593–1603', in Dutton (ed.), *Oxford Handbook of Early Modern Theatre*, pp. 66–70

   Playing Companies and Commerce in Shakespeare's Time (Cambridge University Press, 2001)

The Repertory of Shakespeare's Company, 1594–1613 (Fayetteville: University of Arkansas Press, 1991)

Korda, Natasha, *Labor's Lost: Women's Work and the Early Modern English Stage* (Philadelphia: University of Pennsylvania Press, 2011)

'Trade, Work and Workers', in Gossett (ed.), *Thomas Middleton in Context*, pp. 75–82

Kyd, Thomas, *The Spanish Tragedy*, ed. J. R. Mulryne (London: Arnold, 1989)

Lancashire, Anne, 'London Street Theatre', in Dutton (ed.), *Oxford Handbook of Early Modern Theatre*, pp. 323–9

Leonard, Nathaniel C., 'Embracing the "Mongrel": John Marston's *The Malcontent, Antonio and Mellida* and the Development of English Early Modern Tragicomedy', *Journal for Early Modern Cultural Studies*, 12:3 (2012), 60–87

Levin, Harry, *The Overreacher: A Study of Christoper Marlowe* (Cambridge, MA: Harvard University Press, 1952)

Levine, Laura, *Men in Women's Clothing: Anti-Theatricality and Effeminization, 1579–1642* (Cambridge University Press, 1994)

Lindley, David, 'Blackfriars, Music and Masque: Theatrical Contexts of the Last Plays', in Catherine M. S. Alexander (ed.), *The Cambridge Companion to Shakespeare's Last Plays* (Cambridge University Press, 2009), pp. 29–46

Lowe, Eleanor, 'Clothing and Fashion in Jonson's Plays', in Sanders (ed.), *Ben Jonson in Context*, pp. 330–7

Lupton, Donald, *London and the country carbonadoed and quartered into seuerall characters* (London, 1632)

Lyly, John, *Galatea and Midas*, ed. George K. Hunter and David Bevington (Manchester University Press, 2000)

Mardock, James, *'Our Scene is London': Ben Jonson's City and the Space of the Author* (London: Routledge, 2007)

Marlowe, Christopher, *Doctor Faustus and Other Plays*, ed. David Bevington and Eric Rasmussen (Oxford University Press, 1995)

Marrapodi, Michele (ed.), *Italian Culture in the Drama of Shakespeare and His Contemporaries: Rewriting, Remaking, Refashioning* (Aldershot: Ashgate, 2007)

Marston, John, *Histriomastix* (London, 1610)

The Selected Plays of John Marston, ed. MacDonald P. Jackson and Michael Neill (Cambridge University Press, 1986)

Massinger, Philip, *The Guardian* (London, 1633)

A New Way to Pay Old Debts, ed. T. W. Craik (London: A. & C. Black/Norton, 1999)

McDonald, Russ, Nicholas D. Nace and Travis D. Williams (eds.), *Shakespeare Up Close: Reading Early Modern Texts* (London: Arden Shakespeare, 2012)

McManus, Clare, 'Rank', in Sanders (ed.), *Ben Jonson in Context*, pp. 245–53

Women on the Renaissance Stage: Anna of Denmark and Female Masquing in the Stuart Court (1590–1619) (Manchester University Press, 2002)

McMillin, Scott and Sally-Beth McLean, *The Queen's Men and Their Plays*
(Cambridge University Press, 1998)

McLuskie, Kathleen, 'The Shopping Complex: Materiality and the Renaissance
Theatre', in Edward Pechter (ed.), *Textual and Theatrical Shakespeare:
Questions of Evidence* (University of Iowa Press, 1996), pp. 86–101

McMullan, Gordon and Jonathan Hope (eds.), *The Politics of Tragicomedy:
Shakespeare and After* (London: Routledge, 1992)

McRae, Andrew, *Literature and Domestic Travel in Early Modern England*
(Cambridge University Press, 2010)

Middleton, Thomas, *Thomas Middleton: The Collected Works*, gen. eds. Gary
Taylor and John Lavagnino (Oxford University Press, 2010)

Middleton, Thomas and William Rowley, *The Changeling*, ed. N. W. Bawcutt
(Manchester University Press, 1977)

Morison, Fynes, *An Itinerary . . . containing his ten yeeres travel through the twelve
dominions*, 3 vols. (London, 1617)

Mullaney, Steven, 'Affective Technologies: Toward an Emotional Logic of the
Elizabethan Stage', in Mary Floyd Wilson and Garrett A. Sullivan, Jr
(eds.), *Environment and Embodiment in Early Modern England*
(Basingstoke: Palgrave Macmillan, 2007), pp. 71–89

   The Place of the Stage: Licence, Play and Power in Renaissance England (Ann
Arbor: University of Michigan Press, 1995)

Mulryne, J. R. and Margaret Shewring, 'The Repertoire of the Swan', in Mulryne
and Shewring (eds.), *This Golden Round: The Royal Shakespeare
Company at the Swan* (Stratford-upon-Avon: Mulryne and Shewring
Ltd, 1989), pp. 23–36

Munday, Anthony and others, *The Book of Sir Thomas More*, ed. Vittorio Gabrieli
and Giorgio Melchiori (Manchester University Press, 1990)

Munro, Lucy, *Archaic Style in English Literature, 1590–1674* (Cambridge
University Press, forthcoming)

   Children of the Queen's Revels: A Jacobean Theatre Repertory (Cambridge
University Press, 2005)

   'Music and Sound', in Dutton (ed.), *Oxford Handbook of Early Modern
Theatre*, pp. 543–59

Nashe, Thomas, *Pierce Pennilesse, His Supplication to the Devil*, ed. G. B. Harrison
(Edinburgh University Press, 1966)

Neill, Michael, *Issues of Death: Mortality and Identity in English Renaissance
Tragedy* (Oxford: Clarendon Press, 1997)

Nelson, Alan H. (ed.), *Records of Early English Drama: Cambridge*, 2 vols.
(University of Toronto Press, 1989)

Nelson, Alan H. and John R. Elliott, Jr (eds.), *Records of Early English Drama: Inns
of Court*, 3 vols. (Cambridge: D. S. Brewer, 2010)

Nicholl, Charles, *The Lodger: Shakespeare on Silver Street* (London: Penguin,
2008)

Oakley-Brown, Liz, *Ovid and the Cultural Politics of Translation in Early Modern
England* (Aldershot: Ashgate, 2006)

O'Callaghan, Michelle, 'Thomas Middleton and the Early Modern Theatre', in Hoenselaars (ed.), *Cambridge Companion to Shakespeare and Contemporary Dramatists*, pp. 165–80

Ornstein, Robert, 'Marlowe and God: The Tragic Theology of *Doctor Faustus*', *PMLA*, 83:5 (1968), 1378–85

Ostovich, Helen, Holger Schott Syme and Andrew Griffin (eds.), *Locating the Queen's Men, 1583–1603: Material Practices and Conditions of Playing* (Aldershot: Ashgate, 2009)

Palfrey, Simon and Tiffany Stern, *Shakespeare in Parts* (Oxford University Press, 2007)

Patterson, Annabel, *Shakespeare and the Popular Voice* (Oxford: Blackwell, 1989)

Pearson, Meg F., 'Audience as Witness in *Edward II*', in Jennifer Low and Nova Myhill (eds.), *Imagining the Audience in Early Modern Drama, 1558–1642* (Basingstoke: Palgrave Macmillan, 2011), pp. 93–111

Peck, Linda Levy (ed.), *The Mental World of the Jacobean Court* (Cambridge University Press, 2005)

Perry, Curtis, *The Making of Jacobean Culture: James I and the Renegotiation of Elizabethan Literary Practice* (Cambridge University Press, 1997)

Pincombe, Mike, *The Plays of John Lyly: Eros and Eliza* (Manchester University Press, 1996)

Platter, Thomas, *Travels in England, 1599*, trans. Clare Williams (London: Jonathan Cape, 1937)

Pollard, Tanya, 'Drugs, Remedies, Poison and the Theatre', in Gossett (ed.), *Thomas Middleton in Context*, pp. 287–394

  Drugs and Theatre in Early Modern England (Oxford University Press, 2005)

Postlewait, Thomas, 'Eyewitnesses to History: Visual Evidence for Theatre in Early Modern England', in Dutton (ed.), *Oxford Handbook of Early Modern Theatre*, pp. 575–606

Power, Andrew, 'What the Hell is Under the Stage? Trapdoor Use in the English Senecan Tradition', *English*, 60 (2011), 276–96

Poynting, Sarah, '"In the Name of all the Sisters": Henrietta Maria's Notorious Whores', in Clare McManus (ed.), *Women and Culture at the Courts of the Stuart Queens* (Basingstoke: Palgrave Macmillan, 2003), pp. 163–85

Quarmby, Kevin, *The Disguised Ruler in Shakespeare and His Contemporaries* (Aldershot: Ashgate, 2012)

Rackin, Phyllis, 'Androgyny, Mimesis, and the Marriage of the Boy Heroine', *PMLA*, 102 (1989), 29–41

Rackin, Phyllis and Jean E. Howard, *Engendering a Nation: A Feminist Account of Shakespeare's English Histories* (London: Routledge, 1997)

Richardson, Catherine, *Shakespeare and Material Culture* (Oxford University Press, 2011)

Robson, Mark, *Stephen Greenblatt* (London: Routledge, 2007)

Rowley, William, Thomas Dekker, John Ford, &c', *The Witch of Edmonton*, in Peter Corbin and Douglas Sedge (eds.), *Three Jacobean Witchcraft Plays* (Manchester University Press, 1986)

Rutter, Carol Chillington, 'Remind Me: How Many Children Had Lady
  Macbeth?', *Shakespeare Survey 57* (2004), 38–53
  (ed.), *Documents of the Rose Playhouse* (Manchester University Press, 1984)
Rutter, Tom, *The Cambridge Introduction to Christopher Marlowe* (Cambridge
  University Press, 2012)
Sanders, Julie, 'Beggars' Commonwealths on the Pre-Civil War Stage', *Modern
  Language Review*, 97 (2002), 1–14
  Ben Jonson's Theatrical Republics (Basingstoke: Macmillan, 1998)
  Caroline Drama (Plymouth: Northcote House, 1999)
  The Cultural Geography of Early Modern Drama, 1620–1650 (Cambridge
  University Press, 2011)
  '"The day's sports devised in the Inn": Jonson's *The New Inn* and Theatrical
  Politics', *Modern Language Review*, 91:3 (1996), 545–60
  'Geographies of Performance: An Early Modern Midlands Case Study', in
  Susan Bennett and Mary Polito (eds.), *Performing Environments: Site
  Specificity in Medieval and Early Modern Drama* (Basingstoke: Palgrave
  Macmillan, forthcoming)
  (ed.), *Ben Jonson in Context* (Cambridge University Press, 2010)
Seaver, Paul S., 'Thomas Dekker's *The Shoemaker's Holiday*: The Artisanal World',
  in David L. Smith, Richard Strier and David Bevington (eds.), *The
  Theatrical City: Culture, Theatre and Politics in London, 1576–1649*
  (Cambridge University Press, 1995), pp. 87–100
Sennett, Richard, *The Craftsman* (London: Allen Lane, 2008)
Shakespeare, William, *The Oxford Shakespeare: The Complete Works*, gen. eds.
  Stanley Wells and Gary Taylor (Oxford University Press, 1988)
  Richard III, ed. John Jowett (Oxford University Press, 2000)
Shapiro, I. A., 'The Bankside Theatres: Early Engravings', *Shakespeare Survey 1*
  (1947), 25–37
Shapiro, James, *1599: A Year in the Life of William Shakespeare* (London: Faber
  and Faber, 2005)
  '"Tragedies naturally performed": Kyd's Representation of Violence', in
  David Scott Kastan and Peter Stallybrass (eds.), *Staging the Renaissance:
  Reinterpretations of Elizabethan and Jacobean Drama* (London:
  Routledge, 1991), pp. 99–113
Shevlin, Eleanor F., '"To Reconcile Book and Title and Make 'em Kin to One
  Another": The Evolution of the Title's Contractual Function', *Book
  History*, 2 (1999), 42–77
Shirley, James, *The Cardinal*, ed. E. M. Yearling (Manchester University Press,
  1986)
  Hyde Park, ed. Simon Trussler (London: Methuen, 1987)
  The Lady of Pleasure, ed. Ronald Huebert (Manchester University Press,
  1987)
Smallwood, Robert L., '"Here in the Friars": Immediacy and Theatricality in *The
  Alchemist*', *Review of English Studies*, 32:126 (1981), 142–60

Smith, Bruce R., *The Acoustic World of Early Modern England: Attending to the 'O' Factor* (University of Chicago Press, 1999)

Phenomenal Shakespeare (Oxford: Wiley-Blackwell, 2010)

Smith, Emma, 'Shakespeare and Early Modern Tragedy', in Garrett A. Sullivan, Jr and Emma Smith (eds.), *The Cambridge Companion to English Renaissance Tragedy* (Cambridge University Press, 2010), pp. 132–49

Smith, Nigel, *Literature and Revolution in England, 1640–1660* (New Haven, CT: Yale University Press, 1994)

Sofer, Andrew, 'Properties', in Dutton (ed.), *Oxford Handbook of Early Modern Theatre*, pp. 560–74

Solga, Kim, 'Playing *The Changeling* Architecturally', in Susan Bennett and Mary Polito (eds.), *Performing Environments: Site Specificity in Medieval and Early Modern Drama* (Basingstoke: Palgrave Macmillan, forthcoming)

Stallybrass, Peter and Ann Jones, *Renaissance Clothing and the Materials of Memory* (Cambridge University Press, 2000)

Steggle, Matthew, *Richard Brome: Place and Politics on the Caroline Stage* (Manchester University Press, 2004)

Wars of the Theatres: The Poetics of Personation in the Age of Jonson (Victoria, BC: English Literary Studies, 1998)

Stern, Tiffany, *Documents of Performance in Early Modern England* (Cambridge University Press, 2009)

'The Dumb Show in *Hamlet*', in McDonald, Nace and Williams (eds.), *Shakespeare Up Close*, pp. 273–81

Making Shakespeare: From Stage or Page (London: Routledge, 2004)

'"On each Wall / And Corner Post": Playbills, Title-pages, and Advertising in Early Modern London', *English Literary Renaissance*, 36 (2006), 57–85

Streete, Adrian, *Protestantism and Drama in Early Modern England* (Cambridge University Press, 2011)

Strong, Roy, *The Cult of Elizabeth: Elizabethan Portraits and Pageantry*, 2nd edn (London: Pimlico, 1999)

Henry, Prince of Wales and England's Lost Renaissance (London: Pimlico, 2000)

Sullivan, Jr, Garrett A., 'Land', in Sanders (ed.), *Ben Jonson in Context*, pp. 289–95

Taylor, Gary and Michael Warren (eds.), *The Division of the Kingdoms: Shakespeare's Two Versions of 'King Lear'* (Oxford University Press, 1983)

Taylor, John, *The Carriers Cosmography* (London, 1636)

Todorov, Tzvetan, *Genres in Discourse*, trans. Catherine Porter (Cambridge University Press, 1990)

Tomlinson, Sophie, *Women on Stage in Stuart Drama* (Cambridge University Press, 2005)

Waith, Eugene M., *The Pattern of Tragicomedy in Beaumont and Fletcher* (Newhaven, CT: Yale University Press, 1952)

Walker, Jonathan, *Early Modern Academic Drama* (Aldershot: Ashgate, 2008)

Walsh, Brian, 'Performing Histories in Dekker's *Shoemaker's Holiday*', *Studies in English Literature*, 46 (2006), 323–46

Webster, John, *The Duchess of Malfi*, ed. Leah S. Marcus (London: Arden Shakespeare, 2009)

  The White Devil, ed. John Russell Brown (Manchester University Press, 1985)

  Women Beware Women, ed. J. R. Mulryne (Manchester University Press, 1975)

Weimann, Robert, 'Performance-Game and Representation in *Richard III*', in Edward Pechter (ed.), *Textual and Theatrical Shakespeare: Questions of Evidence* (University of Iowa Press, 1996), pp. 66–85

Westfall, Suzanne, *Patrons and Performance: Early Tudor Household Revels* (Oxford: Clarendon Press, 1990)

White, Martin, *Renaissance Drama in Action: An Introduction to Aspects of Theatre Practice and Performance* (London: Routledge, 1998)

Wickham, Glynne, Herbert Berry and William Ingram (eds.), *English Professional Theatre, 1530–1660* (Cambridge University Press, 2000)

Wilder, Lina Perkins, *Shakespeare's Memory Theatre: Recollection, Properties, and Character* (Cambridge University Press, 2010)

Wilson, Richard, *Will Power: Essays on Shakespearean Authority* (Detroit, MI: Wayne State University Press, 1992)

Wiseman, Susan, *Drama and Politics in the English Civil War* (Cambridge University Press, 1998)

Womack, Peter, *English Renaissance Drama* (Oxford: Blackwell, 2006)

Zucker, Adam, *The Places of Wit in Early Modern English Comedy* (Cambridge University Press, 2011)

Index

act breaks, 11, 39, 75, 152
adaptation, 3, 33, 50, 196, 237
Admiral's Men, 6, 22, 23, 24, 33, 129, 214, 216, 223
Alleyn, Edward, 1, 3, 5, 11, 22, 23, 24, 27, 28, 29, 30, 42, 48, 57, 221, 223, 224
Alleyn, Joan, 5, 29
Anna of Denmark, Queen, 13, 194, 195, 204, 206
Appadurai, Arjun, 80
Arden of Faversham, 46, 112, 214
Aristophanes, 112
Aristotle, 35, 44, 225
  Poetics, 35
Armin, Robert, 5
asides, 8, 23, 36, 54, 69, 71, 86, 120, 121, 165, 168, 196
Astington, John, 202, 239
audiences, 8, 11, 27, 28–9, 31, 38, 39, 131, 143, 144, 163, 174, 183, 187, 209, 211

Bacon, Sir Francis, 65
  'On Revenge', 65
balconies, 42, 77, 164, 165, 236
Banqueting House, 15, 204, 210, 217, 219
bear-baitings, 56, 59, 167, 206
Beaumont, Francis, 110, 124, 150, 182, 183, 184, 186, 188, 189, 190, 203, 205, 206, 209, 217, 227, 232, 237
  Knight of the Burning Pestle, The, 209, 217

Masque of the Inner Temple and Grays Inn, 205
Beaumont, Francis and John Fletcher, *Philaster*, 110, 124, 150, 152, 180, 182, 183, 184, 185–9, 190, 191, 196, 217, 227, 237, 239
Bednarz, James, 153, 235
Bevington, David, 124, 232
Billingsgate, 139
Bishops' Ban, 159, 160
Blackfriars precinct, 10, 204
Blackfriars Theatre, xii, 5, 10, 11, 14, 15, 19, 43, 44, 67, 72, 74–7, 127, 136, 175, 190, 201, 203, 205, 211
Blundeville, Thomas, 148, 213
boy actors, 77, 119, 122, 128, 142, 183, 195
Bradbrook, Muriel, 36, 46, 187, 220
Bradley, A. C., 27–8
Brayne, John, 2, 3, 6
Brome, Richard, ix, 15, 19, 46, 107, 112, 126, 127, 132, 133, 135, 140, 144, 147, 150, 151, 182, 184, 191, 193, 194, 195, 197, 200, 204, 207, 208, 218, 219, 225, 228, 232, 233, 236, 237, 238, 239
  Antipodes, The, 208
  City Wit, The, 147, 218
  Jovial Crew, A, 8, 126–7, 208, 212, 219, 232
  Queen and Concubine, The, 180, 182, 185, 189, 191–4, 197–200, 236

253

Cambridge Introductions to...